Annual Review of Cultural Heritage Informatics

EDITORIAL BOARD

College of Arts and Sciences
816 Bull Street
Columbia, SC 29208
JPRZYBYS@mailbox.sc.edu

Abebe Rorissa, Ph.D.
Associate Professor
Department of Information Studies
College of Computing and Information
University at Albany, State University of New York
Draper Hall, Room 116
135 Western Avenue
Albany, NY 12222
arorissa@albany.edu

Anna Maria Tammaro
Presidente Comitato Scientifico UNIPR CoLab
Università di Parma
Chair IFLA Library Theory and Research Section
Via Montebeni 9
Fiesole 50014 (Firenze)
Italy
annamaria.tammaro@unipr.it

Colin F. Wilder, Ph.D.
Associate Director
Center for Digital Humanities
Thomas Cooper Library
University of South Carolina
Columbia, SC 29208
wildercf@mailbox.sc.edu

Greg Wilsbacher, Ph.D.
Curator, Newsfilm Collections
Moving Image Research Collections
University of South Carolina
Columbia, SC 29208
gregw@sc.edu

Annual Review of Cultural Heritage Informatics

2015

Jennifer Weil Arns

ROWMAN & LITTLEFIELD
Lanham • Boulder • New York • London

Published by Rowman & Littlefield
A wholly owned subsidiary of The Rowman & Littlefield Publishing Group, Inc.
4501 Forbes Boulevard, Suite 200, Lanham, Maryland 20706
www.rowman.com

Unit A, Whitacre Mews, 26-34 Stannary Street, London SE11 4AB

British Library Cataloguing in Publication Information Available

Library of Congress Cataloging-in-Publication Data

Library of Congress Cataloging-in-Publication Data Available ISBN 978-1-4422-6370-3 (cloth : alk.
paper) — ISBN 978-1-4422-6371-0 (electronic)

∞™ The paper used in this publication meets the minimum requirements of American National Standard for Information Sciences—Permanence of Paper for Printed Library Materials, ANSI/NISO Z39.48-1992.

Printed in the United States of America

Contents

List of Figures

List of Tables

Acknowledgments

The need for a publication that centered on cultural heritage and related fields for library, archive, and museum professionals and scholars was originally recognized by Dr. Samantha Hastings, director of the University of South Carolina School of Library and Information Science, and Charles Harmon, editor at Rowman & Littlefield. Their encouragement and expertise continue to be important factors in the success of this series. Many, many thanks to both!

We also want to thank our contributors. Their good work is the heart of this volume, and without their enthusiasm, expertise, and persistence, this volume could not have been completed. Among these, special thanks go to Dr. Anna Maria Tammaro for introducing us to the IFLA Turin Conference contributors.

The editorial board also played an important role in this process, and their contributions as advisors, contributors, and peer reviewers are greatly appreciated. The list of the board members and their affiliations found in this volume reflects the diversity of their interests and the academic accomplishments—both of which were crucial to producing a volume that would be of interest to scholars from a variety of locations and disciplines. Among these, special thanks go to our Perspectives contributors for their thought-provoking questions and essays.

Lastly, we all know that no one works alone. In this case, the ideas that populate this volume and have guided its development clearly come from a rich and growing community of scholars and many formal and informal conversations. We are also very fortunate to have a great copyeditor among us, and Karen Miller deserves all of the praise and credit for this task as well as her many intellectual contributions. Karen, your expertise and assistance are greatly appreciated, and we look forward to working with you, our contributors, our advisory board, and our devoted scholarly community again!

Introduction

Now in its third edition, *The Annual Review of Cultural Heritage Informatics* continues to pursue its original objectives. The volume in hand is intended to shed light on the ways that we access, store, and preserve our cultural heritage. The contributions of our authors focus on the research and practices that nurture the field of cultural heritage informatics. Taken together, their work is intended to advance scholarly knowledge, keep reports of advances timely, and foster profitable discussion that will be of interest to scholars from a variety of locations and disciplines. The volume's mission, to provide an annual compilation that brings together current work in this field, is as important today as it was three years ago. We also persist in our commitment to maintaining an international perspective and encouraging the work of emerging scholars.

Former readers will also see some departures from the organization of earlier volumes. The first is the addition of a new *Perspectives* section intended to provide a forum for cultural heritage informatics scholars, practitioners, and leaders to share their insights on important issues. The guidelines for this section suggest that submissions reflect the authors' thoughts on an important challenge facing the cultural heritage field or pose a question of particular personal interest. Viewpoints are expected to be supported by observations and grounded in the authors' scholarly record or personal experience. Topics are expected to range widely from the preservation, study, and promotion of cultural heritage materials to issues related to responsibility, representation, collaboration, and leadership.

Three important submissions from our advisory board members met these criteria. In the first, Carr poses two fundamental questions related to user experiences. How does an institution enact the values and practices of open access and transmit them to users? How can the transactions begun in collections—and the reflections that follow these beginnings—serve the intellect of the place, the community, and the nation? Marty points to a related paradox: as collections become more open and easier to access, the less likely it is that people will understand and value the work required to make these resources available. Tamarro looks with more detail at the work required to produce cultural heritage resources with a particular focus on the theoretical and professional obstacles that hinder converging interests.

Issues related to the institutional convergence of libraries, archives, and museums (LAMs), as well as continuing public discourse (Erway, Hill, Streams, and Harmon, 2015; Berthiaume and Ryan, 2014; Marty, 2014), suggested the need for a section on this topic. Several of those submissions were originally presented at the peer-reviewed IFLA Turin Satellite Conference, and all approach their topic from a different perspective. Pattuelli's history of LODLAM development describes the emergence of a rich web of semantically linked data and suggests that productive solutions to problems in areas such as licensing, data trust and quality, and scalability of query processing are near. Aparac-Jelušić explores the possibility of developing a cross-theoretical foundation that provides a conceptual meeting place for converging practices. Crumpton's literature review combines references to the thoughts of important scholars with reflections concerning the use of strategic planning for curriculum development. Colombati, De Carolis, and Galeffi, and Russo and Leonardi offer case studies exploring successful convergence projects, while Michetti's analytic contribution uses a multidimensional matrix to provide a provocative look at current LAM education practices, the areas that suggest shared learning objectives, and those that appear to be clearly and perhaps necessarily distinguished from one another.

Rising interest in *big data* (Davenport and Patil, 2012; Ekbia et al., 2015; Frické, 2015), also suggested the need for exploration of this topic as it applies to cultural heritage informatics. Pymm, Carroll, McCausland, and Kennan provide several points of departure, beginning with the suggestion that big data poses particular challenges for the cultural heritage sector, including issues created by unstructured data, the inherent complexity of large datasets, and the possibility that current programming skills and educational initiatives may be inadequate to take full advantage of large-scale cultural heritage collections. Rorissa, Assefa, and Alemneh use sequence and thematic analysis of cultural heritage tweets related to the African tourist industry to provide an intriguing example of big-data research linking cultural heritage interests and economic development agenda.

Three submissions bring interesting perspectives to issues related to digital archives and special collections. In the first, Ayala presents a helpful theoretical typology that makes sense of the problems web archivists encounter when building and managing web archives. Schull's literature review approaches its subject from the community archives perspective, noting the need for more research in her discussion of successful projects. Welland's qualitative study provides a somewhat less sanguine observation when she notes that the New Zealand community archives she visited were appreciated by their communities but appeared to lack the resources needed to manage born digital materials effectively.

Finally, two submissions draw upon the wider definition of informatics provided by He (2003): an amalgamation of academic fields that links diverse perspectives concerning the nature of information and technology and the way that individuals bring these together to create and manage knowledge (p. 118). Pierce and Smith's chapter provides an unusual example of this type of informatics scholarship, as well as an intriguing glimpse at a late-nineteenth-century writer who used a relatively new technology, serial publication, to create a cultural icon that figured widely in the lives of young readers during that period. Returning to the present, Vamanu considers how media technologies and counter-narratives can be used for artistic purposes and better depiction and understanding of Native cultural heritage.

As a group, the contributors to the third edition share an optimistic stance. They agree that the technologies driving cultural heritage informatics will continue to mature and, in time, provide the robust infrastructure needed to support open access to cultural heritage resources and enrich the lives of those who live in small and large communities. On a more cautionary note, they also suggest that improvements in educational curricula are needed, that more original research is required, and that the availability of financial resources to support these activities will be critical to the success of future efforts.

REFERENCES

Berthiaume, G., and Ryan, P. (2014). Bibliotheque et Archives nationales du Quebec: Convergence and the path of innovation. *IFLA Journal*, *40*(3), 182–85.

Davenport, T. G., and Patil, D. J. (2012, October). Data scientist: The sexiest job in the 21st century. *Harvard Business Review*, 70–76.

Ekbia, H., Mattioli, M., Kouper, I., Aravel, G., Ghazinejad, A., Bowman, T., Sugimoto, C. R. (2015). Big data, bigger dilemmas: A critical review. *Journal of the Association for Information Science and Technology*, *66*(8), 1523–45.

Erway, R, Hill, C, Streams, S., and Harmon, S. (Eds.). (2015, April 28). *IMLS focus: The national digital platform for libraries, archives, and museums*. Washington, DC: Institute of Museums and Library Services. Retrieved from https://www.imls.gov/sites/default/files/publications/documents/2015imlsfocusndpreport.pdf

Frické, M. (2015). Big data and its epistemology. *Journal of the Association for Information Science and Technology*, *66*(4), 651–61.

He, S. (2003). Informatics: A brief survey. *The Electronic Library*, *21*(2), 117–22.

IFLA Turin Satellite (2014). *Theory and research on the convergence of professional identity in cultural heritage institutions (libraries, museums, and archives) beyond technology*. Library Theory and Research Section with ALISE, EUCLID, and Città di Torino, Biblioteche civiche, Torino. August 13–14, 2014.

Marty, P. (2014). Digital convergence and the information profession in cultural heritage organizations: Reconciling internal and external demands. *Library Trends*, *62*(3), 613–27.

Part I

PERSPECTIVES

Chapter One

Reflections on Practice in an Open Cultural Institution

Thinking Together in Provocative Places[1]

David Carr

When it opens itself to its users in a diverse community of knowledge, the capacity of a rich cultural institution is simultaneously formidable and promising, as complex and daunting to its users as it is intriguing and convivial. It is also formative and constructive. Strong institutions transmit concepts of evidence and experience, inquiry and experiment. People are thinking individually and becoming themselves here, each invisibly different from another. Museums, libraries, and archives construct complex situations for understanding the possibility of knowing more. When a cultural institution proclaims an embrace of openness and clear access, the visibility of knowledge and the formative intentions of a rich collection will expand. Openness, by its nature, is pervasive. Whatever its content or character, an open place will actively affect the future of knowledge and judgment among its present and virtual users, and awaken their tendency to reflect. But it is essential to ask, how does an institution enact the values and practices of open access and transmit them to users? How can the transactions begun in collections—and the reflections that follow these beginnings—serve the intellect of the place, the community, and the nation? How might conversations that begin with the objects and documents, and the traces of knowledge and experience, offer both continuity and inspiration for progress?

Everything I do or say about cultural institutions stands on my belief that there are thoughtful, capable, common people in this society whose horizons include complex, powerful, and lasting unknowns that do not inspire fear. In fact, they inspire something far different, an intellectual fearlessness embracing the intellectual, the historical, the ethical, the moral, and the aesthetic. I believe that such motives are more powerful than the economic and political motives in our headlines, and they have qualities to be touched, grasped, and trusted.

Such people, the many who live with wanting to know more, live authentic lives in a world that is neither remote nor ideal. They are visible every day, and certainly apparent in knowledge collections. Their questions may be humble and inarticulate, but their longing to know and understand something has power and value to them, and beyond them. There is a national value in the need to know more and seek more. Knowledge of the library, museum, or archive kind is best when it helps such people over time to be more engaged, more curious, more empathetic, and more reflective; less judgmental; more aware of the fragile; and less afraid of ambiguity. Such knowledge leads us to that rare thing: the long view of life on earth. The long view is the better, harder view; it is more difficult and requires a deeper world. Cultural institutions deepen the long view of history, and a long view of the self.[2]

If my reflections have the quality of a summary, it is perhaps due to an absence of work in a classroom. After leaving forty years of teaching, I found that I had also left a daily opportunity to create a reflective space together with my students, something between us in the themes we needed to define. Each class meeting was an opening that we could fill, where we might separate and organize our understandings. At best, a classroom is invented by each of us in response to the experience of thinking with others on a particular day. And now, retired, I believe that what happened in that space each day was for me the play and the promise of the possible.[3] Library practice was that way for me as well; service was a form of play, unpredictable and consequential. Without such days, I work at understanding what they contained, what they were.

Perforce, I take a long view. Whenever the day begins in a museum, a library, or an archive, I imagine the reality of the space that has just now appeared. It contains nothing before we speak and think with each other in it. And by our presence, the openness is immediately occupied and enlarged by everything we carry with us, and everything we think. Whether we use the cultural institution for scholarship or explore it for fresh experiences, we bring our entire lives, holding the many possessions that define us but we may find difficult to describe. I mean past experiences and proven expertise, the maze of things we may believe or doubt, the more forthright ideas we trust and value. Things we care for and tend in our memories, we may not yet have come to understand in full.

What is the state of curiosity in this space? How will we stir and deepen it? When a person arrives to use collections, the most important part of the mind's experience is also imminently present: the moment we recognize something never seen before. And then the mind connects and recalls, and thinks of questions, imagines contexts and finds words to say. So begins something that is not present unless the human being is present and thinking. As a museum user, I always try to begin with some small event or fresh discovery, a moment of attention for an object that draws me. This moment was not possible in my life before. That object did not exist in my experience before my attention. And then I ask, what am I to do with it? What has now become possible for me to do or think? How will the moment be unlocked and opened?

"Open" in my thinking means unfinished, improvisational, incomplete. A cultural institution is always an open work, completed in a particular way as it is experienced, a way that cannot be reproduced because it is woven into a private performance as we gaze in the presence of the new.[4] I have come to believe that what we casually and uncritically call *learning* is not a part of it; it is experiencing what is before us that matters before anything else matters. And it is thinking well, not learning something, that makes us different. Here is a place where content and its value are first performed by the user who stands inside the event, thinking. And then these experiences are re-performed (perhaps for the rest of one's life) as memories or stories or insights, in imaginations and recollections. *This thought*, we might say in the future, *was opened for me in the library (or museum, or archive) one day, and here is the difference it has made.*

So I want to turn the idea of the *open* from its relatively narrow meaning in the world of scholarly access to a concept much larger. Open access to a cultural institution includes its accumulated knowledge, responsive tools, and practitioners who live in a constant flow. It means that knowledge produced in the institution is open to all eyes, as evidence of its power and depth. Professionals and scholars, too, are living vessels of knowledge and instruments of change, serving and inspiring something that is always unfinished, always in process, mostly invisible, and certainly impossible to measure. How should we grow to think of ourselves as open, how to make practice visible and responsive, how to address unknowns that are not routine? Now I am thinking about the openness of an institution, the openness of its practices, and the idea of its service to the many unfinished, open lives in our nation.

My intention is to extend the ideas and values of an open-access environment to every user. I want to suggest that through its professionals, an institution's voice expresses the value of thinking and questioning freely. For the user, the experience of being here is also an experiment, and its possible effects are unknowable. After the experience of knowing an object or a document, I think it is possible that a user's story will differ just a bit, and—because of you—the user might have felt or seen the beginnings of a slightly different intellect. People use the museum in order to experience something, to see and sense something, and—uncertainly, tentatively, cautiously—to become something they have not been before.

I hope to recompose—to reconjure, if that is possible—a conversation around the concept of open access. I hope to draw your thinking toward the implications of an open environment for professional service, scholarship, and authentic advocacy for the user. The term, of course, is redundant. "Open" means accessible. "Access" implies openness. So it needs a better noun, and perhaps a different adjective as well.[5] As a librarian turned museum observer, when open access is talked about as a new information concept, I think of John Cotton Dana, who seems to have practiced it for the people of Newark at the start of the twentieth century, another time of excessive privilege and narrowed public access to resources and possibilities.

To reconjure the idea, I need to expand the lexicon: "open" means more than "freely shared." I think its most important meanings are "unformed," "malleable," "permeable," "expansive," "generative," "possible." These are also the characteristics of a democracy at its best, living up to its original promise, something unfinished and always under our design and construction. In a democracy, I think that the highest work of institutions is to create an open field for citizens to do the building, and to provide some of the lumber that democratic conversations require. This is what cultural institutions do. I dare to think it is never too late for this in a distressed society. If any institution is the place where our culture is made clear, where intellectual fear and mistrust are abated, where the oversimplification of the complex is revealed, where knowledge is not remote but imminent and permeable, and where our resistance to difficult conversations about ambiguities in a democracy can erode, I trust that place must be a museum, or it is a library.

In places created for knowledge, users appear, and they are alive with invisible, unspoken things. They bring all that has happened to them so far and all that they want to have happen still. Their lives appear in the open spaces of the museum and the library today. For all of us, an open world is arriving and waiting to be created and acknowledged. We have no idea what it will contain. We have no idea what will happen. We are all as one, observing, pausing, questioning, improvising. For me, this is where authentic experiences begin.[6]

The idea of openness is an environment of possibility that we occupy, not a place or a collection, so much as it is an invisible thing that is always about to happen. This invisible, impalpable concept fills the open space between us with immanence and anticipation. Our presence together makes this space new. Users of a great collection encounter a formidable, challenging space apart from their lives of predictable experience. Because both its content and situation are extraordinary—virtually limitless—it is a place where the capacity of lives and the integrity of thoughts can be proven. The invisible, inviting dimension of the museum asks us to be present and true to a given moment, even though what we want and what moves us forward in the open space may be difficult to see. No one anticipates this open place without questions and hopes.

In service as a librarian, I found that no matter what information or tools I gave to library users, it was the quality of the giving, the encouragement, what was said, how we talked together that always seemed to be at least equal in value.[7] As a teacher, and as an observer in museums, I came to learn that it is similarly the quality of the openness between us that defines our reciprocal and conversational transactions of knowledge and practice. The opportunity to approach and imagine, to pause and go back, to disassemble and reconstruct assists thinking and creates the promise of some active possibility. *Something*, we think, *could come of this*.

And something does. When a cultural institution proclaims an embrace of openness and clarity, the visibility of knowledge and the formative intentions of its collection should expand and unfold with more encounters, more talk, more exchange. In an open environment, the museum user looks for conviviality, landmarks, places of conversation, and common experiences that help to form questions. Never doubt that the journey to the collection is consequential to the user who undertakes it. Each life comes here to make and revise part of a cautious, tentative narrative of its own, original to the self that lives it, in a space that has been defined and constructed for them. To come here means that a person is creating something new in the story of one life, and the integrity of the place is an essential part of it.

For me, cultural institutions complete and repair the fragmented world. When our previous constructions of a life are pierced or broken, or inadequate, or when they are overturned by complex events, knowledge is a form of restoration, solace, and reconciliation. Among families and others, knowledge is a form of binding together, even if it is not joyous. In communities, without transmissions of fresh knowledge and art, entropy abides and stagnation takes us down. But knowledge restores; knowledge consoles. The open, active institution can change the model of the world we bring with us and compel us to take a fresh and maybe rougher view of our lives from a different angle. By changing our cognitive geometry, the museum or the library alters the mirror of the self. *How must I think in the presence of the complex, or in the presence of the unknown?* When any of us can speak within ourselves about changing our capacity to know things and think things, we have begun to write a new story of the self. The great collection, the great museum, is also an opening in the lives of its users.

My work in this reflection is to address what that opening in users' lives might mean, and to bring to mind the value of cultural institutions in a democracy. I want many things to happen in museums, archives, and libraries. Here are some of them:

- I believe that **conversations** should occur in cultural institutions that address matters of ethics, government, and public life; we can address the tensions of history as experienced in the lives of Americans; we can talk about the nature of knowledge and the reflective intellect; we can alter our reading practices and our talking practices. We can learn to see processes that we cannot otherwise see: narratives of exploration and courage that can make empirical differences in how we imagine other lives than our own. We can discuss the historic fabric of ideas, and how we have gotten things wrong and sometimes right, and (in the long view) how every person encounters the challenge of telling the difference.
- It is a purpose of information professionals, collections, and tools to assist users to **go beyond** the information and the place, to other collections, and to cultural institutions worldwide. There are reference tools that assist in constructing bold maps, and there are handheld tools to be designed—a social or civic Wikipedia—that explore the nature of knowledge and its applications in public life. Thinking in this way, a museum can develop public awareness of current explorations and recent discoveries; it can describe the many unknowns that still claim us. Here, knowledge, knowing, and acts of minding—John Dewey used the word "mind" as a verb—can be the primary theme of every experience.
- Whenever a cultural institution brings **the day's news** and **the ongoing crises of human experience** into the building—explorations of health, languages, environment, folkways, migrations, domestic lives worldwide—a compelling case for knowledge can be made, based on the idea that the world beyond the museum continues to evolve. In my view, institutions or collections should curate large and small evidence of the daily state of changing populations, communities in both erosion and triumph, the losses of languages and cultures, the signs of endangered nature and the worldwide biosphere, explorers of frontiers on earth and above it, historic discoveries and reinterpretations, archaeological finds, and worldwide biological and health research. Much of what happens in the living world today should be brought to awareness in our cultural institutions, where its contexts and antecedents are documented and where we might stimulate an increase in thinking for the long run of human life and civilization.
- For the strongest themes in a collection, I advocate that we **curate the progress of information**, explore the most important open research ques-

tions, identify major research tools and databases, and reveal how specialists and scholars think. An institution should lead users to provocative ideas and breakthrough publications. It should demonstrate the infrastructures of knowledge and inquiry that create new knowledge and nurture fresh thoughts. Throughout this space, questions ought to appear: *How do we know this? How important is this? What remains unknown? What is the difference to be grasped? How do I find out more?*

- Any librarian knows that the most compelling intellectual activity does not respect academic disciplines, but draws from an interdisciplinary world. Among its sponsored conversations, an institution's open aspect ought to sponsor settings where scholars in dialogue can pull out the most interesting threads that tie common themes. And yet, such interaction will address the complexity of living systems and social interactions. For all citizens, a grasp of complexity and context can be a revelation. In these contexts, where there are no easy answers, children need to see curious adults thinking and talking together.
- Collections should select a public bookshelf of guides to the ideas that form collections and the inquiry that happens in them. What concepts cross these collections? Migration, community, tools, families, adaptation? What ways of thinking—historical, anthropological, aesthetic—inform the world addressed here? A **selective, well-stocked bookstore** nearby could provide current, diverse, accessible nonfiction and history works in affordable formats, tied to concepts at hand. Live and virtual **book conversations** would naturally follow. The intellect at the center of the cultural institution can take on a public face in this way.

To these advocacies, I will later add one more *desideratum*, and it is a simple idea: the creation of **an open heuristic**, a sequence of naïve but essential questions for useful thinking in the presence of the unknown, applicable by any user in any institution anywhere.

I think we live in an ambiguous sphere where much that is vital has been made unstable and unpredictable, national ethos is in flux, and we have become distant from common strengths and capabilities. For me, the questions we need most to address have no answers online and only partially on paper. And so, a lifetime after starting out as a teacher in my open classroom—a failure of hubris and inexperience—I have come to see that we still require an open place for contemporary thinking, with all the slowness and deliberation needed to think well, and all the information and depth only thoughtful citizens and committed professionals in great cultural institutions can bring to the conversation. The values of my classroom fifty years ago might well be useful for adults today.

Think of what begins each day in our cultural institutions. Human beings enter with bundles of memories and anticipations of fresh experiences; the museum draws them right up to the edge of what they know and what they can say. Perhaps they can step beyond that edge to think again or recombine what they know with something new. To think clearly of other lives, think first of your own life: how you remember and anticipate, and how you mind each other and mind the world. So much of our vast collections of the visible and tangible is about the purely imagined thing, a concept or a principle, a motive or a symbol—diversity, recovery, injustice, invention, daring—and so it is always useful to consider what you cannot see. How do these invisible things appear in the experiences of others? Think of the mind moving from the visible evidence to the invisible suggestion, connecting and broadening, finding a metaphor or an image, then asking a question, or restoring briefly the situations and contexts of other times and places. There are invitations to think beyond the moment everywhere.

When I imagine other lives, I think of a personal process—or struggle—to find words, to hold images in mind, to connect fragments, and to link them to the continuing themes of one life. The purpose of being in a cultural institution is not to *learn* anything but to *think* anything and to follow the thought. It is a formidable institution. More important, it is a formative institution, an instrument of opening and unfolding something in the human imagination that remains beyond the moment.

We must think more closely about lives and their aspirations. When I began to observe in cultural institutions, I thought of them as public settings left open for people to walk in and out, making observations and having thoughts. Then I began to see them less as brilliant gatherings of collections, and more as forums for the collective mind stirring among users, all of them thinking and becoming something together at once, each engaged in "the play of the possible." In any museum or library, it was the quality of the stirring among its users that enticed me to think about them, to think with them, and this still remains for me the objective of my observations.

Among users, I too became a different person, I imagined the unfinished lives of others, and the unfinished issues that configured their experiences, just as I did my own. These are the matters that shape us over time, that come to us early perhaps, in our families, our schools, in our experiences of faith and ethics, our caring for others, the subtle complexities and confusions of feeling, the losses and successes of becoming adult, of enduring experiences. Because these unfinished issues are complex and definitive for us, they do not disappear and they retain their power for us regardless of how vigorously we pursue them. In some ways, they design our attention and the events that give us a sense of agency and purpose. Every person who enters any cultural institution carries an array of unfinished issues. They are not simple, and they are not accidental.

I came to believe that people want knowledge in their lives and in their own hands, not because knowledge is power, but because knowledge is possibility. Here, the contexts of human lives are always in play, never static. As I moved through museums, I asked myself questions in search of those contexts and how to respond to the possibilities. *Is this something I have the capacity to understand? Is knowledge of this kind within my reach? How has my life prepared me to grasp it? How must I change my thinking?* I do not doubt that my grandchildren, three and younger, ask questions of this kind in some form, and look for someone nearby, as we all do, to be a source of courage and fearlessness.[8]

My intention still is to inspire questioning lives, people finding their edges and moving across them fearlessly. I believe that it is an ethical necessity for cultural institutions to do this, because it is clearly a critical time for intelligence in our democracy. A difficult time for being in public schools as teacher or student.[9] A difficult time for science and effective public policy. A difficult time for knowledge and decisions related to public health, the degraded environment, the preservation of life. A difficult time for ethics, trust, empathy, generosity. A difficult time for higher education. And as always, a difficult time for adults, out of school, who want to change their minds and lives for reasons of work and prosperity, but also for vitality, self-renewal, and personal integrity. Personally, I worry about the many appearances of small thinking and the generalized fear of intellect in American life, especially fear that nourishes undemocratic impulses. These are all parts of what a cultural institution addresses in a democracy.

And so: think of lives. What would be the effect of Americans across the nation who suddenly have an increased tendency to say, "I have the capacity to ask this question." Or, "I am capable of being a critical thinker." Or, "I need to know more about that." Or, "I need to find a book (a trusted source, an expert who knows) about that." Think of what it would mean to any museum or library if each user, each day, uttered one previously unspoken question aloud. Think with me of lives in one more way. Think of your mother's life, your father's life. Think of your grandparents and their parents. Suddenly, we are now deep into the past by one or two centuries. Do not think abstractly about their lives; think of what they experienced and how these experiences created their anticipations of the world, their frames of reference, challenges and sorrows, the schooling they completed or did not get, the work they loved or endured, the jobs won and lost, their families and marriages and relationships, the places they called home, the variables of family structure, and their lasting challenges and comforts.

When we do this, we understand that lives are composed of variable, continuous strands of experience, inevitably interwoven and at once potentially empowering and demonstrably fragile. They are different for each of us. Embedded in these strands, they shape us and guide our thinking. We know the contexts that have most meaning and the parts of our lives we must continue to explain to ourselves. And from these places, we ask questions and look for connections to what we know and what we might still become.

The continuities of one life cannot be fully observed or known, except from within the life. All the strands that compose one life evolve differently. All strands are connected and potentially equivalent in holding power over our aspirations. Events in the context of one strand have effects on other life strands. Consequently, no plan will last for long, no awareness will be untouched by others. When people arrive in need of knowledge, they may be in the midst of crises, accidents, and aspirations because they are alive and their questions and unfinished issues make them ready and open for new information. All of these desires will remain unknown until we think and ask about lives and offer ways to deepen and extend their grasp.[10]

Openness is our great virtue. For me, what is definitive about our nation's experience is its open character, our audacious exploration of knowledge unmitigated by privilege or ownership. Where that impulse exists, it refreshes our scholarship, inspires our art and language, and writes a fluent record for our culture. Every cultural institution has a place in that ethos because each one is devoted to honing the edge of an evolving life. We steadily try out our knowledge of the world; we use it to build more and make more out of what we have been given and what we have hewn ourselves. It appears to be part of our historic character to reimagine everything, to remake and reinvent and possess the past on our own terms.

We imagine and build institutions because we are part of the American impulse to engage in an open way with forms and practices. Cultural institutions are ways we have created to think with each other in the presence of our great narratives of hope and possibility. My thinking in libraries and museums has caused me to reimagine the capacity of these institutions for sponsoring self-renewal, especially among American adults whose voices and experiences are rarely expressed in dialogue with each other.

I can offer no blueprint for the convivial thinking that has not yet happened in American life. However I believe that we will see evidence of one soon, in the opening of the National Museum of African American History and Culture on the National Mall. I cannot imagine a more necessary place at a more necessary time. In addition to the evidence of experience it will offer to us all, there is a fresh record to be made of museum users naming the salience of that place for themselves, anticipating the conversations it will provoke with their peers and their families because of what they have seen of the past and themselves there. If you do not believe in the collective vitality of thinking together and becoming something together, that museum might cause you to think again, as that large building will become an intimate personal space for countless citizens. They will go to the museum on a particular day and use the unfinished parts of history to find themselves, and to look deeply around for resonance and wholeness that cannot be erased. Here, as everywhere in cultural institutions, the objects and narratives will mean most in their traces. In my view, the sudden unexpected transfer of past experiences, past voices, and still unforgotten aspirations into the moving and living currents of the present is the purpose of great museums.

Assume that every person who enters this new space wants something to occur in it that deepens and sustains them and evokes something elusive or lost in the past. An insight, a connection, a revelation, a suggestion, something overlooked, something forgotten and worth recovering and reexamining. Such fresh moments can become parts of the individual's future: a conversation with family, a new book to be read, an unexpected idea that persists over time. A voice, a vibration, an image. Assume as well that we do not often have the words to say what it is we are looking for, or what it is that might change our understanding of our experience. Recognize that not one of these persons who will arrive at the museum is likely to predict or describe the event or moment that needs to happen for them, because no one can. But those moments will happen in places of trust—places of ambiguity and tension, certainly—but also places for fearless thought. We are stronger and more competent than we think, once we are open to possibility. As Annie Dillard says, "We live in all we seek."[11]

Consequently, our lives say this: when we know something, we can become something, we can do something, we can think something. My advocacy is for steady steps to assure that the democratic motive inevitably ascends in all cultural collections. The means of ascension are common. Knowledge needs voices and contexts beyond the labels, giving less data but more story. Data must be given context and origins. Voices and traces should be present to offer contexts, neither curatorial nor didactic in tone. What will the voices say, and what paths will they trace? What thinking should they stir? What does the museum want to stimulate in its users? Nothing happens here unless something provocative is stirring the intellect in the unexpected privacy created by a museum voice.

Even in great collections, something is meant to be overturned. As readers, we are drawn to works about overturned lives. If we want to see aspects of the infinite in the consequences of everyday lives and understandings, we need to overturn something that is conventional in order to see its underside.[12] Our understandings of ourselves can change and challenge us best when conventions and expectations are overturned.

No dedicated inquirer is still, within. A question is a way of moving forward. And in the great collections we keep, something is always open and continues to move. Human lives are changing, permeable, variable, and consequential as they move forward in inquiry. Something is always moving along the strands of an individual life, in intellect and values and in the imagination of the possible. Without a place for this motion, our lives would not grow. Without this place and its collections, certain events would never occur, deep experiences would be lost. What knowledge, what curious questions would disappear? What connections would be missed?

Our institutions and their greatest powers in service to the nation thrive best in the open conversations that can take place in them about knowledge and its origins in inquiry and connection. Inquiry and connection: because knowledge has neither meaning nor use without an active knower, one who holds it and acts on it and explores its combinatory qualities. I believe that connection to a user's imagination, ethics, and consciousness will gradually loosen the grasp of magical and uncritical thinking and open the complexity of an authentic world to view. The democratic motive, realized, invites engagement and thought toward self-renewal and the rise of the free intellect among us, with deep and continuous implications for public life and thought.

And so, as I would ask of my students, how do you practice to serve intellect in a cultural institution? How do you nourish other minds? What is the tension of the unknown in your lives? What is your capacity to ask good questions, where "good" means "useful and provocative"? What do others ask? What is the value of thinking about differences among us? What happens when two minds meet? When we understand differences in the thoughts and experiences of others, how do our lives become more complex? What is the value of ambiguity and questioning to the intellect? We may learn the open ways of cultures for ourselves when we craft a process.

Our questions are instruments for breaking through routine performances and uncritical observations whenever they occur. If our work might transfer a useful question—or a set of useful questions—to those who are its users, it is a great gift that follows and inspires. Look around in the collection and ask, "How does knowledge matter here? What questions does it illuminate?" How do you want to provoke the play of the possible that good questions inevitably generate? What effect do you want to have on public discourse about science, the social and historical record, the health of our conversations, our fearlessness before art, our courage in the complex world? These are decisions to think of every day, even knowing that there is no end to them.

A librarian knows that a question is an engine of language that moves and directs attention in probing ways, starting at the surface of things, but then going deep. Long ago, I wrote a user's heuristic to be applied in any museum, following the idea that a problem-solving challenge can be opened up by thinking.[13] A heuristic is a way to manage hesitation, uncertainty, and complexity. It allows us tentative, experimental, even improvisational thoughts, especially useful when we are looking at something we have never seen before.

> *What has been brought here? What ideas accompany it? How promising are these ideas in the light of my interests? What is nearby? How does my thinking change when looking at more than one thing? Where is the center of the collection? How will I recognize the difficult parts of this experience? How have I met such challenges before? What are my new questions now?*

Our most naïve questions often work best. What is going on here? What memories are brought to mind? How might I use them to move forward? Naïve questions, assuming nothing, turn the inquirer into a stranger, say, someone who has never seen a seashell before.[14] They take away easy assumptions and subtract the element that obscures much of our lived reality, the taken-for-granted, and the mass of knowledge grounded in self-assurance alone. What is expected of me here? How can I think of this experience? Where are the words I need most?

As a librarian and as an observer in cultural collections, I know I asked these questions repeatedly over time. Here are users observing objects and speaking about them to each other. How might their experience be deepened and extended? How do people who ask large and challenging questions think? What do they see hidden among ordinary possibilities and mundane explanations? What evidence do they see that promises something more to be known? How does an intellect become engaged by a problem? How does inquiring attention differ when its object is a natural, historical, social, or aesthetic idea? How fully must conventional thinking be overturned for a mind to work well in this open space? What questions will engage users here, cause them to pause, and challenge them most?

I believe that evidence, when accompanied by imagination and courage, can evoke the unexpected steps we require in order to explore the strands of our lives. Complexity is what we are given every day and every day our insights grow from exploring it. It is possible to think that a mind is infinitely renewable, and in the midst of knowledge always capable of extending itself in order to find itself. Capable of using a museum collection, a library, an archive in order to think without limits. Capable of discovering its undercurrents. Capable of going beyond the museum and thinking elsewhere. Capable of breaking through, using evidence to discover a compelling story for the unexpected, evolving self.

Among the great complexities of service to the intellect and integrity of a community and a nation, I have hoped to address the need for cultural institutions to be permeable and generous in their invitations to citizens, and to make the changing presence and influence of knowledge essential to their everyday thoughts and deliberations. I see the evidence everywhere that the professionals of museums, libraries, and archives are uncompromising advocates for intellect, thought, and connection and that their ethos of generosity is undiminished. It is an extension of our responsibility to give fitting and useful knowledge to users without restriction as a right of free inquiry in a democracy. This is, to me, how a great cultural institution regards itself as an instrument of living culture, stimulating progress, identity, and the responsibly informed self in a culture that has sometimes denied them. In my thinking, if citizens are to become something together, it will be by what we think and say to ourselves and to others in safe, open spaces where knowledge is most alive. And this is how the trust of great public cultural institutions is linked fundamentally to justice.

NOTES

1. This chapter was first delivered as an address to the librarians of the Smithsonian Institution, at the S. Dillon Ripley Center on February 26, 2015.

2. *The History Manifesto*, by Jo Guldi and David Armitage (Cambridge: Cambridge University Press, 2014) argues for the long view of history, asserting that new ways of managing historical data allow "new patterns of imagination" and critical perspectives never possible before. The book can be downloaded without cost at the Cambridge University Press site: http://historymanifesto.cambridge.org/download/.

3. Martin Buber refers to play as "the exultation of the possible." Among the most important books in my library is *The Play of the Unmentionable*, the monograph accompanying Joseph Kosuth's installation at the Brooklyn Museum in 1990. My use of "play" is similarly an adult use, intended to imply improvisation and the imprecise variables essential to open places and conversations.

4. For more on this theme, see my essay, "A Museum Is an Open Work," first published in *The Journal of Heritage Studies* in 2001 and republished in *The Promise of Cultural Institutions* (Walnut Creek, CA: AltaMira Press, 2003).

5. Here is a situation where replacing a phrase might do wonders for the idea it attempts to capture. (See also "net neutrality" and "educational achievement" as examples of public terms whose meanings have been made elusive by the politicization of the words themselves.)

6. Throughout this text, I use collective pronouns like "we" and "us" without specifying their antecedents with sufficient clarity. My audience for this talk com-

prises museum and library professionals, but "we" also will refer to museum users and those who dwell apart from museums. "We are all as one" means that each of us possesses curiosity, recollection, and aspiration, though our relationships to the museum may differ.

7. See Carr, D. (1986, Fall). Meanings of the adult independent library learning project. *Library Trends*, *35*(2): 327–45.

8. The theme of a helping agent in museums, parallel to the agency of librarians in libraries, has been important to me in every way. The importance of Lev Vygotsky's description of the "zone of proximal development" is, in my experience, unequaled in the literature of teaching. (See *Mind in Society: Development of Higher Psychological Processes* [Cambridge, MA: Harvard University Press, 1978.]) The larger and more documented concept of apprenticeship is superbly developed by Barbara Rogoff in *Apprenticeship in Thinking* (New York: Oxford University Press, 1990). A related concept, situated learning, is addressed by Jean Lave and Etienne Wenger in *Situated Learning: Legitimate Peripheral Participation* (Cambridge: Cambridge University Press, 1991). I strongly recommend two works of importance to my thinking: Jerome Bruner's *Actual Minds, Possible Worlds* (Cambridge, MA: Harvard University Press, 1986), and Maxine Greene's *The Dialectic of Freedom* (New York: Teachers College Press, 1988).

9. Commentaries about the political status of schooling in America are abundant and worthy of debate. One might begin with the recent work of Diane Ravitch, "Making Schools Poor," *New York Review of Books*, June 13, 2014, examining state funding for education (http://www.nybooks.com/blogs/nyrblog/2014/jun/13/making-schools-poorer/). Other topics mentioned here are also documented widely. On these and other issues, including the public understanding of science, economic disparity, communication habits, and demographic changes, the work of the Pew Research Center (http://www.pewresearch.org) is worthy of professional attention. Its recent report on U.S. adult perceptions of science (http://www.pewinternet.org/2015/01/29/public-and-scientists-views-on-science-and-society/) describes disparities between scientists' beliefs and those of the public. For all cultural institutions, I strongly recommend its April 2014 report about emerging profiles of the American population, "The Next America" (http://www.pewresearch.org/next-america/).

10. This paragraph is largely taken from a chart titled "Strands: Continuities and Possibilities of One Life," on page 60 of my book, *Open Conversations: Public Learning in Libraries and Museums* (Santa Barbara, CA: Libraries Unlimited, 2011). A version of this chart was added to the web announcement for this lecture.

11. Annie Dillard, *For the Time Being*, New York: Vintage, 2000, p. 172.

12. See my essay, "An Aspect of the Infinite: New Zealand Talks," *Curator*, *53*(1), 51–70, January 2010.

13. The idea of a heuristic for the museum is based on G. Polya's book, *How to Solve It* (second ed., Princeton, NJ: Princeton University Press, 1957). I first discussed the concept in an essay published in the Fall 1991 issue of *Teachers College Record*, and republished in my book, *A Place Not a Place: Reflection and Possibility in Museums and Libraries* (Walnut Creek, CA: AltaMira Press, 2006). The relevance and value of Frank Smith's book, *To Think* (New York: Teachers College Press,

1990) are difficult to overstate. Readers interested in relationships between thinking and creativity should see, among other works, Vera John-Steiner's *Notebooks of the Mind: Explorations of Thinking* (Albuquerque: University of New Mexico Press, 1985).

14. I first read Paul Valery's essay, "Man and the Seashell," published in his collected works, when I was an undergraduate. A grounding in aesthetic questions, it can be read here: http://monoskop.org/images/e/ed/Valery_Paul_An_Anthology.pdf.

Chapter Two

The Cobbler's Children

Invisible Work and Information Professionals in Museums

Paul F. Marty

In January 2003, Florida governor Jeb Bush, facing severe budget cuts, proposed that the State Library and Archives be disbanded, its staff fired, and its collection of nearly a million books and documents given away. Fortunately, the professional community responded quickly, rallying sufficient support to save the State Library and Archives from the budget axe.

As a relatively new transplant to Tallahassee, I followed the events with some trepidation, because the building that housed the State Library and Archives also housed the Museum of Florida History, a fact that had apparently slipped the minds of the rallying public. Why, I wondered, was nobody asking what was going to happen to the museum?

It was rarely mentioned in newspaper articles at the time (Associated Press, 2003; Roberts, 2003). People knew about the museum; they loved the giant armadillo and dugout canoe, the steamship replica and Spanish artillery. But when push comes to shove, "Save the museum too!!" does not make for a good rallying cry. Again, why?

The answer to my question, I believe, lies firmly rooted in the field of cultural heritage informatics. Information professionals in libraries (and to a lesser extent, archives) have worked hard to help the public understand what happens in those institutions. Information professionals in museums, on the other hand, are often more focused on providing information about their collections than explaining their role in modern society. Thus, while people had some sense of what they might lose if the State Library and Archives closed, it was harder to say what would happen if they lost the museum. What do they do in there anyway? If we need to save money, couldn't the staff be replaced by security guards to keep the exhibits safe, and janitors to keep the cases clean? If not, why not?

Why not, indeed. Over the past few decades, museum professionals of all types, and information professionals in particular, have worked tirelessly to make themselves invisible, while simultaneously enabling their visitors to access information about their collections, anytime, anywhere. As a result, museum information professionals face a stark paradox: the easier they make it for people to access their museum's information resources, the harder they make it for people to understand how much work is involved in making those resources available (Marty, 2012, 2014).

To be fair, all memory institutions, including libraries, archives, and museums, face this problem; many people falsely believe that "if it's free for me to access, it must be free for you to create." But with libraries, people at least think they know what librarians do (they are usually wrong, of course, but at least they think about it), whereas with museums, people happily admit they have no idea what goes on in there. Everyone loves museums, but few people know what museum professionals actually do, especially behind the scenes, and while one might love a good mystery, it can be hard to support something one doesn't understand.

Connecting people and information about cultural heritage collections is an admirable goal, but it can also be dangerous if one's efforts to create high-quality, well-organized information resources remain relatively invisible and largely uncredited (especially to funding agencies and governing bodies). As long as people believe their easy access to your museum's collections just magically appeared—no thanks to your invisible work—there is always the danger that someone will ask, "Why are you important? What were your contributions? and Who are you anyway?"

Much has been done to try to change this. From the #AskACurator tag on Twitter (Pearson, 2014) to museum outreach programs in bars (Kiessner, 2009), there have been many attempts to raise public consciousness that museum work matters. But whether any of this raises awareness of the actual work that happens in museums is another question. To be sure, when a museum is directly attacked, such as Governor Rauner's recent attempt to shut down the Illinois State Museum (Burnett, 2015), people flock to support it. But do they really understand what happens in museums?

Much of what museums do has been invisible for a long time. Every museum professional has a story about someone who visits a museum with free admission, and comments, "These exhibits are great! You could totally charge for this!" Even worse, the invisible nature of museum work has done little to address the growing divide between people who feel museums are for them and people who feel museums are for someone else—a problem that Michelle Obama recently addressed when she argued for museums to be more inclusive (Incluseum, 2015).

Unfortunately, the more we look at visitors' understanding of information work in museums, the worse things get. In the late 2000s, when many museums were uploading images to the Flickr Commons project, there was hope that such efforts would increase understanding of museum information work. Sadly, while Flickr users were delighted to have these images available—the Smithsonian, for example, found that their images received more views in three months on Flickr than they had during the previous five years on the Smithsonian's website (Kalfatovic, Kapsalis, Spiess, Van Camp, and Edson, 2009)—almost no one bothered to find out who created them or where they came from.

At this point, one might well ask, does it matter? Many museum professionals prefer to let their objects speak for themselves, and work hard to make themselves invisible to the general public. Unfortunately, while individually it might be fine to say, "I'm just happy that people are using my stuff," institutionally it is an entirely different ballgame, especially when public funds are involved. When tough budgetary decisions need to be made, it's easy to attack things people don't understand.

Many who are good at sharing information about the things that others have done resist sharing information about their own efforts to make those same resources available. Is it possible to encourage museum information professionals to make their own contributions clear, while simultaneously meeting the information needs of a general public that wants increasingly unlimited access to everything, with as few barriers as possible, and all of it for free? Cannot information professionals in museums highlight their own contributions and admit that they too have an influence on the society they serve? Or are museum information professionals doomed to become like the cobbler's children, constantly providing information about others for others while their own contributions to the betterment of humanity go unrecognized?

To achieve this goal, we need to stop pretending that our nation's cultural heritage information resources are created by magic elves—armed with enchanted scanners and paid in floor sweepings. It is my belief that the solution to the challenge we face exists within us all, museum professionals and museum visitors alike. The best way to make information work in museums visible is to develop connections with museum visitors that align with those of museum professionals, thereby involving everyone in the co-curation process as consumers and producers of museum information resources. By leveraging the ways in which visitors use collections information resources outside the museum, we can find new ways to make information work inside the museum more visible.

REFERENCES

Associated Press. (2003, January 25). Gov. Bush proposes closing state library to save money. *Gainesville Sun*. Retrieved from http://www.gainesville.com/article/20030125/NEWS01/201250318

Burnett, S. (2015, August 31). Illinois State Museum is latest target in political fight. *State Journal-Register*. Retrieved from http://www.sj-r.com/article/20150831/NEWS/150839930

Incluseum. (2015). Michelle Obama, activism, and museum employment. *The Incluseum*. Retrieved from http://incluseum.com/2015/05/12/michelle-obama-activism-and-museum-employment-part-i/

Kalfatovic, M. R., Kapsalis, E., Spiess, K. P., Van Camp, A., and Edson, M. (2009). Smithsonian team Flickr: A library, archives, and museums collaboration in web 2.0 space. *Archival Science*, *8*(4), 267–77.

Kiessner, E. (2009). Drinking it up: Museum outreach extends to the pub. *Museum*, *88*(3), 56–59. Retrieved from http://aam-us.org/resources/publications/museum-magazine/drinking-it-up

Marty, P. F. (2012). Unintended consequences: Unlimited access, invisible work, and the future of the information profession in cultural heritage organizations. *Bulletin of the American Society for Information Science and Technology*, *38*(3), 27–31.

Marty, P. F. (2014). Digital convergence and the information profession in cultural heritage organizations: Reconciling internal and external demands. *Library Trends*, *62*(3), 613–27.

Pearson, G. (2014, September 16). It's ask a curator day! *Wired*. Retrieved from http://www.wired.com/2014/09/ask-curator-day/

Roberts, D. (2003, February 8). Bush winces at price tag on state history. *St. Petersburg Times*. Retrieved from http://www.sptimes.com/2003/02/08/Opinion/Bush_winces_at_price_.shtml

Chapter Three

Convergence or Cooperation?

An IFLA Satellite about Professional Identity in Cultural Heritage Institutions (LAM—Libraries, Museums, and Archives) beyond Technology

Anna Maria Tammaro

DIGITAL CONVERGENCE

About twenty years ago, Rayward (1998) was the first to anticipate the issue of digital convergence, challenging today's librarians, archivists, and museum curators with the need for them to deliver the integrated, seamless level of service that tech-savvy users were increasingly coming to expect. Jenkins has recently further analyzed the concept of digital convergence (2006), describing it as on three levels: convergence of support-like instruments of transmission, participatory culture, and collective intelligence. For Jenkins, digital convergence is a sector wherein diverse actors find that they must collaborate in a different way from the traditional print artifacts workflow tested over centuries. It is thus necessary to not only consider the technological impact but also to rethink entirely the traditional relationships among the players involved, implicating social, organizational, cultural, and industrial changes. Leaders of the private sector of cultural heritage see opportunities in aggregating digital content accessible directly by the user through many channels, in order to increase earnings and expand markets. At the same time, the users continue to look for increased access to a public sphere and "open access," free of passwords and network controls in a broad digital environment. At times, the tendencies of private enterprise and public institutions reinforce each other, creating closer relationships and with results advantageous to the creators of content, suppliers of services, and users. At other times, the private businesses, public cultural institutions, and the users are at loggerheads.

Today cultural institutions find themselves facing this completely changed context, which is difficult to understand for conservative and traditional structures like libraries, archives, and museums. Digital convergence is seen above all in the first technological sense: convergence of digital content. Some disciplinary boundaries, such as the types of artifacts in the collection, books or documents, text or artwork, or archival folders, have been overruled by the increasing access and use by users of digital copies or digital resources.

Above and beyond the technology there is the risk of overlooking the users' change of perspective, wanting to be free to choose and to be more involved in the managing as well as accessing and use of the digital heritage. Recently Paul Marty (2014) affirmed:

> In a world where the traditional assumptions we take for granted about information organization and access in libraries, archives, and museums are simply not shared by our users, the future of the information profession depends on the ability of cultural heritage information professionals to transcend the traditional boundaries between libraries, archives, and museums to meet information needs in the digital age.

Trant (2009) adds that professionals will survive positioning themselves as trusted sources and avoiding the risk of getting lost in the meandering labyrinths of social media. Who are the protagonists to consider for the libraries, archives, museums? They are now professional information technology operators, archivists, librarians, conservators and curators, jurists, and experts in the economy of culture: all of them involved in the organization of information and knowledge creation.

During the first UNESCO Conference in Vancouver (2012), it became evident that there are diverse obstacles to cooperation among these actors in the cultural heritage sector. There remains a culture of "isolated silos," divergent interests between creators of content in private industries and in cultural institutions that decide to undertake preservation, and also little ability to manage the technological and organizational changes. Thus, digital convergence poses a series of challenges to cultural institutions, requiring changes that go far beyond technological adjustments.

IFLA AND DIGITAL CONVERGENCE

IFLA (International Federation of Library Associations) in 2007 set up a "working group on convergence," initially headed by Ingrid Parent. When Parent became president of IFLA, Lynne Rudasill assumed the chair of the Professional Committee. IFLA's approach to convergence is well stated in its ethical code: the profession of librarian is to provide access to information. Convergence is thus intended as understanding how digital technologies can provide better access to cultural heritage. The IFLA Working Group decided that the goal of digital convergence is to employ the fullest potential of digital technology to enrich the user experience by enabling seamless access to all types of information without limits to format or geography.

The first step of the working group was to invite collaboration among professionals in the cultural heritage sectors in order to encourage digital convergence, and in 2008, the group began a collaboration with other international professional associations such as ICA (Archives), ICOM (Museums), ICOMS (Monuments and Sites), and CCAAA (Audiovisual Archives). In fact, all the international professional associations are facing the same challenge.

In 2009, the working group took the title *LAMMS Co-ordinating Council* and began a series of periodic meetings. The results of the LAMMS group have been concentrated on common political problems. The first collaborative project looked at copyright exceptions for cultural institutions, in which the LAMMS Group collaborated in obtaining exceptions for cultural institutions by negotiating with WIPO (World International Property Organization). Another communal effort has been in putting pressure on politicians for correct management of cultural goods within the activity carried out with UNESCO's Blue Shields. The LAMMS Group also dealt with technical procedures such as preservation and standards for global digital libraries. For example, in its first convention in The Hague the LAMMS group discussed a roadmap for preservation as defined in the Vancouver Declaration, together with UNESCO and the University of British Columbia.

One early investigation by the IFLA Working Group showed that collaboration between the three professions is mostly based on projects. The report by IFLA at the end of the study identified numerous projects among archives, libraries, and museums carried out for the most part at a local level and only in the more developed nations. All the projects were concentrated on online access as, for example, search engines for integrated searching of material held or for the collaborative construction of digital collections. The majority of collaborative projects among archives, libraries, and museums were meant to accompany temporary events, like expositions of resources in the collection. Another common type of collaborative project lies in integrated services such as, for example, creating virtual spaces for learning, especially for projects of mass digitization. Using these results, IFLA identified the different roles and responsibilities of the actors involved, advantages and disadvantages of collaboration, and some elements to be taken into consideration to ensure the success of the projects.

In synthesis, is there an advantage to converging the three professions? Certainly the greater benefit of convergence as evidenced in all the projects studied is in the sharing of resources, whether human, instrumental (viz.

infrastructures), or financial. The increased efficiency resulting from sharing brings improved user service.

If convergence, understood as the sharing of resources, is so advantageous, what are the obstacles to its use? The IFLA Working Group on convergence of the IFLA governing board in 2012 held a conference at Helsinki, "Libraries, Archives, Museums—Exploring the Changing Landscape," in which projects of mass digitization and the impact of indigenous knowledge were discussed. The Helsinki Conference pointed up the difficult balance between local and international interests: the cultural heritage is often housed in historic buildings that have a symbolic meaning for cultural identity, and in some cases the aggregation of digital content is perceived as having a negative impact on local culture.

Another obstacle to digital convergence is seen in the identity of the professions of archivist, librarian, and curator. What are these professional divergences? A study of the different situations in Europe and the United States presented in the Helsinki Conference seems to suggest that they derive from the differing organization of professional education. The conference of the Helsinki working group further determined a consequence of digitization for professionals in cultural institutions like libraries, archives, and museums (LAM): an increase in the convergence of expertise needed from the professionals in all three institutions. Increasingly the workflow of the three professions overlaps, with expertise common to all the professionals who concentrate on the ability to use information technology critically in order to furnish better service. Continuing education and basic education is thus one of the critical points to analyze for digital convergence. The working group on convergence decided to sign this work after the Helsinki Conference.

IFLA Satellite Conference in Turin

The IFLA Satellite Conference in Turin took place as an ideal continuation of the Helsinki Conference and the working group initiative on convergence by exploring the impact of digital convergence "beyond technology." The object of the Turin Satellite was to gather an international community of scholars, researchers, and professionals from the three areas in order to continue the conversation on the theme of convergence.

The initiative began in the IFLA Library Theory and Research Section, to the end of exploring the results of both research on, and the best practices of, digital convergence and the impact on the identity of the professionals in cultural institutions. The choice to hold the conference in Turin was guided by the MAB-Italia experience begun in Piedmont in 2010 and the long Italian tradition of university higher education shared—or at least united—in the one disciplinary sector of archive and library school.

The Satellite's objectives were:

- understanding the theoretical foundations underlying separated but related disciplines;
- opportunities and barriers to achieving the convergence of education for libraries, archives, and museums; and
- broadening the scenario to data curation and big data.

The questions in hand were the following:

- What are the fundamental theories of each different discipline? Does digital convergence influence disciplinary convergence?
- How are professional trained for models of digital convergence? Have new academic programs been developed?

During the second day, the satellite conference organized a round table on education to discuss experiences of success in convergence and of innovation in formative curricula with the protagonists.

MAIN TRENDS IN DIGITAL CONVERGENCE

The Turin Satellite underlined some trends, including the real tensions between the different professions. Theoreticians such as Rayward, Marty, Zorich, and Trant have noticed a necessary change in philosophical perspective for the profession. In the last twenty years, it has often been claimed that the future of the information profession depends on the ability of cultural-heritage-information professionals to transcend the traditional boundaries between libraries, archives, and museums in order to meet information needs in the digital age (Marty, 2014).

Convergence seems to be the end point of a continuum that ranges from cooperative projects to closer forms of collaboration, up to a "confluence" in which the new digital context of the professions leads to a common theory.

To interpret the tendencies that showed up during the Turin Satellite, and following the approach suggested by Tatjana Aparac in her presentation, we will use the four approaches to convergence issues in the study of Borgman and Schement (1990), which served as an intellectual challenge due to its clear distinction between different convergence models:

- the model of paradigmatic shift,
- the model of disciplinary crossing,
- the model of fields overlapping, and
- the model of common theory.

The first and second models (paradigmatic and disciplinary crossing) are based on the new paradigm of the user. The change in paradigm is stimulated by the need to engage the audience, so as to create connections and sharing among collections, institutions, and users in information spaces. The urge behind disciplinary crossing is guided by participatory culture in answer to the need for greater user participation.

The cultural institutions find themselves sharing the challenge of this new digital context, which entails a change from the traditional approach of organization as noncommunicating "silos." To cite the OCLC (Zorich, Waibel, and Erway, 2008) report: "LAM professionals who understand issues surrounding different types of collections and collecting institutions . . . bring an open-mindedness that allows them to embrace ideas from other professions in the interests of the collaboration." This phase, or model, of "fields overlapping" is the current prevailing situation in Europe. The more recently established Europeana Foundation, seen by the European Union (EU) as one of Europe's most ambitious cultural projects, has a very clear vision, which states:

> We believe in making cultural heritage openly accessible in a digital way, to promote the exchange of ideas and information. This helps us all to understand our cultural diversity better and contributes to a thriving knowledge economy.

Changing mindsets are necessitating a change in the ways the cultural organizations interact with visitors, prompting the need for more active engagement of users with resources, reuse, and even collaboration in developing resources. While technological change is fairly easy, sociological change is harder. Information professionals must challenge long traditions and deeply held philosophies to meet public expectations for expanded access to museum resources. But they must also advocate for their own contributions, using socio-technical skills to leverage their work through new platforms and channels to gain broader community recognition, respect, and value.

A common theoretical foundation is still missing, however, and consequently there is no real convergence of cultural heritage professionals. A discussion on interdisciplinary issues of the digitization of cultural heritage is desirable and possible—leading toward a common theory of digital heritage professionals in digital society.

Special attention was given during the Satellite of Turin to common issues such as Linked Open Data (LOD) and Big Data. LOD, in particular, demonstrates where digital cultural heritage becomes an integral part of an extended and expanded web in which data can be discovered and used in both new and unanticipated ways.

The changing nature of cultural heritage professionals and the overwhelming impact of information technology (IT) on all aspects of work (and life generally) suggest that a greater focus on IT should be integral to the learning and training program in these fields, and is inevitable. Digital technologies are a game changer for libraries, archives, and museums even if it is highly debatable how they are a part of the evolution of these institutions and their societal context.

Convergence of technology and making of the digital and nondigital stuff in archives, libraries, and museums is demonstrating that "all tech jobs are conceptual jobs," as affirmed in a presentation by Isto Huvila (2012). During the Satellite, Huvila described a survey of LAM literature revealing that there tends to be a divide between technical literature and conceptual literature about technology in particular contexts with only a limited convergence between these two strands of research and practice. A similar divide can be seen in how professionals conceptualize their institutions and their future.

CONCLUSION

The presentations at the Satellite evidenced different trends covering collecting and presenting, as well as preserving and using digital assets. Those assets are designed upon a multilayered concept of the communication of cultural memory as a complex phenomenon that foresees the synergies between LAM studies and IT, and several of those synergies form a part of the education and training in the curricula.

In conclusion, cultural heritage institutions have to go beyond explicit and implicit dichotomizing of technical tasks and conceptual tasks. The tasks such as digital preservation and digital curatorship are less technical than conceptual and theoretical enterprises in how professionals develop and adapt new technical solutions for the broader cultural and societal endeavors of the LAMs.

The new digital context brings LAM professionals to the model of a common theory, which is approaching the challenge of participatory culture. Some questions remain open and need further consideration: What role do professional organizations have to play in the redesign of digital heritage services? Are we to offer new education and training programs? Are we to offer specializations within existing courses or programs?

REFERENCES

Borgman, C., and J. R. Schement (1990). Information science and communication research. In J. M. Pemberton and A. E. Prentice (Eds.), *Information science: The interdisciplinary context* (pp. 42–59). New York: Neal-Schuman.

Huvila, I. (2012). Navigators, debaters or information architects? How library, museum and archive professionals perceive their role in the future society. In W.-F. Riekert and I. Simon (Eds.), *Information in e-Motion: Proceedings of the BOBCATSSS 2012 20th International Conference on Information Science Amsterdam, 23–25 January 2012* (pp. 190–94). Bock + Herchen. Retrieved from http://www.istohuvila.se/files/IstoHuvilaNavigatorsPrePrint.pdf

Jenkins H. (2006). *Convergence Culture: Where Old and New Media Collide*. New York: New York University Press.

Marty, P. F. (2014) Digital convergence and the information profession in cultural heritage organizations: Reconciling internal and external demands. *Library Trends*, *62*(3), 613–27. Retrieved from http://diginole.lib.fsu.edu/cgi/viewcontent.cgi?article=1023&context=slis_faculty_publications

Raynard B. (1998). Electronic information and the functional integration of libraries, museums and archives. In Edward Higgs (Ed.), *History and Electronic Artefacts* (pp. 207–26). Oxford: Clarendon Press.

Trant, J. (2009, December) Emerging convergence? Thoughts on museums, archives, libraries and the training of [information] professionals. *Museum Management and Curatorship*, *24*(4), 369–86. Retrieved from http://www.archimuse.com/papers/trantConvergence0908-final.pdf

UNESCO. (2012). *The Memory of the world in the digital age: Digitization and preservation.* Proceedings of the International Conference on September 2012 in Vancouver, British Columbia, Canada. Retrieved from http://ciscra.org/docs/UNESCO_MOW2012_Proceedings_FINAL_ENG_Compressed.pdf

Zorich, D. M., G. Waibel, and R. Erway. (2008). *Beyond the silos of the LAMs: Collaboration among libraries, archives and museums*. OCLC. Retrieved from http://www.oclc.org/content/dam/research/publications/library/2008/2008-05.pdf

Part II

CONVERGENCE

Chapter Four

LAM From the Trenches

The LODLAM Community and the Building of LAM Culture, Practices, and Education

M. Cristina Pattuelli

ABSTRACT

Linked Open Data in Libraries, Archives, and Museums (LODLAM) is an international community of information professionals, researchers, and educators working toward the application of Linked Open Data (LOD) principles and technology to digital cultural heritage. Emerging in 2011, LODLAM has gone from a small grassroots effort to a movement at the forefront of fostering the culture of integration and sharing across different cultural heritage domains through LOD research and implementation. This chapter discusses the role and activities of LODLAM from the perspective of an active participant in the community.

INTRODUCTION

Linked Open Data in Libraries, Archives, and Museums (LODLAM)[1] is an international community of information professionals, researchers, and educators engaged in the research and implementation of Linked Open Data technology to digital cultural heritage. LODLAM can best be described as an open movement that emerged in the last few years rather spontaneously, driven by the goal to transition cultural content to the LOD ecosystem and realize the vision of the Web of Data, the semantic extension of the web as we know it. Self-organized and acentric, LODLAM is rapidly growing through a string of activities, off-line and online, global and local, that bridge different cultural contexts and strengthen the ties of various research and professional communities. As the LODLAM movement is too novel and evolving to be captured in its complexity, in this chapter, I intend to simply highlight its cultural and technological context as well as some of the stages that have been pivotal to its development and consolidation.

WHAT IS LODLAM?

A practical outgrowth of the Semantic Web, the LOD initiative provides the context for fostering greater collaboration among libraries, archives, and museums (LAMs), as well as other cultural institutions such as galleries, which inspired GLAM, the acronym often used interchangeably with LAM. The Linked Data initiative is defined as a set of practices for publishing structured data on the web in ways that make this data machine readable, interlinkable, and open to novel and enhanced uses. Technically, linked-data methods rely on a few common open standards including the HyperText Transfer Protocol (HTTP) and the Unique Resource Identifier (URI). The Resource Description Framework (RDF) serves as the unifying model to structure the data (Bizer, Heath, and Berners-Lee, 2009).

As a subset of Linked Data, LOD focuses specifically on freely sharable and re usable data. This open model works as a catalyst for data and metadata from distributed and heterogeneous sources to be shared, connected, and reused. The linked-data "technology stack" addresses well-known challenges such as data interoperability and integration and makes it possible to steer this data into the web to support open and seamless access and use. In other words, the web itself becomes the management platform and the global and unified space for data discovery and navigation. We have only begun to envision and understand the potential for cultural heritage organizations to offer integrated access to their content.

A HISTORY OF THE LODLAM SUMMITS

Jon Voss (2012b), one of the driving forces behind the movement and the cofounder and chair of the LODLAM Summit, recalls that the idea of gathering together a group of information professionals working in the domain of cultural heritage emerged in 2009. The initial goal was to interconnect heterogeneous datasets of American Civil War archival content. It was then that the group realized that there was "an appetite for educating the broader community of libraries, archives, and museums about the concept of Linked Open Data" (p. 41). The next step was the creation of the LODLAM logo and the organization of the first summit, which took place in San Francisco in June 2011.[2] Though originally intended for fifty attendees, the call for participation raised significant interest, and the number of summit delegates doubled. A diverse mix of librarians, archivists, researchers, developers, and technologists came together for a two-day event from around the world (seventeen countries were represented).[3]

This first LODLAM Summit is reminiscent of the pioneering spirit of the Dublin Core Metadata Initiative (DCMI)[4] of 1995, when an international and heterogeneous community self-described as "freaks, geeks, and people with sensible shoes" flocked to Dublin, Ohio (Weibel, 2005). Their aim was to find a solution that would overcome the limitations of the search engines of the time and improve online discovery. Over the years, the Dublin Core community has grown and evolved, almost organically, through annual meetings and other venues, and their focus and activities have expanded well beyond the universal metadata schema they developed.

Hosted by the Internet Archive and funded by grants from the Alfred P. Sloan Foundation and the National Endowment for the Humanities, the first LODLAM Summit was organized as an "unconference," and was thus not bound by the conventions of academic and professional meetings. Without a preset agenda or paper presentations to attend, participants were free to self-organize and discuss the burning issues of the day. A facilitator and an easel were all that were needed to aggregate people around topics of their interest. Delegates were encouraged to move around and join the discussions that inspired them. This level of spontaneity and openness made it possible to engage people with varying degrees of expertise and technical experience on different approaches to the challenges facing LOD in the cultural heritage arena. Vocabularies were a particularly hot topic because of the critical role they play in the construction of RDF triples—the building blocks of LOD. Concerns related to vocabulary expressivity, issues of dealing with different levels of granularity, and the need for mapping and alignments were all part of defining a common space for sharing semantics among different cultural domains and representation practices. Data quality and the need to deal with the messiness that comes with heterogeneous datasets were paired with discussions on provenance and trust. The user side of LOD development also began to emerge in discussions of new modes for data consumption, including the lack of usable and intuitive interfaces for LOD-driven services targeted at new user communities. The realization that we were converging around questions that we were all facing or thinking about, regardless of the different practices and traditions, was a strong element of cohesion and an indicator that a community was emerging.

A second summit followed two years later in June 2013, this time hosted by the National Library and Archive of Quebec in Montreal. Once again, more than one hundred participants from sixteen countries came together.[5]

The agenda was created freestyle during the conference with only a few sessions proposed in advance. This time it felt to some extent like a reality check where people shared the progress they had made on their work as well as lessons learned. A number of developments had occurred in the intervening two years that impacted the kinds of problems addressed at the summit. As Voss (2012a) points out, the amount of linked open data had increased exponentially.

Libraries had continued to release their bibliographic and authority data as LOD at a high rate (according to Neubert and Pohl, 2011, the Linked Open Data cloud had grown by 1,000 percent with library data in 2010). Europeana had integrated Linked Open Data capability into its framework and announced plans to publish the metadata for over two million resources as LOD. The Library of Congress BIBFRAME project announced in the fall of 2011 that it would leverage semantic web and LOD principles and methods to represent and connect bibliographic data.

A good deal of conversation at the summit was devoted to the methods and tools needed to implement the LOD model. Key initiatives such as the upcoming release of a handful of Getty's vocabularies as LOD were announced and discussed. This time the summit included a new component—the "LODLAM Challenge" competition.[6]

LODLAM PROJECTS

Intended to highlight use cases, the LODLAM Challenge solicited submissions from projects at various stages of completion and encompassing visualizations, tools, and prototypes. This showcase offered a range of current approaches to LOD development and demonstrated that the implementation of LOD for domains like cultural heritage was still highly experimental. Regardless of the scale of the projects and their level of maturity, prototyping remains common practice, and efforts continue to be put into building use cases that can demonstrate the potential of LOD applications.

Teams were asked to submit a video and description of their project. Two rounds of online voting took place from September 2012 through February 2013. Eighteen projects participated and a total of five finalists were selected to receive travel stipends, delegate seats at the summit, and eligibility to compete for a prize. Submissions included tools and efforts to convert legacy data of various types to LOD, projects to visualize collections, map and text annotators, and initiatives related to access to specific archives.

The winning project was a web tool called Pundit; originally created by the Semblib project, the tool is currently developed by Net7 and partially funded by the Digital Manuscript to Europeana project.[7] A semantic annotating tool, Pundit's focus is on giving users the ability to create a linkable data layer on top of web content including text or images. Annotations are stored on a server and can then be leveraged to create visualizations and graphs.

Linked Jazz, a finalist in the competition, is another independent research project focused on creating broadly applicable tools for LOD development and use.[8] Directed by the author of this chapter, the project's aim is to use LOD to represent and visualize the relationships among the densely interconnected network of jazz musicians, as described in digital oral histories.

Several applications have been developed to accomplish this goal, including a name-mapping and curation tool that allows for automated and human disambiguation of personal names through mapping with name authorities, an analyzer for name recognition and extraction from textual documents, a crowd-sourcing tool that allows users to contribute by determining relationships between musicians, and an interactive visualization tool for social network analysis (Pattuelli, Miller, Lange, Fitzell, and Li-Madeo, 2013).

Another finalist, the MisMuseos project, is an example of an application of LOD to museum content.[9] Focused on Spanish public institutions, MisMuseos gathers metadata from multiple museums and libraries as well as the CER.ES collection in Europeana composed of Spanish art and artists. Using the GNOSS (see GNOSS.com) as its publishing platform, it combines museum and Europeana metadata with data from Dbpedia, Geonames, and Didactalia, a social network and user-contributed open dataset of educational resources. It currently presents over 17,000 pieces of art and 2,650 artists. Works of art can be browsed by facets including collection headings (based on traditional museum department divisions), location (museum), artist/author, time period, movement, school, type, technique, and medium. Artist entries can be browsed using the collection, movement, and school facets as well as a birthplace facet.

In the domain of archives, ReLOAD (Repository for Linked Open Archival Data), a project of Regesta.exe, takes data from the Istituto dei Beni Culturali Regione Emilia Romagna and the Archivio Centrale dello Stato and makes it available as Linked Open Data.[10] Leveraging archival descriptions in the form of XML EADs and authority records in EAC-CPF, the project's aim is to display the connections between the material using authority records and geo-referencing. Not conceived of as a portal, the current iteration of ReLOAD has developed a shared space for archival description metadata, which at this phase can be browsed by various facets.

The WWI Linked Data project, which received an honorable mention in the competition, also seeks to mash up archival data. In its initial stages, the project is developing an ontology for describing events and linking places and agents to documents. The specific dataset under consideration is an online collection at the University of Colorado, Boulder, and the project grew out of practical concerns about resource discovery in the university environment.

Rounding out the challenge finalists, Free Your Metadata is an outreach project focused on building best practices and providing training for the creation of Linked Open Data.[11] A collaboration between Multimedia Lab (ELIS Ghent University/iMinds) and MaSTIC (Université Libre de Bruxelles), the project attempts to make LOD accessible to the LAM community. As an example, they provide a step-by-step participatory exercise using metadata downloaded from the Powerhouse Museum so users can follow the process of metadata cleaning in action.

LODLAM EDUCATION AND OUTREACH

The Free Your Metadata project touches on the broader issue of the need for education about LOD principles and applications, also reflected in one of the sessions at the summit devoted to the topic of teaching LODLAM. One of the educational initiatives discussed during the session was the IMLS-funded (Institute of Museum and Library Services) project led by the University of Washington's iSchool, titled Learning Linked Data. With different types of audiences in mind—from professionals seeking to understand Linked Data on the job to library and information science (LIS) students and educators—the project identified key topics to introduce the theoretical and technical aspects of LOD development and envisioned a learning environment including videos, micro-tutorials, and virtual courses.

In addition to this more traditional pedagogical approach, the Learning Linked Data project also emphasized the importance of peer-to-peer community engagement—which has been part of LODLAM from the beginning. LODLAM has been actively engaged in community building and outreach with regional meetings, workshops, web presence, and social media. The LODLAM Training Day, which was a part of the 2014 Semantic Technology and Business Conference,[12] is one example of the type of informal education taking place, while the Twitter hashtag #LODLAM, heavily used for sharing news and projects related to LODLAM, demonstrates the effective use of social media. The LODLAM Challenge itself was an integral part of the efforts to educate the community about LOD by showing compelling real-world applications. Its relevance extends beyond the event as the volume of documentation generated by those projects offered a valuable resource for those interested in learning about LOD in the LAM context.

THE LODLAM VISION

As a self-organized and distributed community, LODLAM has evolved through an array of initiatives, events, biannual international summits, and regional meetings that have brought together professionals, researchers, and enthusiasts from different cultural contexts and organizations. The new and boundless scenario envisioned and enabled by the LOD initiative calls for a strategic reconsideration of our traditional documentation, curatorial, and discovery methods. Libraries, museums, and archives have historically developed diverse, and to some extent divergent, descriptive practices that are tailored to modes of access and use of resources rooted in the analog world. LOD technology offers a common framework for data structure and representation where both newly created and legacy metadata can converge and connect. To permeate the web with "radically open cultural heritage data" Voss (2012a), it is essential to depart from the "walled garden" model of siloed data and metadata. Back in 2009, Berners-Lee, founder of the LOD initiative, had urged everyone to "stop hugging your data" and to start connecting data to each other in order to enable unprecedented opportunities for data analysis and interpretation.

The culture of openness and sharing across domains drives LODLAM leaders, innovators, and enthusiasts to create the conditions for overcoming invisible institutional walls and to contribute to the expansion of traditional access to cultural content. From the humanities to the sciences, it is the mashup culture that underlies the idea of interlinking granular content from diverse sources and mixing and matching open vocabularies from different communities to create new meaningful pathways to inquiry and discovery. This is a culture of cooperation that does not necessarily require coordination, as everybody works within the same data representation paradigm.

It is also a culture of experimentation as a new array of methods and sets of tools are needed to build this new scenario. LOD is considered the practical implementation of the grand vision of the Semantic Web and it is driven by a very pragmatic approach. This means a good deal of crafting original tools and learning by doing. "Start small and progress through piloting and prototyping" is a LODLAM mantra, especially for small-scale independent projects. Such an iterative process makes LOD research and implementation less intimidating and more pervasive, while the LOD framework provides the thread that ties all the efforts together.

CONCLUSION

There is an exciting feeling today of being on the cusp of a profound cultural shift in the way digital cultural heritage is managed and "consumed," while a staggering volume of cultural linked data is being made available by memory institutions and organizations worldwide. As part of these developments, LODLAM is contributing to the emergence of a rich web of semantically linked data while at the same time addressing an array of challenges, such as licensing, data trust and quality, and scalability of query processing, that still prevent a large-scale adoption of LOD. The ultimate goals, implementation of the radical LOD vision, and creation of a world where digital cultural heritage materials can become integral parts of an extended and expanded web, will allow data to be discovered and used in new and unanticipated ways. This chapter highlights some of the key aspects and developments that have and are now moving LODLAM in this important direction.

ACKNOWLEDGMENTS

I would like to thank Alexandra Provo and Hannah Sistrunk for their assistance in the preparation of this paper.

NOTES

1. http://lodlam.net
2. http://lod-lam.net/summit/
3. The list of delegates can be found at http://lod-lam.net/summit/participants/
4. http://dublincore.org
5. The list of delegates can be found at http://summit2013.lodlam.net/about/participants-flat/
6. http://summit2013.lodlam.net/challenge/
7. https://thepund.it/
8. http://linkedjazz.org/
9. http://mismuseos.net/comunidad/metamuseo
10. http://labs.regesta.com/progettoReload/en/
11. http://freeyourmetadata.org/
12. http://semtechbizsj2014.semanticweb.com/LODLAM

REFERENCES

Berners-Lee, T. (2009). *The next web.* TED2009. [video online] Retrieved from http://www.ted.com/talks/tim_berners_lee_on_the_next_web.html

Bizer, C., Heath, T., and Berners-Lee, T. (2009). Linked data—The story so far. *International Journal on Semantic Web and Information Systems*, *5*(3), 1–22 Retrieved from http://tomheath.com/papers/bizer-heath-berners-lee-ijswis-linked-data.pdf

Neubert, J., and Pohl, A. (2011). *SWIB11 28–30 November 2011 in Hamburg; Focus: Scholarly Communication in the Web of Data* [conference announcement]. Retrieved from http://swib.org/swib11/index_e.html

Pattuelli, M. C., Miller, M., Lange, L., Fitzell, S., and Li-Madeo, C. (2013). Crafting linked open data for cultural heritage: Mapping and curation tools for the linked jazz project. *Code4Lib Journal.* Retrieved from http://journal.code4lib.org/articles/8670

Voss, J. (2012a). Radically open cultural heritage data on the web. In *Museums and the Web 2012.* San Diego, California, April 11–14, 2012. Retrieved from http://www.museumsandtheweb.com/mw2012/papers/radically_open_cultural_heritage_data_on_the_w

Voss, J. (2012b). LODLAM state of affairs. *Information Standards Quarterly*, *24* (1/2) Retrieved from http://www.niso.org/publications/isq/2012/v24no2-3/voss/

Weibel, S. L. (2005). Border crossings: Reflections on a decade of metadata consensus building. *D-Lib Magazine*, *11*(7/8). Retrieved from http://www.dlib.org/dlib/july05/weibel/07weibel.html

Chapter Five

The Convergence Paradigm as the Basis for the Design of New Programs in the Field of the Information Sciences

Tatjana Aparac-Jelušić

ABSTRACT

The Department of Information Sciences at the University of Zadar has recently submitted its new program for accreditation at two university levels—the undergraduate and the graduate. These programs were designed according to the needs of the library, archival, and museum (LAM) community. Together with the existing PhD program, these programs approached educational issues from a twofold perspective: first, the authors intended to offer new content, knowledge, and skills, as represented by a number of optional and elective courses and workshops that could answer the needs of the LAM sector in both Croatia and the region; and second, the authors were aware of the fact that the educational programs for the LAM sector, which sometimes tend to be atomized and situated in different academic surroundings, should be managed in a different way.

Reflecting those perspectives, special attention in this chapter will be paid to issues concerning the digitalization of cultural heritage. Different models for the collection and presentation, preservation, and use of digital assets have been designed. All are based upon a multilayered concept of the communication of cultural memory as a complex phenomenon that foresees the synergies between LAM and ITC (information technology and computers) studies, and several of them form a part of the courses in the curricula. This chapter will also focus on convergence issues as a basis for the understanding of the relationship between several LAMs and other disciplines, such as communication, semantics, and cognitive sciences, among others, as well as the theoretical boundaries of the information sciences in relation to the disciplinary traditions of archival, library, and museology studies. This will shed light on the unifying principles of information disciplines and fields of practice that could provide a new framework for disciplinary theory, as well as on the barriers that sometimes affect the planning process. Also included will be a discussion on interdisciplinary issues (as something to be desired), as these can lead toward a new paradigm of information science (IS) in a digital society, as well as how these issues might influence overall discipline identities.

INTRODUCTION

In recent years, library and information science (LIS) and information science schools worldwide have been involved in the development of a certain curriculum that offers pathways and certificates that should prepare students for work in a digital environment. Some of these schools focus on "digital libraries," "digital humanities," "the management of heritage institutions," "digital curation," or "data curation," among others. Yet it remains difficult to investigate the extent to which these new programs are able to answer the needs of a changing environment in the libraries, archives, and museums (LAMs) sector.

Useful research has been presented by a joint effort of the editors of the *Library Quarterly*, *Archival Science*, and *Museum Management and Curatorship* when they agreed to publish three special issues (one for each journal) exploring the shared information needs and challenges facing libraries, archives, and museums in the information age. It was clear that the LAM sector required more information in order to shed light on the overlapping educational goals of library and information sciences, archival studies, and museum studies programs (Marty, 2008, p. 247). From the perspective of tertiary education, this is a very challenging era, and what is required is a new approach to the design of curricula and the management of educational programs.

Croatian professionals and academics from the LAM sector began discussions on a joint venture within a global environment at a relatively early date (Willer, 1998). They approached this venture from two perspectives:

1. from a perspective of everyday needs, to increase the quality of services, to modernize working methods and management practice, and to co-ordinate activities toward rationalization of financial resources; and
2. from the perspective of the redesign of existing educational programs, to ensure that heritage studies approximate and equate their requirements to those studies in similar academic fields.

Until recently, according to traditions in Croatia and other European countries, archival studies were situated in departments of history, whereas museology was taught in departments of art history, for example. At the same time, library science education was offered as a separate program at separate and independent departments. As an academic discipline, information science began in Croatia and other countries of ex-Yugoslavia in the early 1960s, with a formal postgraduate educational program at the University of Zagreb for information professionals in various fields—in science and medicine in particular (Pehar and Aparac-Jelušić, 2012). Later in the decade, a postgraduate program in documentation, library science, and museology was established at the Referral Centre of the University of Zagreb, and the first graduate program in Croatia began in 1976, when full and part-time students of library science enrolled at the Faculty of Philosophy of the University of Zagreb (Horvat, 2000). Several years later, at the same faculty, the Chair of Library Studies and the Chair of Social and Humanities Informatics merged and became the Department of Information Sciences, at first offering students a number of academic courses in library science and informatics, and later, courses in archival science and museology.

There are three departments of information sciences currently in Croatia at the university level (Zagreb, Osijek and Zadar); one program is offered by the Department of Croatian Language and Literature at the University of Rijeka, and one, as a segment of Cultural Studies, at the University of Osijek. The initiative to conceive a new program emerged at the Department of Information Sciences (formerly Department of Librarianship) at the University of Zadar. The approved program in 2005 was in library science, since the job market in Dalmatia was in need of library professionals with high-level diplomas.

The underlying reasons for a thorough reconstruction of the existing program in 2013 were twofold:

1. Considering that this program was designed and accredited at a time when the department was lacking in teaching staff, the accredited program was oriented toward library science only. This program was modified almost every academic year, as staff numbers had increased (from two positions in 2004, to sixteen in 2013, with eleven staff members with a scientific degree). After a process of a self-evaluation and a consideration of the pros and cons of the program, modifications were made in accordance with the endorsed changes and the approval of the University's senate.
2. Taking into account the opportunities for staff training in the field of information sciences, and seeing that they are expected to function in an unpredictable environment in information and heritage institutions, as well as to encounter new forms of communication and the provision of information services online, it was concluded that the program should be thoroughly updated in order to master the knowledge and skills of future professionals in the LAM sector that will contribute to the social and eco-

nomic development at both the local and national levels, and to acquire a modern educational foundation to further their studies in the field of social sciences and the humanities, particularly in the field of the information sciences (Aparac, 1998).

This issue of the education of LAM information professionals at the university level has already been dealt with in a number of countries worldwide. Bearing in mind the current process of globalization and advances in technology (IT and web), developments in the education of LAM information professionals had to be considered in the light of their adherence to principles; these include the international or global scope of curricula, the creation of value-added information, the mastery of new information skills, and the application/implementation of a broad-based approach, which will enable graduates to work in a variety of information environments (Horvat, 2004).

THEORETICAL BACKGROUND

Convergence issues as a basis for the understanding of the relationship between several LAMs and other disciplines, such as communication, semantics, cognitive sciences, and so on, provoked a number of discussions (during LAM conferences in Croatia, for example). An agreed-on point of departure was that the theoretical boundaries of the information sciences, when viewed in relation to the disciplinary tradition of archival, library, and museology studies (which form a part of both historical and contemporary traditions), will be better understood if the unifying principles of information disciplines and fields of practice are seen as an advantage. They might provide a new framework for a disciplinary theory. Accepting such an approach should make it possible to recognize the barriers that sometimes affect the planning process for cooperation in various fields, including aspects of education. A discussion on interdisciplinary issues as desirable and as something that can lead toward a new paradigm of IS in digital society, and how these attempts might influence disciplinary identity, is another way of looking at convergence problems.

Discussions on the convergence of disciplines within the wider field of information sciences gained greater prominence in the 1980s. What had surrounded these discussions was a society of global communication and information in which "individual disciplines began to take a greater interest in more general questions, albeit interpreting these questions from the perspective of their own fields of interest, yet also expecting that, should this permeation prove effective, they would be able to strengthen their scientific foundation and affirm their place in the family of sciences" (Aparac, 1998). Seen from the perspective of LAMs, their field of research consisted of a myriad of diverse activities by which certain relations were reflected, also taking into account the totality of knowledge at any given moment, as J. Nitecki (1968) would say. Should we use his interpretation of library science as an example, we could also prove that the reality of LAMs occurs at three different levels: at the procedural (empirical), contextual, and conceptual level. Rayward (1998), on the other hand, examined early on how changes from physical to digital media affect the traditional distinctions between information organizations and thus introduced the term "digital convergence."

As noted by Marty (2008), the common features of libraries, archives, and museums have also served as a theme for several different conferences, including RLG 2005 and RBMS 2006. More recently, OCLC published a study (Zorich et al., 2008) that inspired several authors to continue working on theory. Trant (2009) offered some interesting insights concerning emerging convergence issues and Zorich (2008) pointed out that "the endpoint of the collaboration continuum is convergence, a state in which collaboration around a specific function or idea has become so extensive, engrained and assumed that it is no longer recognized by others as a collaborative undertaking."

In my opinion, it is possible to propose that the central thesis of the discussion concerning the nature of the activities under research, and the need to found a plausible theory on a conceptual level in which the library, archival, and museum disciplines, can be considered in the sense of the constant permeation of the metaphorical relationship between the given and newly attained dimensions of knowledge. In order for this to succeed, the role of both professional and academic institutions, which are responsible for the activities just cited, must be based on the effective dissemination of knowledge. This can be achieved by a reliance on the two following aims, which ultimately derive from their inherent value: the first aim, without a doubt, is to assist users in discovering concepts that appear to be new to them, unknown, and unrecognized until now; and the second is to ensure the sources required to understand those concepts that were discovered earlier yet have not been fully understood. Since one of the themes of debate in recent years concerns disciplinary convergence within the field of information sciences, two approaches have come to the fore. On one level, leading theoreticians and experts in particular disciplines attempt to seek out the best solutions for similar, general problems, despite the fact that they begin their work with different goals and develop a different terminological "apparatus." Basically, their approach is based upon an understanding that the disciplines inside a wider IS and communication science should develop closer connections. On another level, more attention is given toward ITC as a strong connective element for the design and offering of modern information products and services, the purposeful connection of different information activities, quality bibliographic control, and the insurance of the availability of information resources at global/local levels (Aparac-Jelušić, 2009). In a context such as this, it is certainly necessary to recognize, select, and interpret what may be the general principles, so that certain authors have asked if they exist and also whether it is possible to recognize the general principles that should lead to a better understanding of the principles of the field of information sciences.

A digital environment has, without a doubt, led certain institutions to implement new library services that aid the user in receiving a more complete, correct, and professional answer to what he or she might ask. Unique and coherent access to various digital products and services has certainly led to a professional curiosity among practitioners and academics in the LAM sector and has also emphasized the fact that, without the proper awareness of the strident changes in such an environment, one cannot be encouraged to find one's "own" place in the changing conditions of contemporary life.

T. Šola (1990) stated that information studies—which in his opinion include museology, archival, and library studies, all tend toward the same—to study information that reflects past human experience, its creation, and acquisition in any given format, organization and analysis, and preservation and dissemination. It is because of this that they must all be based on the same theoretical framework. He later proposed a new discipline—heritology, mnemosophy in fact, which has the phenomenon of a total heritage at its center and also attempts to unify the knowledge and methods of which the foundations of the scientific interpretation of the processes of the organization, curation, and utilization of heritage consist. This would bring together various related disciplines (some of which have been mentioned above) under one collective roof (Šola, 2003).

Despite the relatively long tradition and the annually held LAM conferences (established in 1997) in Croatia, systematic investigations are still lacking on the ways in which these three professions are interconnected and influence one another. One such investigation was carried out by Aparac-Jelušić, Faletar Tanacković, and Pehar (2010) based on a corpus of works of the LAM conferences proceedings (from 1997 to 2007), during which a surprisingly high degree of professional cooperation was maintained. Following suggested sources of data that could be used to determine the extent to which two (or more) fields are converging (such as research questions in common, theorists shared, citation links, and overlapping membership in professional organizations [Borgman, Schement, 1990]), they could prove cooperation in organizing conferences and working together on joint professional projects, but not support for the elements that would lead toward a more successful method of citation between sectors and a research project consensus between the authors from three different disciplines.

CONVERGENCE AND EDUCATIONAL PROGRAMS

Why is convergence an important issue in the process of designing academic programs? In my opinion the reasons are twofold:

1. Although earlier (bibliometric) research did not show much interest in the notion of convergence in the field of information sciences, some cross-disciplinary journal citation patterns were found (for example, Borgman and Rice, 1992; Pehar, 2012; Aparac-Jelušić, Faletar Tanacković, and Pehar, 2010).
2. Investigation by Borgman and Schement (1990) into some of the likely common theoretical grounds for information (and communication) sciences has shown that a small corpus of theoretical literature exists; other authors suggested that there are different approaches for the design and performance of academic education in the wider field (Tibbo and Lee, 2010).

These results are useful as indicators of scientific communication patterns when considering interdisciplinary problems or possible new research topics, such as the organization of information or collection management and digital services. Yet they are also solid ground for the design of academic programs, as Tibbo and Lee (2010) indicated, because of the growing interest in, and actuality of, LAM convergence, so that there is a pressing need for the educators of LAM professionals to consider the implications of this new reality for changes in educational requirements and programs.

There are even more disciplines bordering the LAM sector (such as media theory, human and human-computer theory, as well as the theory of communication) that, in a digital environment, are opening new vantages and collaborative projects that will be able to investigate the closer ties in the education of professionals from all three institutions, as well as those from communication institutions and agencies within schools of information. Together they could contribute to a dynamic integration of traditions and to the enhancement of professional training as currently offered for each of the separate disciplines. Nevertheless, "coordinated" should not mean "identical" because distinct user models for many of the differences that fostered these institutions remain in the networked world (Trant, 2009).

For our approach to convergence issues in program design, the study by Borgman and Schement (1990) served as an intellectual challenge due to its clear distinction between different convergence models: the model of paradigmatic shift, the model of disciplinary crossing, the model of fields overlapping, and the model of common theory. The authors noted that there are certainly not a great number of convergence-based articles and data about the convergence between two disciplines they observed, at least in relation to co-citations. This is also obvious nowadays in regard to the LAM sector. Professional literature is growing, many projects are being presented, but we are lacking co-citations between disciplines and theoretical considerations based on common ground. Nevertheless, almost every academic department in LIS is considering not only merger with other departments (often as a result of the university's policy and rationalization rather than a more natural closeness) but also a redesign of existing programs to accommodate higher numbers of common themes that will offer knowledge and skills useful for students who might find their jobs in any of the information/heritage institution. Such an approach tends to be directed toward:

- traditional themes and topics connected to "memory institutions" when researchers seek out the best solutions for problems raised out of daily performances inside libraries, museums, archives, and information and documentation centers;
- themes and topics not related to a particular institution, but to problems that ultimately derive from the intention to assure a better access to knowledge and information, which also focuses on the notion of "information needs" and "information demands" as well as on the possibilities of cooperating within a network environment;
- theoretical phenomena with the separation and interpretation of basic phenomena as its goal, as well as the search for common principles and the origins of information, mostly provoked by the requirements of an academic community where PhD programs are allowed and scientific grades in information sciences have been established—the status of this young academic field has to be measured by commonly accepted academic norms; and
- the technological trend toward globalization that has to be investigated on three basic levels of functioning institutions (because traditionally established concepts and procedures are not functioning any more): conceptual, operational, and technical.

NEW CURRICULA AT THE UNIVERSITY OF ZADAR

It is often claimed that the future of the information profession depends on the ability of cultural heritage information professionals to transcend the traditional boundaries between libraries, archives, and museums in order to meet information needs in the digital age (Marty, 2012). Educational institutions have increasingly stepped up to this challenge, and the Department of Information Sciences in Zadar is no exception.

The Department of Information Sciences at the University of Zadar has recently submitted a new program at two university levels for the accreditation process—the undergraduate and the graduate. These programs were designed according to the needs of the LAM community. Together with the existing PhD program, these programs approached educational issues from a twofold perspective:

1. The authors intended to offer new content, knowledge, and skills represented by a number of optional and elective courses and workshops that could answer the needs of the LAM sector in Croatia and the region.
2. The authors were also aware of the fact that educational programs for the LAM sector, which sometimes tend to be atomized and situated in different academic surroundings, should be managed in a different way.

Special attention in the new program was given to issues of the digitization of cultural heritage. Different courses covering collecting and presenting, as well as for preserving and using digital assets, have been designed upon a multilayered concept of the communication of cultural memory as a complex phenomenon that foresees the synergies between library, archival, and museum studies (LAMs) and information technology and computer studies (ITC), and several of them form a part of the courses in the curricula.

In an attempt to face the challenges of academic education in a new era, we considered the necessary changes at several different levels: at the organizational, structural, conceptual, and methodical levels. Organizational changes depend mostly upon a department's policy and the university's strategic goals. Structural changes should certainly have an effect on the quality of education as closer ties to other departments should ensure that the same academic course has not already been offered by them (some examples are Introduction to Logic, Introduction to Cognitive Science, Research Methodology, Introduction to Museology, and Introduction to Archival Studies, which are currently offered at least by two departments), as well as providing the opportunity for teaching staff to concentrate on the core subjects of the information sciences.

Structural changes are also tied to the study level, which was in accordance with the demands of financing bodies that the same educational program must not be offered at the graduate level if it does not exist at the undergraduate level. This proved to be an encumbrance for our teaching staff because teaching hours increased more than expected. It was also difficult for students to master the habits required for study in an academic environment as they were lacking the skills for critical and analytical thinking, computer and information literacy, and problem solving, as a consequence of the secondary schools' organization. Introductory workshops, and a consideration of the first year of study as a year in which the student will learn to adapt to a new environment, will certainly prove advantageous; and this applies to all the social sciences and particular subjects in the humanities and technical sciences (stronger foundations in general knowledge, mathematics, statistics, etc.).

Conceptual changes were also in the focus of our interests, for two reasons in particular: first, we have, on the basis of our research (Aparac-Jelušić, Dragija Ivanović, Faletar, and Pehar, 2005), gained greater insight into what we would like and what we need to change in order to create a flexible and attractive program that will ensure the competence required to work in the shifting environment of the heritage sector; and second, we were independent when preparing and making the decisions at this level. The challenges of convergence for the heritage sector were our guiding light when we discussed the content of the core subjects of the wider field of information sciences. We also attempted to conceive of the needs of individual professions active in a small country with a rich cultural heritage to be able to design a flexible program that would accommodate knowledge and skills necessary to future LAM professionals. A theoretical base was founded on the achievements of single disciplines' theories—LAM, IS, and the closeness of research topics and themes, and our methodology was extracted from approaches and methods of collaborative projects.

In the process of remodeling the existing curricula, expected outcomes of the program lead toward students' competencies:

- To ensure services that will optimize the availability of all material despite its origin and endurance—on the basis of this outcome the core contents linked to information services were gathered;
- To offer information services as a social good, which aims to maximize the societal role of the objects of symbolic culture for the good of mankind—on the basis of this outcome the core contents linked to the formation, supply, and insurance of information products and services are constructed;
- To constantly improve the methods by which information is passed from the human being who produces it to the human being who uses it—on the basis of this outcome the core contents linked to the acquisition, organization, maintenance, and preservation of various collections is constructed;
- To protect cultural heritage in order to assist the development of civilization as our aim—on the basis of this outcome the core contents linked to

digitization and digital born items, the formation of digital collections and the management of their content is constructed; and
- To be able to elaborate information with a supplementary value as the foundation for the improved organization and direction of the user through the *selva selvaggia* ("wild forest") of an abundance of information in a network environment—on the basis of this outcome core contents linked to the new approaches of the organization and management of information in a semantic web are constructed.

The methodological approach has been founded on the basis of the recommendations of the European Commission Bologna Working Group (*Framework*, 2005), which expects a clear articulation of the outcomes of learning, the inclusion of students in teamwork, problem solving, the application of theory to practice (field work), the acquisition of organizational skills (the preparation of national and international conferences), and so on. The majority of these demands were successfully met earlier in relation to library studies, but were also required to consider the extension of the learning outcomes to other fields within the information sciences that were embedded into the new program. In order to approximate theory and practice, we turned toward a method of critical collaborative inquiry, for which we selected teachers and reflective practitioners in order to discuss the necessary changes, and carried out a self-evaluation of our existing programs (Riding, Fowell, and Levy, 1995).

CONCLUSION

Seeing that both the programs and tools used for work with information are changing at an accelerated pace, it is essential that educational programs at all levels, including those that see professional improvement as a lifelong task, be proposed as flexible, of wide scope, and attractive to professionals in the LAM sector. This is the way in which they will yield rewards (especially in regions with a small number of professionals) in individual, separate professions and ensure a better exchange of knowledge and skills.

One cannot easily ascertain how LAMs will develop, yet it is possible, with Borgman's and Scherman's models as a basis, to conclude that in Croatia, the model of permeation already points toward the migration of individual scientists/practitioners between different fields, and not to the convergence at the level of an entire field (experience of a LAM seminar, for example). Yet the model of the convergence of fields points toward the existence of certain fields of research that all disciplines share (communications theory and user behavior theory, for example). Whereas the model of a common theory finds its vantage point in the modes of practice in particular areas in which certain disciplines are independent at the academic program level, there is also a common corpus of theory on the basis of which every discipline finds its specific themes of investigation. The new doctorate program is a witness to this. Although its foundations are still in individual disciplines, the doctorate program is open to interdisciplinary themes and problems.

REFERENCES

Aparac, T. (1998). Informacijske znanosti: temeljni koncepti i problemi. (Information Sciences: basic concepts and problems). In M. Willer et al. (Eds.), *Seminar Arhivi, knjižnice, muzeji* (pp. 14–28). Zagreb: Hrvatsko bibliotekarsko društvo.

Aparac-Jelušić, T. (2009). Konvergencija disciplina u polju informacijskih znanosti: izazovi, trendovi i dileme. (Convergence of disciplines in the field of information sciences: challenges, trends and dilemas. In Ž. Vučković, G. S. Simončić, and V. Crnogorac (Eds.), *Temeljne vrednosti savremenog bibliotekarstva: zbornik radova sa međunarodne naučne konferencije održane u Beogradu*, December 14, 2009 (pp 9–22). Beograd: Bibliotekarsko društvo Srbije.

Aparac Jelušić, T., Faletar Tanacković, S., Pehar, F. (2010). Struktura trostruke uzvojnice AKM- a: bibliometrijska analiza priloga objavljenih u razdoblju od 1997. do 2007. (Structure of triple helix of LAM seminar: Bibliometric analysis of papers published in the Proceedings from 1997 to 2007). In M. Willer, S. F. Tanacković (Eds), *Seminar Arhivi, knjižnice, muzeji: mogućnosti suradnje u okruženju globalne informacijske infrastructure* (pp. 13–29). Zagreb: Hrvatsko knjižničarsko društvo.

Aparac-Jelušić, T, Dragija Ivanović, M., Faletar, S., and Pehar, F. (2005). *LIS programs reflecting the needs of ALM community.* In L. Achcroft (Ed.), Coping with continual change—Change management in SLIS—ALISE/EUCLID joint meeting (pp. 46–58). Radford, UK: Emerald Group.

Borgman, C. L, and Rice, R. E. (1992). The convergence of information science and communication: A bibliometric analysis. *American Society for Information Science and Technology*, *43*, 397–411.

Borgman, C. L, and Schement, J. R. (1990). Information science and communication research: An essay on convergence. In J. M. Pemberton and A. E. Prentice (Eds.), *Information science as a discipline* (pp. 42–59). Chicago: Neal-Schuman.

Framework for qualifications of the European Higher Education Area: Bologna Working Group on qualifications frameworks. (2005, February). Ministry of Science, Technology and Innovation. Retrieved from http://www.ond.vlaanderen.be/hogeronderwijs/bologna/documents/050218_QF_EHEA.pdf

Horvat, A. (2000). Library legislation and free access to information as new topics in library and information science education. *Information Research*, *5*(2). Retrieved from http://InformationR.net/ir/5-2/paper72.html

Horvat, A. (2004). Continuing education of librarians in Croatia: Problems and prospects. *New Library World*, *105*, 370–75.

Lee, C. A. (2011). A framework for contextual information in digital collections. *Journal of Documentation*, *67*(1), 95–143.

Marty, P. F. (2008). An introduction to digital convergence: Libraries, archives, and museums in the information age. *Archival Science*, *8*, 247–50.

Marty, P. F. (2012). Unintended consequences: Unlimited access, invisible work, and the future of the information profession in cultural heritage organizations. *Bulletin of the American Society for Information Science and Technology*, *38*(3), 27–31.

Marty, P. F. (2014). Digital convergence and the information profession in cultural heritage organizations: Reconciling internal and external demands. *Library Trends*, *62*, 613–27.

Nitecki, J. (1968). Reflections on the nature and limits of library science. *Journal of Library History*, *3*, 103–19.

Pehar, F., Aparac-Jelušić, T. (2012) *On the Origins and Development of Information Sciences as an Academic and Research Field in Croatia*. In T. Carbo and T. B. Hahn (Eds.), *International perspectives on the history of information science and technology* (pp. 74–82). Medford, NJ: Information Today.

Rayward, W. B. (1998). Electronic information and the functional integration of libraries, museums and archives. In E. Higgs (Ed.), *History and electronic artefacts* (pp. 207–24). Oxford, UK: Oxford University Press.

Riding, P., Fowell, S., and Levy, P. (1995). An action research approach to curriculum development. *Information Research*, *1*(1). Retrieved from http://www.informationr.net/ir/1-1/paper2.html

Šola, T. (1990). *Muzeološki prilog teorijskim osnovama informacijskih znanosti* (Museology Contribution to the Theory of Information Sciences). In Z. Dovedan (Ed.), Informacijske znanosti i znanje (pp. 147–53). Zagreb: Filozofski fakultet.

Šola, T. (2003) *Eseji o muzejima i njihovoj teoriji-prema kibernetičkom muzeju* (Essays on museums and their theory: Towards a cybernetic museum). Zagreb: Hrvatski nacionalni komitet ICOM.

Tibbo, H. R., and Lee, C. A. (2010). Convergence through capabilities: Digital curation education for libraries, archives and museums. In *Archiving 2010: Final Program and Proceedings, June 1–4, 2010, Den Haag, The Netherlands* (pp. 53–57). Springfield, VA: Society for Imaging Science and Technology.

Trant, J. (2009). Emerging convergence? Thoughts on museums, archives, libraries and professional training, *Museum Management and Curatorship, 24*(4), 369–87.

Waibel, G., and Erway, R. (2009). Think globally, act locally: Library, archive, and museum collaboration, *Museum Management and Curatorship, 24*(4), 323–35.

Willer, Mirna. *Predgovor* (Introduction). (1998). In M. Willer and T. Katić (Eds.), *Arhivi, knjižnice, muzeji: mogućnosti suradnje u okruženju globalne informacijske infrastrukture: zbornik radova* (Archives, libraries and museums: Possibilities for collaboration in a Global Information Infrastucture environment) (p. xi–xiii). Zagreb: Hrvatsko bibliotekarsko društvo.

Zorich D. M, Waibel G, and Erway R. (2008). *Beyond the silos of the LAMs: Collaboration among libraries, archives and museums*. Report produced by OCLC Programs and Research. Retrieved from http://www.oclc.org/programs/reports/2008-05.pdf

Chapter Six

Convergence of Skills through Theory, Practice, and Strategy

Michael A. Crumpton

ABSTRACT

Changes within the information and library science profession have required professional positions to have a convergence of skills that can better enable a more complex, dynamic, and expanding role within the home institution. This includes combining specialized areas of traditional functions, including the cultural heritage positions with roles in libraries, archives, and museums. The debate over specialization of skills compared to the benefits of collaborative sharing and convergence of professional skills and duties continues but within a technology-rich environment that in most cases produces a higher level of financial investment. A review of literature will be provided for discussion of skills that are learned in a broader fashion, but can be specialized into organizational needs with a multidisciplinary approach to learning, through professional development and enhanced curriculum offerings. Strategic human resource planning can facilitate the convergence of skills needed to transcend traditional concepts among libraries, archives, and museums as well as address some of the challenges and conflicts regarding philosophical differences between library, archive, and museum organizations. Finally, research work conducted over the past four years demonstrates a new internship model that helps a student shape their professional identity and develop an understanding of the importance of collaboration and convergence for ongoing cultural heritage sustainability.

INTRODUCTION

Changes within the information and library science profession have required professional positions to have a convergence of skills that can better enable a more complex, dynamic, and expanding role within the home institution. This includes combining specialized areas of traditional functions, including the cultural heritage positions with roles in libraries, archives, and museums. Other considerations are:

- trends in LIS programs that recognize and address the impact of these changes in the earlier stages of development, during the education process;
- how post-education human resource models are changing to reflect a new professional identity for librarians in whom hard skills are merged with the intelligence to utilize those skills in different ways, based on current organizational needs; and
- an expectation of how these skills need to have a practical approach and perspective, as demonstrated through the problem-solving side of applying theoretical knowledge.

Research work has been conducted that demonstrates a new internship model, tested over the past four years, that helps a student shape their professional identity for selected areas of librarianship, including work in a library archives.

Almost twenty years ago, in an opinion paper by Thomas J. Galvin (1995), the debate over specialization of skills compared to the benefits of collaborative sharing and convergence of professional skills and duties was just beginning to see the impact of technology on individual jobs and research. Galvin recognized that technology would change the professional's focus from "keeper of content" to "instructor and curator of content and access" and that, ultimately, there would be a need to first collaborate and then converge processes, skills, methods, and infrastructure. Twenty years later, this debate continues, but within a much more technology-rich environment that in most cases produces a higher level of financial investment.

A review of literature will be provided for discussion of skills that are learned in a broader fashion but can be specialized into organizational needs with a multidisciplinary approach to learning, through professional development and enhanced curriculum offerings. Strategic human-resource planning can facilitate the convergence of skills needed to transcend traditional concepts among libraries, archives, and museums. This approach can also address some of the challenges and conflicts regarding philosophical differences between LAM organizations.

A CHANGING ENVIRONMENT

The world is changing at a rapid pace, with significant impact on many professions and lifestyles. Technology is the driver in most cases, influencing services, collections, and their contents, and the ability to have instant access to knowledge and information. But technology alone does not sustain a profession nor uphold its core values and standards for incumbent employees doing the work of the various organizations. New professionals entering the field with a defined set of skills may not match up with existing circumstances within the workplace without a flexible understanding of how skills can be utilized in various ways based on need.

Emerging trends of work processes in professional fields must also undergo a convergence of skills, from old to new, from educational theory to practical application, and from individual existing knowledge platforms to shared knowledge using a variety of formats. This convergence has implications across economic and financial concerns, services and user expectation concerns, and the staffing models of the professionals employed in the field from a human-resources strategic point of view.

The focus here is the human-resource equation of convergence of skills, both convergence of skills based in a changing environment along with changing needs, and the advantages gained and expected within the profession from collaboration between libraries, archives and museum organizations. As it was identified in 2008 by an OCLC research report (Zorich, Waibel, and Erway, 2008), successful endeavors will see staff who incorporate collaborative efforts into their work, as well as maintaining the support of administrators who are challenged to find creative solutions to financing and developing their organizations for the future. And it is the collaborative efforts that will ultimate result in a convergence of ideals that are no longer seen as collaborative but instead are a known part of the infrastructure or system(s) of operations.

An example can be seen from an article about educational services from the cultural departments in museums in France. Marie-Christine Bordeaux (2013) writes about the educational value and missions of museums and recognizes that libraries are not figured predominately with regard to cultural services offered. But they are regarded as cultural agents that provide a link to the social mission of the public cultural institutions, thus collaboration. Determining what actions libraries could take, and recognition of the advantages of a shared mission, could move this relationship from collaborative to convergent.

Given and McTavish (2010) offer another point of view in that much of modern-day convergence of skills has already occurred but became divergent with new technologies and gender (male) interest in the profession. Whether motivated from financial need or collaborative content sharing, they view current efforts of convergence by institutions and organizations to be a re-convergence with new players and technologies. Thus, basic principles and similarities in the work to be performed already exist, and it is a matter of redesigning the core missions of cultural heritage institutions to reimage their shared visions.

A changing environment also occurs at the organizational level before it can successfully guide changes at the individual professional level. Davidson and Davis (1990) compare organizational changes for business models with the expansion of an information economy. Some of those principal changes to an organization apply to the professions of libraries, archives, and museums—most commonly, the shift from prioritized efforts at production and collecting, to a more customized approach of broader and easier access and outreach for addressing individual needs. As they stated in 1990, flexibility will be the key for driving organizational change for staff and the related issues of managing the human-resource side of the organization. Technology ultimately will impact the economic factors that sustain the organization, thus staff must be flexible enough to embrace the technologies that will have a positive economic impact.

The question of "how?" is echoed by Paul Marty (2014) with regard to maintaining traditional distinctions of work within cultural heritage institutions in lieu of new demands by users and more complex relationships with partner organizations and institutions. Extending the work of W. Boyd Rayward, Marty associated the traditional values of cultural heritage workers with the increased exposure and use of materials and resources by a broader spectrum of users who do not have the same loyalty or disposition toward the benefactor institution. He raises the question of organizational identity with regard to delivering information and services, which can ultimately translate into individual professional identity for professionals seeking to advance their careers or research interests.

Bob McKee (2005) expressed similar thoughts about the future of information organizations and how the need for flexibility and the recognition that we are a global society is important. This modern-society trend toward personalization and consumer choice changes the traditional point of view from collectivism to individual consumption. And although, as professionals, individual specializations and interests are still important and valued, finding ways to share and collaborate within similar contexts is not only important but part of the emerging trend for our profession.

There are motivating factors that support convergence and the process in which that could occur. In addressing the convergence of skills in an information economy, Christopher Barth (2011) outlines these motivations as follows:

- alignment of institutional goals and objectives;
- changes that occur in common service models;
- preexisting collaborations;

- leadership attributes, supportive or missing;
- models set by others;
- financial benefits;
- more efficient organizational structure; and
- improvement of services for stakeholders.

This list was modified to fit the current discussion, but the principles remain the same. Today's environment provides many reasons to seek collaborative and convergence solutions to staffing needs and responses.

Cultural heritage professionals have an advantage regarding issues that have surfaced within the organizations and other professions performing the activities listed above. That is, many cultural heritage professionals have "gone before," and a lot has been learned. For example, information management first needed to address convergence of skills as technology created convergence through systems and product development. This led the way for organizations to invest in strategic approaches for changing employee skill development from specialized to cross-trained.

J. E. Herring discusses this in the information-management arena, and in particular within health sciences (Herring, 1991). This is where it was recognized that employees needed to be given broader responsibilities that included a mixture of specialization but also included general knowledge. Competencies such as the ability to communicate effectively and focusing on the big picture of organizational goals and objectives become important at this point. This calls for a greater level of strategic direction with regard to employee competencies.

STRATEGIC INTELLIGENCE FOR PLANNING AND CHANGE

Strategic intelligence is most often associated with military actions, plans, and policies to lead resources toward a successful conclusion of a conflict or potential conflict. Wells (2012) discusses strategic intelligence as the purposefully "steering" in a winning direction. This purposeful steering can be considered for driving change toward developing skills that become useful and desired across the broad spectrum of cultural heritage organizations. Technology and systems enhancements that provide data faster, changing formats that are marketed commercially, a rise in user expectations, and parent organizational demands of sharing costs or adding services are examples of changes being made consistently in the last twenty years. Much of the change is facilitated by professionals who did not experience these types of curricula in library school or worked on the development of those changes internally.

The human-resources consideration within institutions of higher education is also undergoing change and is impacted by current economic conditions. Evans and Chun (2012) point out that by drawing the elements of human resource consideration into strategic planning, an advantage can be gained with proactive contribution and leadership. This trend allows for the elements and activities related to human resources to become part of the strategic planning process and demonstrate a higher level of strategic intelligence by recognizing these advantages.

Strategic planning in itself is not new to libraries or museums. Traditionally, long-term strategic plans are developed and put into place to provide guidelines as to the organization's output for the larger institution or constituency. Then short-term strategic planning can recognize changes when needed to protect the integrity of the institutional mission. In Wells's (2012) definition, he discusses the following three different levels of strategic intelligence:

1. Least intelligent—does not recognize the need to make changes.
2. Higher or smarter intelligence—recognizes the need to change based on external factors and reacts accordingly.
3. Highest intelligence—foresees the upcoming need for change and faster change, thus influencing external factors to their advantage.

Part of preparing for strategic planning activities is to address where the institution stands with regard to organizational development. Strategic planning can cover many elements, depending upon the level of detail needed or desired. Obviously, the more detailed and extensive an effort that goes into the planning process, the more likely it is to be successful in the execution and overall results.

Convergence of skills, processes, systems, or ideals within an organization or organizations can have a formal component of addressing needs or risks to the organization that is making changes. Sometimes called *due diligence*, this is the process of determining the impact future actions will have on individuals and the organization. This can be related to organizational culture, structure, technology, financial, and sometimes even legal concerns. An example of legal concerns could be found in a unionized environment. This review or investigation is necessary to find the proper path of strategic action.

A strategic process should be followed in making changes as well. For example, the need for change should be communicated, and a clear explanation of the reasons and associated benefits should be stated. Plans should be developed with contingencies developed as alternatives if needed. The changes should be communicated to all stakeholders and then assessed for effectiveness. This provides the opportunity to be flexible or make changes if problems occur.

The depth or quality and method by which a strategic plan is developed and enacted can be linked to the strategic intelligence of the parent organization. Proactively seeking dialog and communication regarding emerging trends that will move cultural heritage institutions further toward a positive influence to their constituency will help ensure support and commitment to strategic initiatives that seek to converge process, systems, and skill sets.

TRENDS IN LIBRARY AND INFORMATION SCIENCE EDUCATION

The traditional literature for coursework in LIS programs related to introducing archives and the work of museums into the curriculum focuses on the logistics of staffing and administrative hierarchy or authority. *Museum Librarianship* (Bierbaum, 2000) details staffing in terms of structure and how it relates to planning and budgets from the point of view of a library student. This does provide a good basis for expectations but stops short of identifying skills that could be developed for use in both library and museum environments.

However, some writings are starting to recognize the shared interest and common elements inherent in libraries and museums, even if they are defensive in nature. For example, in 2004 Dilevko and Gottlieb published *The Evolution of Library and Museum Partnerships*, in which they discuss factors impacting both organizations. They address the issue of organizational mission and justification for existence in terms of education, impact on community, and the controversial topic of entertainment. This does imply the specific skills related to instruction, outreach, and marketing, as well as public service attributes for keeping clients and patrons engaged.

This leads to a more specific focus for organizations developing learning communities in which learning outcomes, growth, and sustainability are considered and how post-object care, deeper study of object topics, and display of unique themes make a difference in public perception. These issues have been highlighted and supported by the Institute of Museum and Library Services through funding and programming efforts that both elevate the work of these institutions and provide clarity as to the appropriate skills needed by professionals working in these areas. In their report titled *21st Century Skills* (IMLS, 2009), the Institute of Museum and Library Services clearly outlines the skills, such as literacies and competencies, that will be required for successful twenty-first-century professionals working in museums and libraries.

Paul F. Marty and Michael B. Twidale (2011) explore the work of their own institutions with regard to courses they have offered on museum informatics. They describe museum informatics as the sociotechnical interactions between people and information and technology within museums (Marty, 2011). Their analysis of how these courses have developed includes the introduction of project-based work into the course design. This seems to help demonstrate the value of practical work experience within the educational process, as will be discussed later.

Marty and Twidale (2011) conclude that the benefits of their course go beyond learning more about museums. Instead, they feel they have gained a means for teaching students a broader scope of technologies needed in cultural heritage institutions, but also and more importantly, nontechnical skills. Those skills are listed as *critical thinking for design*, *addressing multidisciplinary issues*, *project development*, and *assessment*—skills that can be common to professions in libraries, archives, and museums.

Jeonghyun Kim (2012) conducted a study and published an article that highlights the integration of museum-related courses into LIS programs across the United States. This study shows a general acceptance by museums to embrace LIS education as a credential for professional work on that side of the house and shows that interdisciplinary approaches to developing the skill set are working and valued.

PROFESSIONAL AND EMOTIONAL INTELLIGENCE FOR CONVERGENCE

With a trend toward specialization for library positions, education and training for the convergence of skills for cultural heritage organizations might seem counterintuitive. But the need for economies of scale from economic and financial concerns, along with the shared issues of advocacy and the need for justification of support from parent organizations, demonstrates a need for skill convergence. In addition, the goals and missions of cultural heritage organizations have developed similarities in their execution, so skills sets needed and desired begin to look similar.

An example of this is taken from O*NET, a partner of the American Job Center Network. This program produces standardized descriptors for a wide variety of jobs across the country in order for educators and employers to react and plan accordingly. Table 6.1 contains a comparison of knowledge, skills, and abilities (KSAs) for the categories of librarians, archivists, and curators. These are the top three listings in each category, and they demonstrate the similarities for each professional category. KSAs become evaluation factors for matching jobs and positions with the appropriate individual.

Other attributes that can be a factor in the individual's success are listed in table 6.2. Work activities, styles, and things people value can also be fac-

Table 6.1. Knowledge, Skills, and Abilities

	Knowledge	*Skills*	*Abilities*
Librarians	English Language	Reading Comprehension	Oral Comprehension
	Service Oriented	Active Listening	Written Expression
	Technology Enabled	Speaking	Information Ordering
Archivists	English Language	Reading Comprehension	Information Ordering
	History and Archaeology	Active Listening	Written Comprehension
	Technology Enabled	Writing	Written Expression
Curators	English Language	Speaking	Oral Comprehension
	History and Archaeology	Reading Comprehension	Oral Expression
	Education and Training	Active Listening	Written Expression

tors in an individual's success at a particular profession. Once again for these three professions, the attributes are similar and can be applied to the strategic planning process.

With strategic planning, the organizational goals are realized through the individual performance objectives of the professionals producing the work. Investment in employee skill development is linked to the organizational goals based on need. If the needs are comparable, then education and training of staff is more appropriately done broadly instead of separately.

It is worth noting that asking incumbent employees to make job changes, merge concepts, and reconsider some of their basic beliefs and values can be stressful and create a high sense of anxiety. This provides opportunity for some emotional-intelligence training that would support self-reflecting of individual ideals for the benefit of the organization. Teaching employees how to understand and manage their own emotions, which can positively influence

Table 6.2. Success Attributes

	Work Activities	*Work Styles*	*Work Values*
Librarians	Getting Information	Cooperation	Relationships
	Computer Use	Adaptability/Flexibility	Working Conditions
	Communication	Attention to Detail	Independence
Archivists	Doc/Record Information	Attention to Detail	Independence
	Getting Information	Integrity	Achievement
	Computer Use	Dependability	Recognition
Curators	Thinking Creatively	Integrity	Independence
	Judging Quality	Attention to Detail	Achievement
	Outside Communication	Dependability	Working Conditions

their emotional responses to others, will help build the relationships needed in a converged environment. By providing emotional-intelligence training, anxiety can be reduced as folks explore their emotions related to change.

A review of cases in Canada and New Zealand recognized the impacts that convergence, or even collaboration, might have on professionals, as well as anxieties that can be produced (Duff, Carter, MacNeil, and Howart, 2013). These case studies demonstrate the complexity of the processes needed for collaboration and convergence by highlighting the diversity and uniqueness of the different institutions. This produces a need to balance the professional expertise of any given institution and its strength of content with the process or system that is causing it to merge with others who have different interests and expertise. The authors identify two common areas that can improve the opportunity to converge; (1) unified or shared access to collections and data, and (2) raising the support of clients and users along with scholarship support. This could also provide the need for emotional support and creating an intelligence model that provides respect for the differences between professionals and celebrates the gains and benefits of collaboration.

PRACTICE VERSUS THEORY FOR SUSTAINABLE PROFESSIONAL IDENTITY

So what are the components of this convergence for all of the aspects of libraries, archives, and museums? What commonalities will afford them to come together with shared goals in a practical, yet sustainable and successful environment? Deborah Wythe (2007) addressed the differences, primarily between libraries/archives and museums as they related to different organizational models. She described these differences for users in terms of an individual experience versus an interpersonal experience based on the service models and organizational support provided. But she also clearly saw how convergence was not only possible but also advantageous, as technology provides a means to merge concepts and ideals. Building upon the shared professional ideals of similar skill sets needed, adoption of standards for effective practice, and providing access to the collections coveted and developed, Wythe proposes that common practices and relationships with users will blend to highlight the advantages of each. Once again this is driven by technology, but must be embraced by the professionals at work to become influential to the users in practice.

As mentioned previously, LIS has begun moving in a direction to blend and combine the skills needed in a converged cultural heritage environment. This blending of advantages could also be served within the venue of practice. This author and his esteemed colleague have conducted research on a shared experiential learning model that not only benefits students learning specific areas of the profession, but also influences curricula decisions and provides a venue for practitioners to update and gain new skills by sharing and engaging projects with students.

The Real Learning Connections project (Bird and Crumpton, 2014) has provided important data to the development of skills for students, librarians, and LIS faculty. Specifically, librarians working with students in this model have gained new insights and acquired new skills through the execution of their own learning objectives within the foundation of each individual project. Projects developed and used in this research are typically related to activities not present in their current state during the practitioner's LIS educational process. Thus, the gain is not only a refreshment of current theoretical concepts being taught, but also an opportunity to learn new perspectives and potentially new technologies being employed, within the framework of the project.

Bird and Crumpton (2014) employ the work of Donald Schon, in *Real Learning Connections*, in which he promotes "reflection" as a key component to integrating theoretical knowledge into a practical environment that requires independent judgment in a changing environment. A project requirement is that each member of the project complete a reflection statement regarding what they have learned. Comments from librarian practitioners include statements related to learning new methods, improvement of the quality of the project, and new knowledge.

Figure 6.1 demonstrates this method of learning with the convergence of the learning objectives into the center "sweet spot." In this model, the library science student can serve as a conduit for a practicing librarian and LIS faculty. In cases and studies conducted, it has been learned that this model

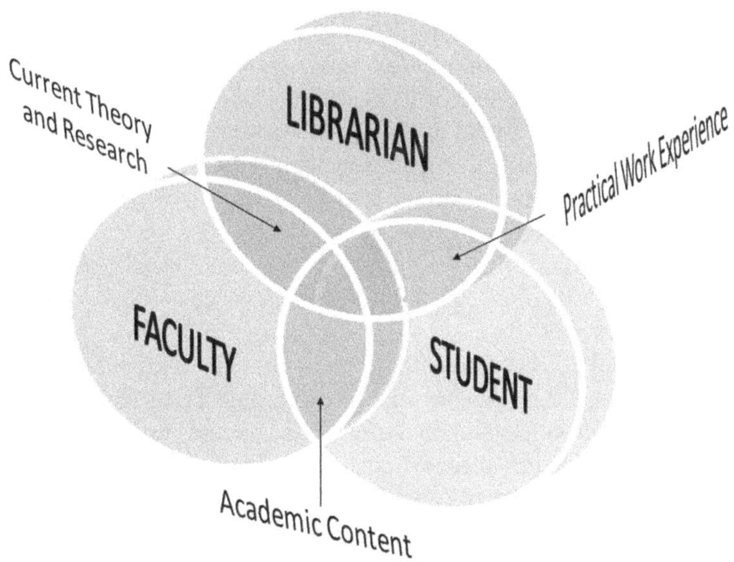

Figure 6.1. Real Learning Connections Model

reinforces and adds new knowledge to the practitioner's frame of reference and also provides constructive feedback through the faculty member involved for updating and/or modifying the curricula.

STUDENT PRACTICUM

A specific project, which related to a manuscript collection in a special collections department, also gave opportunity to address the skills needed for the student working in a setting that crossed into librarianship, curation, and archive of parts of the project. These skills converged in this project to the shared experience of the student, librarian, and faculty with very positive results. This demonstrated that an individual professional can address all elements of a collection, from public service, care, and curation of materials to providing the needed components of archiving appropriate parts.

Although this is a student-practicum model, the benefits to a practicing librarian within this context can be significant. By working with others and with work requiring different skills, the librarian gains a broader sense of skill deployment beyond their specialized area. As has been the case with the project so far, the practitioner's learning objectives are meant to refresh their professional knowledge. Future projects can be studied with this skill convergence in mind.

CONCLUSIONS AND FUTURE CONSIDERATIONS

There are many factors to be considered with regard to convergence of skills needed and used across cultural heritage organizations, such as libraries, archives, and museums. Some of those are economic and financial in nature, as could always be the case, in terms of justification of monies invested. Others will be technological in nature as technologies will continually change to enhance the user experience but also to produce work efficiencies. The skills that produce a unique professional identity for those employed and who promote the work of these institutions will need to be flexible in order to benefit from those financial and technological changes that will come, whether desired or not.

Agnes Vatican (2011) discusses the community and public aspect of convergence from the viewpoint of pooling projects that have general significance of benefit to local communities. She indicates that collaboration on these projects is driven by means, but she also implies that professional duty should motivate professionals working in libraries, archives, and museums to seek convergence for the benefit of the community involved. Institutions should have a shared understanding of the importance of this collaboration for projects or convergence for ongoing sustainability.

Thus, having a mindset or strategic intelligence to proactively create a strategy to embrace change will also provide a desire to modify and enrich job skills as needed by the organization. Organizational leadership should conduct environmental scans at the level of individual contribution and skills in order to determine the benefits gained from seeking different, more blended skills. Individuals will need to demonstrate the desire to match the organization's strategic goals by learning new skills, blending skills and experiences with similar institutions to gain common benefits, and allowing new professionals to influence the creation of new materials and service models.

Library science education has already started to move toward cross-teaching subjects and skills needed by strategically enabled organizations. Many examples exist in which thought has been given to changes in the curriculum that broaden the scope of exposure and learning to subjects and topics meaningful for work in cultural heritage organizations. Coupled with that is the opportunity to gain practical knowledge in work environments that will improve the context of theoretical applications. This can be useful for helping students understand the flexible nature of multiple skill sets and improve long-term career goals and choices.

Future consideration should be given to professional development opportunities in which practitioners in multiple areas of these professional fields are given the chance to work with new knowledge and experiences so as to enable a wider understanding of organizational objectives and goals. But it is not just about the organizations; it is also about the profession and how respect for individual expertise and specialization can be enhanced to include the adoption of new skills that can be shared more broadly.

Additional education and training as it relates to soft skills, such as emotional intelligence, will also increase individual understanding of the benefits of convergence for everyone. This can be done as part of a strategic initiative for seeking change but should also garner new respect for all aspects of the profession.

REFERENCES

Barth, C. D. (2011). *Convergence of libraries and technology organizations: New information support models.* Oxford: Chandos Publishing.

Bierbaum, E. G. (2000). *Museum librarianship.* Jefferson, NC: McFarland & Company.

Bird, N. J., and Crumpton, M. A. (2014). Real learning connections: Questioning the learner in the LIS internship. *Journal of Education for Library and Information Science*, *55*(2), 89–99.

Bordeaux, M.-C. (2013). Educational service of the cultural department in museums. *Bulletin Des Bibliotheques De France*, *58*(3).

Davidson, W. H., and Davis, S. M. (1990). Management and organization principles for the information economy. *Human Resources Management*, *29*(4), 365–83.

Dilevko, J., and Gottlieb, L. (2004). *The evolution of library and museum partnerships.* Westport, CT: Libraries Unlimited.

Duff, W., Carter, J. M., MacNeil, H., and Howart, L. C. (2013). From coexistence to convergence: Studying partnerships and collaboration among libraries, archives and museums. *Information Research*, *18*(3). Retrieved from http://www.informationr.net/ir/18-3/paper585.html#.VfRJpBFViko

Evans, A., and Chun, E. (2012). *Creating a tipping point: Strategic human resources in higher education.* San Francisco: ASHE Higher Education Report.

Galvin, T. J. (1995, August). Convergence or divergence in education for the information professions: An opinion paper. *Bulletin of the American Society for Information Science, 21*(6). Retrieved from https://www.asis.org/Bulletin/Aug-95/galvin.html

Given, L. M., and McTavish, L. (2010). What's old is new again: The reconvergence of libraries, archives and museums in the digital age. *Library Quarterly*, *80*(1), 7–32.

Herring, J. E. (1991). Information management—The convergence of professions. *International Journal of Information Management*, *11*, 144–55.

IMLS (Institute of Museum and Library Services). (2009). *Museums, libraries, and 21st century skills* (IMLS-2009-NAI-01). Washington, DC: IMLS.

Kim, J. (2012). Building rapport between LIS and museum studies. *Journal of Education for Library and Information Science*, *53*(2), 149–61.

Marty, P. F. (2014). Digital convergence and the information profession in cultural heritage organizations: Reconciling internal and external demands. *Library Trends*, *62*(3), 613–27.

Marty, P. F., and Twidale, M. B. (2011). Museum informatics across the curriculum: Ten years of preparing LIS students for careers transcending libraries, archives and museums. *Journal of Education for Library and Information Science*, *52*(1), 9–22.

McKee, B. (2005). Futureproofing our professional association—convergence and CILIP. *Feliciter*, *2*, 72–75.

O*NET Resource Center. (n.d.) *Occupational information network (O*NET)*. US Department Of Labor/Employment and Training Administration. Retrieved from https://www.onetcenter.org/overview.html

Vatican, A. (2011). Convergences and divergences between archives and libraries. *Bulletin Des Bibliotheques De France*, *56*(4), 16–20.

Wells, J. R. (2012). *Strategic IQ: Creating smarter corporations.* San Francisco: Jossey-Bass.

Wythe, D. (2007). New technologies and the convergence of libraries, archives, and museums. *RBM: A Journal of Rare Books, Manuscripts and Cultural Heritage*, *8*(1), 51–55.

Zorich, D., Waibel, G., and Erway, R. (2008). Beyond the silos of the LAMs: Collaboration among libraries, archives and museums. Report produced by OCLC Research. Retrieved from http://www.oclc.org/reseach/publications/library/2008/2008-05.pdf

Chapter Seven

Converging Educational Strategies

An Italian e-Learning Class for Young LAMs Professionals[1]

Carla Colombati, Elena De Carolis, and Agnese Galeffi

ABSTRACT

Converging Education Strategies is a proposed course originated from an e-learning class organized by the Italian Library Association. The outcome of the teamwork for the class was an e-learning course consisting of four themes. The theme chosen by our working group focused on the orientation and education of young students (eighteen to twenty-five years old) to the librarian profession. The proposed course, entitled Reloaded Librarian with the slogan "Break the stereotype!," has prompted interest and received wide praise encouraging us to offer it as a module of the broader course on library, archive, and museum (LAMs) education, adopting a blended and active learning approach and making use of the open learning platform Moodle.

In Italy, at the local level, there are currently many LAM initiatives mainly focused on legislative and management issues. There is not, however, a comparable initiative on education. Our goal is to encourage the establishment of a course, supported by the professional associations, that offers an overview of the LAM approach, including the skills to promote its development. Many institutions have library, archival, and museum collections that require professionals with a background in cultural heritage to consistently perform traditional tasks (e.g., resource selection, description, management, reference services, promotion, etc.) along with new and ever-evolving technical skills (digitization, database development, digital asset migration, linked open data, etc.). Among the open issues to be addressed are: 1) building alliances among the professional associations Associazione Italiana Biblioteche (AIB; libraries), Associazione Nazionale Archivistica Italiana (ANAI; archives), and International Council of Museums (ICOM) to develop common strategies for education and career development; 2) reducing the digital divide between older and younger professionals (e.g., helping professionals transition from traditional competencies to the adoption of new technical skills); 3) engaging students through new learning techniques, such as gamification; and 4) transforming the traditional curriculum through new strategies of engagement.

INTRODUCTION

As part of the international debate on digital heritage, a lively discussion has developed around the repercussions arising from digital convergence in relation to the redefinition of professional profiles in the libraries, archives and museums (LAMs) sector. The changes taking place in this sphere have strongly called into question the individual and well-established professional identities of librarians, archivists, and museum personnel, thereby providing us with a good opportunity to build an "interdisciplinary bridge" (Tammaro, Madrid, and Casarosa, 2013, p. 184).

The objective of this intervention is to propose and explore a possible "converging educational strategies" training course: a blended learning module to be delivered through the e-learning platform, Moodle. Ideally, a project of this kind would involve the various Italian professional associations active in the LAM sphere. We set out from the firm belief that a joint effort made in the area of education represents an effective approach when it comes to the acquisition of new skills, and also for giving fresh impetus to professional advocacy.

BACKGROUND

In the first three months of 2014, the AIB offered an innovative blended-learning course to Italy's community of professional librarians. The course was titled AIB Continuing Education in E-Learning: Teaching and Learning by Means of New Technologies. Structured into four phases and positioned at the sixth level of the European Qualifications Framework for Lifelong Learning (see https://ec.europa.eu/ploteus/sites/eac-eqf/files/leaflet_en.pdf), the goal of the course was to improve the quality of AIB continuing education by means of e-learning.

The course's educational objectives were:

- to impart knowledge in relation to teaching methodologies and e-learning technologies that can enhance learning levels; and
- to develop in enrollees the ability to make choices with an awareness of tools, exercises and content based on the educational objectives and the needs of the participants.

The course was characterized by a constructivist educational approach, and therefore by active and significant learning. All enrollees in the course were allowed to find their own path by freely shifting between traditional resources (lessons presented on slides and Portable Document Format [PDF] documents), informal learning tools, and collaborative learning (forums, participatory glossary building, feedback between peers, and self-assessment through the production of personal portfolios).

Our proposal for a new course was inspired by participation in a work group on the theme of advocacy, which led us to devise and realize an e-learning course titled Reloaded Librarian aimed at young students (eighteen- to twenty-five-year-olds) in order to foster orientation toward the librarian profession. One feature of the course was the shattering of long-established stereotypes associated with the figure of a librarian—stereotypes that have become meaningless in today's technological and communications context. Positive feedback within the learning community prompted us to reflect on the possibility of adopting the course as a starting point for the development of a broader and better structured learning environment for libraries, archives and museums.

The goal is that of offering a new professional model, not only to those who are investigating employment opportunities but also those who are already active in the workplace. By now, it has become clear that there is an urgent need for personnel who are already at work to rethink their established outlook and shift toward a lifelong learning scenario that rapidly evolves and requires a strong aptitude to change and openness to embracing nontraditional learning models. Digital convergence is already giving birth to new professions; Digital Curation (Harvey and Bastian, 2011) is just one example.

WHY TRAIN A LAMS PROFESSIONAL?

By now, the convergence of the world of libraries, archives, and museums has been underway for a number of years. Various projects, conventions, and joint initiatives have taken place. In some instances, there has even been a preference to employ a somewhat "sexier" acronym: GLAM: galleries, libraries, archives, museums (Edson, 2013, slide 7).

In 2008, OCLC published *Beyond the Silos of the LAMs: Collaboration among Libraries, Archives and Museums*, a report that was the fruit of a meeting between the Smithsonian Institution, the Victoria and Albert Museum, and of Yale, Princeton, and Edinburgh Universities, organized by the Research Libraries Group. The section titled "Flexibility" states:

> LAM professionals who understand issues surrounding different types of collections and collecting institutions, and who are not rigidly wedded to their own

> professional traditions, bring an open-mindedness that allows them to embrace ideas from other professions in the interests of the collaboration. Traditionally, [. . .] LAM professionals are schooled, trained and work within respective fields. When brought together, their discussions often focus on the distinctions—rather than the commonalities—among their various domains. . . . While campuses may promote mutual respect among all LAM traditions, they often offer little time and few opportunities to learn about what one participant called "the cultural microclimates of various professional activities" [and] a participant suggested providing cross-domain training for cultural heritage professionals to educate a new generation of professionals who will see the LAM (and not just one if its parts) as their domain. (Zorich, Waibel, and Erway, 2008, pp. 27–28.)

LAM cooperation frequently limits itself to questions in relation to organization, bureaucracy, and lobbying, based on the obvious consideration that cultural heritage institutions concern themselves with the management of collections (Hedstrom and King, 2004). For example, in Italy the constitutive charter of the MAB Coordination (Museums, Archives and Libraries) of 2012 lists among its objectives the proposal to come up with "educational and qualification initiatives for members of the participating associations concerned with the protection, conservation and valorization of cultural heritage" (AIB-ANAI-ICOM 2012, art. 2), but it does not (yet) address training programs that focus on convergence. Furthermore, according to the collaboration continuum described by Waibel and Erway (2009, p. 326), convergence represents the final stage in the evolution of cooperation process.

In training/education, convergence (up to the present) has been placed among digital curation activities (Ray, 2009; Marty, 2008, 2014; Tammaro, Madrid, and Casarosa, 2013), namely the ability to add value to digital assets for use and reuse over the long term. This consideration is undoubtedly motivated by the relative ease of merging digital objects and their descriptions (thus keeping traditional collections in place) in the memory institutions that house them (Robinson, 2012). The role played by the digital curator is unquestionably an important and highly specialized one.

The module we are hypothesizing in this paper is a foundation course, aimed at young people aged eighteen to twenty-five and intended to accomplish two basic objectives:

1. Orientation: demonstrate that careers in the cultural heritage context can be interesting, challenging, and on the cutting edge of high technology; and
2. Training in the area of skills commonly required in the sphere of LAMs, in such a way as to allow individuals to choose a context in which to learn skills relevant to the sector. This second objective may also be of interest to qualified personnel already working within an institution (library, archive, or museum), but who wish to widen their professional horizons.

POTENTIAL THEMES FOR THE COURSE TO ADDRESS

In order to settle on the themes to address during a course intended for LAM personnel, the various tasks performed by a professional librarian serve as a good starting point. Using a table prepared by the AIB in the preparatory stage of creating "A National Index of Educational and Training Titles and Professional Qualifications," one can identify three macro areas of professional activity: (1) management of informational and documentary resources, (2) supply of services, and (3) planning and management of services. Specifically, the anticipated activities (and hence educational contexts) are:

1. Acquisition and inventorying of informational and documentary resources (a);
2. Treatment and physical organization of informational and documentary resources (a);
3. Inventory control of informational and documentary resources (a);
4. Description and other details of resources (a);
5. Revision of collections (weeding) (b);
6. Discarding of resources (c);
7. Drafting of an emergency plan and preventive conservation projects (a);
8. Reproduction (of resources) for the purpose of conservation (c);
9. Maintenance of catalogues and databases (a);
10. Distribution (borrowing) (c);
11. Loan;
12. Document delivery (c);
13. Orientation (front office) and reference both in person and remotely (via telephone, chat, e-mail, etc.) (a);
14. Information literacy;
15. Promotion (book launchings, realization of exhibitions and events, guided visits) (a);
16. Institutional communications (website, online catalogues, social media, newsletter, leaflets, etc.) (a);
17. Analysis of the social context in which the institution operates (a);
18. Drawing up of a collections charter (library selection policy/collection development policy).
19. How to expand collections (a);
20. Management of physical spaces (reading rooms, depositories, service areas, furniture, signposting) (a);
21. Management of informational resources and hardware/software tools (a);
22. Drafting of a service charter (library service policy) (a);
23. Management of human resources (selection, organization, assessment and training) (a);

24. Management of a safety plan (a);
25. Fundraising and management of financial resources (a).

Many of the activities are of an essentially clerical nature, and therefore well suited to young people. The activities tagged (a) are those that, notwithstanding the differences between institutions, are all shared by LAMs; those tagged (b) are activities common to libraries and museums, while those tagged (c) are activities common to libraries and archives.

But what exactly do we mean by training/education in respect to "description and other details of resources" when the methods that have been tried and tested over time in LAMs can vary? Bearing in mind that "coordinated" should not mean "identical" (Trant, 2009), the proposed course would not go into too much detail as regards norms, but instead examine the objectives of descriptive tools in use in libraries, archives, and museums. In the case of the Collections Charter (library selection policy-collection development policy), the course would present different ways of expanding collections (in line with institutional aims).

To the above list we can add a few more themes that are necessary to explore in order to give sufficient weight and depth to the context in which the course enrollee will subsequently work:

- professional ethics;
- concept of "service";
- concept of "cultural heritage";
- support for professionals (Freedman, 2009), support for professional associations, and advocacy; and
- institutional typologies of libraries (national, state, civic, university libraries, etc.), archives (state archives, non-state public archives, private archives, company archives, etc.), and museums (art galleries, civic museums, science museums, etc.).

These themes provide a conceptual framework for the twenty-five activities listed above by pointing to common ground between LAM institutions such as professional ethics, the predisposition of LAM operators toward user services, and cultural heritage as physical objects and an overview of institutions included under the umbrella acronym "LAMs."

WHAT KIND OF SPACE FOR A LAM OPERATOR?

Professional contexts now call for a great capacity to adapt, to solve problems, to be flexible, and for teamwork and creativity as part of a constant process of lifelong learning. A young LAM professional will have to be able to:

- understand what kind of institute best aligns with their preferences in such a way as to guide their subsequent training;
- work in institutions, networks, and consortia that include collections within the whole gamut of LAMs;
- work in a flexible fashion in libraries, archives or museums;
- work on cooperative/collaborative projects, coordination, or convergence programs in the LAM sector; and
- guide users through LAM resources, whether those who seek specific information, or alternatively those who are undertaking research in their free time simply because they feel inspired to do so.

At the same time, the "openness" of this kind of professional figure will make it easier to realize the desired convergence. Training should succeed in anticipating and "capturing" the needs of a context that is becoming ever more interconnected. Very often, and with good reason, the view is expressed that the context best suited to merging is the Web, in other words, resources in digital format, and shared (but virtual) research and consultation environments. On the other hand, we all know how most people feel the need for physical meeting places where they can communicate with each other in person—the so-called third place theorized by Ray Oldenberg (1991) twenty-five years ago: places where people can feel free to circulate and satisfy their curiosity among book shelves or in exhibition galleries, "harvesting" in the process multi-sensory stimuli that can then be built on. The differences between LAMs do not necessarily lead to the erection of barriers, all the more so given that the way users think and their wishes are becoming ever more "fluid." David S. Ferriero, tenth Archivist of the United States, who was formerly director of the New York Public Library, and previously worked at the Massachusetts Institute of Technology, has stated (during a gathering organized by the Harvard Library Strategic Conversation, "We need to focus on user behavior. We don't know enough about how they use resources, users expect to be able to span the scope of knowledge in seconds" (Leddy, 2012). For this reason, personnel able to receive, advise, and guide (users), in addition to being able to work in a cultural context without barriers, are required.

NEW LEARNING TECHNIQUES FOR LAM PROFESSIONALS

Another aspect that should not be neglected in the educational process aimed at new professionals in the LAM sector is without a doubt the development of a capacity to identify the needs of users, above and beyond the custodial histories typical of individual disciplines. The challenge we are presented with is to engage the audience so as to create connections and sharing among collections, institutions, and users in information spaces, firmly positioning ourselves as trusted sources and avoiding the risk of getting lost in the meandering labyrinths of social media (Trant, 2009, pp. 383–84).

Social engagement has always been an integral part of the activities of libraries, archives, and museums, but it is necessary to make strides in terms of quality so as to enlarge traditional core communities: as the OCLC's Report on Social Media underlines, "to move beyond the project and experimental stage, LAMs staff need to know how to incorporate the user generated content generated by social media within their daily workflows" (Smith-Yoshimura, 2011, p. 9). To favor—in an effective way—active learning of this new capacity, we think it will be very useful to exploit new learning techniques, such as game-based learning and other methods based on simulation, which incline toward the acquisition of skills such as problem solving and critical thinking (Harvey and Bastian, 2011).

The goal of this approach is to succeed in engaging students by using as leverage their innate curiosity and the "entertainment" and pleasure they derive from participating, rather than focusing on the necessity to show that an objective has been accomplished as an end in itself. In other words, the emphasis is placed on drilling students in the valuable skill of knowing how to pose questions and how to make effective choices, rather than on the capacity to always and quickly be able to provide correct answers. A playful environment makes it possible for students to proceed at their own pace, testing out, through trial and error, the choices they make and then assessing the consequences of those choices. In this way, the student will acquire the ability to act and an awareness of how to make a difference in the working environment—qualities that we would like to see becoming an integral part of a new LAM professional's profile.

These skills, furthermore, are crucial if we are to establish ourselves as active protagonists, not only in communication and information processes but also in education. More and more we hear talk of "extreme learning environments," environments that must not elude LAM professionals if we are to build relevant communities, both in physical venues and remotely—a future that will be rich in game-like and creative opportunities, and in which MOOCs, live events, augmented reality, and gamification initiatives all blend into a new way of ubiquitous learning (Buck, 2013).

Among the initiatives, we can mention Metadata Games (http://www.metadatagames.org/) as being a particularly interesting experience. Metadata Games is a crowdsourcing project that has created a digital gaming platform (developed by Tiltfactor and Dartmouth Colleges) for collecting metadata on archival images, audio, and moving image artefacts, and which is also developing collaborations with important institutions such as the British Library (Flanagan and Carini, 2012) (figure 7.1).

Figure 7.1.
Source: http://www.metadatagames.org/british-library/

Last, but not least, this new scenario offers the chance to meet the challenge of transforming the traditional curriculum through new engagement strategies, such as the integration of gaming. The NMC Horizon Report: 2014 Higher Education Edition cites an example of gamification that could potentially also be used in our context to incentivize professional development: "Deloitte developed the Deloitte Leadership Academy, a training program that leverages gamification to create curriculum-based missions. Learners earn badges for completing missions, which they can display on their LinkedIn profiles" (Johnson, Adams, Estrada, and Freeman, 2014, p. 43).

A concrete example of development in the area of new learning techniques in Italy is represented by the AIB course that we have already mentioned. The success of the AIB e-learning training experience is a result of a constructivist educational approach: knowledge sharing was emphasized by the community of practice (CoP) which, once the learning method was set in the e-learning mode, could be defined as a community of practice of e-learning (CoPE), endowed with a glossary of communications and specific activities.

These elements can be taken into consideration when one is mulling over the key components of the basic course that we are proposing to offer in the sphere of LAMs convergences, taking into account, of course, that one of the fundamental goals will be to transmit a sense of "professional community" to the students in such a way as to transform their learning into knowledge.

The CoPE philosophy is based on the presupposition that knowledge sharing represents the bedrock of community of practice, today also known as *e-learning communities of practice*; therefore, let us pick up again on some reflections on knowledge management (KM) as proposed by Dalkir touching on the KM cycle. Dalkir (2005) lists several definitions of KM examined from three main perspectives:

1. the business perspective: of no relevance in the current discussion;
2. the cognitive science or knowledge science perspective: "Knowledge—the insights, understandings, and practical know-how that we all possess—is the fundamental resource that allows us to function intelligently. Over time, considerable knowledge is also transformed to other manifestations—such as books, technology, practices, and traditions—within organizations of all kinds and in society in general. These transformations result in cumulated expertise and, when used appropriately, increased effectiveness. Knowledge is one, if not THE, principal factor that makes personal, organizational, and societal intelligent behavior possible" (Wiig, 1993, pp. 38–39, as quoted by Dalkir, 2005, p. 5); and
3. the process/technology perspective.

The various definitions listed by Dalkir make clear how difficult it is to define and encapsulate KM within neat confines. In fact, Dalkir highlights the multidisciplinary side (Dalkir, 2005, p. 6), and reiterates the distinction between "data" and "knowledge," as well as that between "tacit knowledge" and "explicit knowledge." In addition to proposing an analysis of the importance that KM currently places on the categories *Individuals*, *Communities*, and *Organizations*, Dalkir also proposes an integrated KM cycle. An integrated KM cycle makes it possible for different activities related to KM to develop in a concatenated fashion: in this way, information, within the relevant context (whether that of individuals, organizations, or communities of practice), is transformed into knowledge.

Among the three above-mentioned categories, that of *Communities* is perfectly matched to our context. For the community of practice, knowledge management:

- develops professional skills;
- romotes peer-to-peer mentoring;
- facilitates more effective networking and collaboration;
- develops a professional code of ethics that members can follow; and
- develops a common language (Dalkir 2005, p. 20).

The integrated KM cycle that Dalkir proposes develops in three stages: (1) knowledge capture and/or creation, (2) knowledge sharing and dissemination, and (3) knowledge acquisition and application. By moving from one stage to the next, assessing, contextualizing, and updating KM (renewed by means of a continuous process), respectively, are achieved (p. 43). The role played by knowledge sharing is the one of most interest to us since it develops the dimension of "social construction of meaning" (p. 109) and underscores the notion of "community," which is essential to the successful convergence of LAMs: "The establishment of a community identity depends heavily on knowledge sharing" (p. 129). In particular, knowledge sharing is achieved by means of communities of practice (CoPs): "A community of practice refers to 'a group of people having common identity, professional interests and that undertake to share, participate and establish a fellowship'" (Pickett et al., 2000, as quoted by Dalkir, 2005, p. 112).

Dalkir stresses the influence of technology on the development of knowledge sharing: thanks to this influence, continual learning activities take form that differ among themselves according to the technological tools employed and are typified in the context of Web 2.0 (Dalkir, 2005, pp. 109–12). In this setting, the growing phenomenon of CoPs is characterized by a social constructivist approach to learning and knowledge. This knowledge sharing development model based on CoPs is the subject of another transformation. Picking up again on some emerging themes brought to the fore in the *NMC Horizon Report: 2014 Higher Education Edition* (Johnson et al., 2014), noteworthy among trends of fast, mid- and long-range trends we find:

- Fast Trends: the "Growing Ubiquity of Social Media" and the "Integration of Online, Hybrid, and Collaborative Learning";
- Mid-Range Trends: the "Rise of Data-Driven Learning and Assessment" and the "Shift from Students as Consumers to Students as Creators"; and
- Long-Range Trends: "Agile Approaches to Change" and the "Evolution of Online Learning."

Thanks to technology, learning methods can be based on both the content devised by the supplier of the educational material and that created by the students, thus putting into effect the constructivist teaching model. Learning techniques based on "online learning" stimulate interaction within the community, which, as a whole, builds the content.

This strongly interactive and constructivist role is suggested by Chikh, Berkani, and Sarirete (2008), who observe the transformation of CoPs into CoPE—a new model of learning by e-learning. This group of researchers holds the view that "e-learning is seen as a process of learning," in which both the student and the teacher or supervisor learn reciprocally in a constructivist way. The fact that the community described shares a common vocabulary represents another successful element:

> A lot of research has been done to promote and develop good e-learning models, practices, and technological environments. However, fewer efforts were deployed to support e-learning practitioners in performing their job on a day to day basis. There is a need to facilitate communication, collaboration, and coordination amongst e-learning community members. A strategic approach is to solve the problem of capitalization of techno-pedagogic knowledge, tacit and explicit, in the domain of e-learning within the framework of an online community of practice of e-learning (CoPE). The present thesis attempts to solve this problem by creating an individual memory and organizational memory for resources, information, and knowledge that need to be made available to the community members along with an ontology representing a uniform vocabulary for the CoPE. (Chikh, Berkani, and Sarirete, 2008, p. 31.)

The "ideal" model would therefore be to realize a professional community of students that truly becomes a community, a community that takes advantage of a common vocabulary (derived from LAM vocabularies) and that develops shared competences.

OBSERVATIONS AND CONCLUSIONS

The key "common" word, "convergence," invites us to ponder the various ideas and phenomena that foster a transition "from Coexistence to Convergence" (Duff, Carter, Cherry, MacNeil, and Howarth, 2013). Also of great relevance is the development of a common vocabulary and set of competences. By way of a couple of hints, we can cite the studies on the taxonomy of KOS (knowledge organization systems) and the initiatives frequently linked to LAMs institutions of the "wiki" world which, by means of "hackathons," populate Wikipedia in a "structured" (not to say "scientific") way, so as to foster the development of linked data operability for the realization of the Semantic Web.

The typical profile of a new generation of LAMs professional, as envisaged by the training course we are proposing in this intervention, will be characterized by the need to establish a trusted identity and a common language derived from traditional competencies. The acquisition of a range of not strictly technical abilities, such as creative thinking, teamwork and problem solving, will also be necessary. In this way the student, who represents a future LAMs professional, will be able to manage—with a good degree of cognizance—social engagement and will also be proficient in channeling user-generated content into the digital information space of memory institutions, as part of a steady process of collective lifelong learning.

NOTE

1. This chapter reflects the state of the art as of August 2014.

ACKNOWLEDGMENTS

AIB E-learning community and Maria Cristina Pattuelli.

REFERENCES

AIB, ANAI and ICOM 2012, MAB atto costitutivo. Retrieved from http://www.mab-italia.org/images/pdf/MAB-Naz_Atto-costitutivo_2012-06-12.pdf

Buck, T. E. (2013). The massive effect of MOOCs on higher education. *Ed Tech Magazine.* Retrieved from http://www.edtechmagazine.com/higher/article/2013/01/massive-affect-moocs-higher-education

Chikh, A., Berkani, L., and Sarirete, A. (2008). Communities of practice of E-learning 'CoPE'—Definition and concepts. In *Proceedings—International Workshop on*

Advanced Information Systems for Enterprises, IWAISE (pp. 31–37). doi: 10.1109/IWAISE.2008.13.

Dalkir, K. (2005). *Knowledge management in theory and practice*. Burlington, MA: Elsevier.

Duff, W., Carter, J., Cherry, J., MacNeil, H., and Howarth, L. (2013). From coexistence to convergence: studying partnerships and collaboration among, libraries, archives and museums. *Information Research, 18*(3). Retrieved from http://www.informationr.net/ir/183/paper585.html#.VfM8zxFViko

Edson, M. (2013). *Scope, scale, and speed.* Galleries, Libraries, Archives, Museums and Wikimedia Conference, London, British Library. Retrieved from http://www.youtube.com/watch?v=wp_BdHDZW68

Flanagan, M., and Carini, P. (2012). How games can help us access and understand archival images. *American Archivist, 75*(2), 514–37.

Freedman, S. (2009). Effective mentoring. *IFLA Journal, 35*(2), 171–82. doi: 10.1177/0340035209105672

Harvey, R., and Bastian, J. (2012). Out of the classroom and into the laboratory: Teaching digital curation virtually and experientially. *IFLA Journal, 38*(1), 25–34. doi 10.1177/0340035211435072

Hedstrom, M., and King, J. L. (2004). On the LAM: Library, archive, and museum collections in the creation and maintenance of knowledge communities. OECD. Retrieved from http://www.oecd.org/education/innovation-education/32126054.pdf

Johnson, L, Adams, B., Estrada, V., and Freeman, A. (2014). *NMC Horizon Report: 2014 Higher Education Edition.* Austin, TX: The New Media Consortium. Retrieved from http://cdn.nmc.org/media/2014-nmc-horizon-report-he-EN-SC.pdf

Leddy, C. (2012, April 10). Linking libraries, museums, archives. *Harvard Gazette*. Retrieved from http://news.harvard.edu/gazette/story/2012/04/linking-libraries-museums-archives/

Marty, P. F. (2008). An introduction to digital convergence: Libraries, archives, and museums in the information age. *Archival Science, 8*(4), 247–50. doi: 10.1007/s10502-009-9094-1

Marty, P. F. (2014). Digital convergence and the information profession in cultural heritage organizations: Reconciling internal and external demands. *Library Trends, 62*(3), 613–27. doi: 10.1353/lib.2014.0007

Oldenberg, R. (1991). *The great good place.* New York: Paragon House.

Pickett, J. P., et al. (2000). *The American heritage dictionary of the English language* (4th ed.). Boston, MA: Houghton Mifflin.

Ray, J. (2009). Sharks, digital curation, and the education of information professionals. *Museum Management and Curatorship, 24*(4), 357–68. doi:10.1080/09647770903314720

Robinson, H. (2012). Remembering things differently: Museums, libraries and archives as memory institutions and the implications for convergence. *Museum Management and Curatorship, 27*(4), 413–29. doi: 10.1080/09647775.2012.720188

Smith-Yoshimura, K. (2011). *Social metadata for libraries, archives and museums: Executive summary*. Dublin, OH: OCLC Research. Retrieved from http://www.oclc.org/research/publications/library/2012/2012-02.pdf

Tammaro, A. M., Madrid, M., and Casarosa, V. (2013). Digital curators' education: Professional identity vs. convergence of LAM (libraries, archives, museums). In M. Agosti, R. Esposito, S. Ferilli, and N. Ferro (Eds.), *Digital Libraries and Archives—8th Italian Research Conference, IRCDL 2012* (pp. 194–94). Berlin: Springer.

Trant, J. (2009). Emerging convergence? Thoughts on museums, archives, libraries, and professional training. *Museum Management and Curatorship*, 24(4), 369–87. doi: 10.1080/09647770903314738.

Waibel, G., and Erway, R. (2009). Think globally, act locally: Library, archive, and museum collaboration. *Museum Management and Curatorship*, *24*(4), 323–35. doi:10.1080/09647770903314704

Wiig, K. (1993). *Knowledge management foundations*. Arlington, TX: Schema Press.

Zorich, D., Waibel, G., and Erway, R. (2008). *Beyond the silos of the LAMS: Collaboration among libraries, archives and museums*. Dublin, OH: OCLC Programs and Research. Retrieved from http://www.oclc.org.ezproxy.hioa.no/programs/reports/2008-05.pdf

Chapter Eight

Technical Standards on Professional Profiles

An Opportunity for Library and Archives Convergence

Giovanni Michetti

ABSTRACT

The European Qualification Framework (EQF) for lifelong learning is a reference model established by the European Parliament and Council to support improvement of education and training systems. Based on a multidimensional matrix where knowledge, skills, and competencies should be identified as learning outcomes and assigned their proper level of qualification, such a model may serve not only as a translation device between different education systems but also as a tool to qualify a professional profile in a transparent and efficient way. This model has been applied to the archival and library domain: the Italian Standards Organization (UNI), together with the professional associations, has developed two national standards aimed at identifying the relevant features of both archivist's and librarian's profile. For the first time, a technical standard defines the competences, skills, and knowledge needed to be an archivist or a librarian. Such an initiative not only may support updating and redesigning professional curricula and education but may also help identify commonalities and peculiarities of the archival and librarian profiles, hence providing the ground for a possible convergence of libraries and archives. This chapter provides an overview of the EQF model and the Italian standards on the archival and librarian professional profile. Then it will focus on the comparison of the models promoted by these standards in order to highlight any features that may support or hinder convergence and show how technical standards may be an unexpected means of advancement toward convergence.

INTRODUCTION

> New technology and socio-economic phenomena like globalization have dramatically changed the labor market, resulting in a request for new skills and professional figures able to cope with the change. This is more than true for the archival domain: the space in which archivists work, the tools they work with and the way they work have totally changed since the last century, to the point that the archival community is investigating whether the archivist's role and identity needs for a redefinition—rather: a reinterpretation—in light of these big changes. (Michetti, 2014, p. 19)

This is true for the whole LIS domain, a space in which internal boundaries are more and more blurred while external boundaries keep on expanding and overlapping with other domains.

Education and training systems have been affected by these phenomena. All around the world, universities and professional associations "are struggling to be responsive to an increasing demand for new skills and competences" (Michetti, 2014, p. 19): new courses are designed every day, advanced programs are launched, novel professional figures are pushed into the market, and trendy terms are created—after all, jargon is an identifying feature of a professional community because mastering the language is a way to suggest that the underlying reality can be mastered, too. Interdisciplinarity is the rule, and technology is not optional anymore—far from being just a tool, technology has become the glue of many educational and professional initiatives, if not the objective.

The overall result is a rich and stimulating educational and professional environment, but such variety is also an issue when it comes to the need of comparing skills, qualifications, and learning paths. There can be no ambiguity in a common space like the European Union because of its founding principle: people, goods, services, and money can move around the EU without being obstructed by national borders and barriers. EU citizens can study, live, and work in any EU country.

This is the reason why the European Commission supported the creation of a European credit transfer system for vocational education and training (ECVET) integrated with a European credit transfer system (ECTS) in higher education: the idea was to create a European area of lifelong learning where the outcomes of different learning initiatives could be compared. The European Union assumed *competence* as the central feature of any lifelong learning policy and launched a set of initiatives with the objective of reforming agendas in vocational education and in tertiary education in the member states.

Following this approach, the European Parliament and Council established in 2008 the European Qualifications Framework (EQF) for lifelong learning, a reference model to support improvement of education and training systems (European Parliament, 2008). The European act recommends using the European Qualifications Framework as a reference tool to:

- compare the qualification levels of different qualification systems;
- promote lifelong learning and equal opportunities; and
- promote further integration of the European labor market, while respecting the rich diversity of national education systems.

In practice, the EQF acts as a "translation device to make qualifications more readable and understandable to employers, individuals and institutions, so that workers and learners can use their qualifications in other countries" (European Commission, 2008). It has two principal aims: to facilitate mobility and lifelong learning. The architecture of EQF is very simple: it is based on the triad "knowledge, skill, and competence," which are considered to be the fundamental learning outcomes through which any professional profile may be identified.

Knowledge is defined in the EQF as a body of facts, principles, theories, and practices that is related to a field of work or study. It is the outcome of the assimilation of information through learning, "the result of an interaction between intelligence (capacity to learn) and situation (opportunity to learn)" (Winterton, Delamaire-Le Deist, and Stringfellow, 2006, pp. 6–7)—hence its socially constructed nature. Knowledge is based on the ability of acquiring and understanding new knowledge, which in turn requires some cognitive prerequisites and specific knowledge and skills. Therefore, it is not always easy to distinguish between knowledge and skills. As a matter of fact, higher levels of competence are characterized by increasing proceduralization of knowledge, so "at higher levels, knowledge is converted to skills" (Klieme et al., 2004, p. 70).

Skill is defined in the EQF as the ability to apply knowledge and use know-how to complete tasks and solve problems. It may be cognitive or practical. However, even very practical skills "depend upon understanding of results and verbalised knowledge" (Winterton et al., 2006, p. 28): broad cognitive skills (such as problem solving and decision making) affect skilled performance. As noted above, there is a thin line between knowledge and skills: it is difficult to regard cognitive competences as knowledge rather than skill. This is particularly evident when we turn to the LIS domain, since we cannot establish clear boundaries between these two categories—the LIS professions are a complex mix of practical skills and theoretical competences.

Competence is the proven ability to use knowledge, skills, and personal, social, and/or methodological abilities in work or study situations and in professional and personal development. Therefore, it can be described in terms of responsibility and autonomy.

"Call it Knowledge, Skill, and Competence; or Savoir, Savoir faire, and Savoir être: in the end, the European model defines a 3-dimensional space, where archivists can find their own place at the intersection of cognitive, functional and social competences" (Michetti, 2014, p. 22).

The EQF also defines *levels* in order to identify different degrees of qualifications in relation to knowledge, skills, and competences. Levels allow the design of a full range of triads increasing in complexity from Level 1 to Level 8. The overall result is a matrix where knowledge, skills, and competences get a specific meaning with reference to the different levels.

Such a matrix can be a useful tool to reconsider archival activities under a different light: this consideration was one of the fundamental drivers of an Italian initiative launched in 2012, grounded upon the EQF model and aimed at developing a national standard to define the qualifying features of the archivist. The initiative was promoted by the Italian Standards Organization (UNI–Ente Nazionale Italiano di Unificazione) and eventually led to the issue of two national standards: *UNI 11535:2014 Professional librarian's profile. Defining requirements about knowledge, skills and competences*, and *UNI 11536:2014 Professional archivist's profile. Defining requirements about knowledge, skills and competences*. They are probably the first examples of adoption and implementation in the LIS domain of a European recommendation. These standards

> may improve the social and professional identification of archivists [and librarians] as proactive agents not only within their specific domain—as specialists of information and documentation processes—but also in the broader societal context, in their fundamental role as managers and preservers of cultural heritage, hence supporting local communities and societies at large in their ongoing action of self-definition. [. . .] The standard[s] may also improve education processes at graduate and post-graduate level: knowledge, skills and competences defined in the standard[s] may be adopted as a criterion or a guide to design a coherent and comprehensive educational program. (Michetti, 2014, p. 24)

Let's focus first on the standard on the archivist's profile. Its core is a *scheme* where functions, activities, competences, skills, and knowledge are organized in a systematic way. The philosophy that drove the development of the standard may well be expressed using the words of Richard Pearce-Moses:

> *what* information professionals do in the digital era remains the same. They must still work with record creators and publishers to build the collection; manage the

> organization of the materials, their preparation for use, and their preservation; and they must work with the public and other users to provide access to the collections. None of that changes in the digital era. However, [. . .] *how* information professionals do their jobs will change. (Pearce-Moses and Davis, 2008, p. ix)

In other words, "the standard has been developed assuming that the fundamental functions and activities of archival profession have not changed" (Michetti, 2014, p. 25), as can be clearly seen from the very first level of the scheme, which identifies the threefold *mission* of the archivist:

- manage archives through their life;
- communicate archives; and
- manage and run archival services.

Each mission is structured into *functions*, that is, a set of activities aimed at accomplishing a purpose, as depicted in table 8.1.

Please note that records management is considered an archival function: according to the Italian archival theory, there is no ontological distinction between current records and archives, *everything is archives*. Archives are a whole, from creation to preservation stage (Cencetti, 1939, pp. 7–13).

The standard provides a brief description of each function, as shown in table 8.2. All of these functions are considered pertinent to the archival profile, and all together they shape the professional identity of an archivist, but not every archivist is supposed to perform them all in their daily activity: rather, specialization is encouraged, as in any other field.

Table 8.1. Archivist. Mission and Functions

Mission	*Function*
Manage archives through their life, from design, creation, and accumulation to preservation stage	1. Records management 2. Protection 3. Appraisal and disposition 4. Arrangement and description 5. Preservation 6. Design and appraisal of information systems and applications
Communicate archives, providing services for users, promoting knowledge of archival resources, and encouraging skilled training and education	7. User services 8. Promotion, training, and education 9. Research
Manage and run archival services, planning their development and governing their resources	10. Management and administration

Table 8.2. Archivist. Functions

1. Records management	Whole of the activities aimed at governing creation, maintenance, handling, use, and disposition of records.
2. Protection	Whole of the activities aimed at monitoring and safeguarding non-state archives, carried on through a widespread auditing action performed by archival superintendencies.
3. Appraisal and disposition	Whole of the activities aimed at evaluating the historical and legal value of records, in order to identify those records that need to be preserved forever, and those that may be destroyed.
4. Arrangement and description	Whole of the intellectual and practical activities aimed at analyzing, organizing and describing archival materials on the basis of archival principles.
5. Preservation	Whole of the activities aimed at preserving documentary systems and objects along with their relationships, in such a way that their significant properties are not altered. Such an objective is achieved by implementing adequate environmental conditions, carrying on an ongoing control action onto objects, and designing proper strategies for safety and damage prevention.
6. Design and appraisal of information systems and applications	Whole of the activities aimed at designing or assessing information systems or software in the archival domain.
7. User services	Whole of the activities aimed at supporting users in archival research.
8. Promotion, training, and education	Whole of the activities aimed at promoting knowledge of archival resources and delivering training and education initiatives in the archival domain.
9. Research	Archivists put their knowledge at the service of scientific research, but they also have a specific, autonomous role with reference to research on history, historiography, institutions, archives, and more generally any information science topic.
10. Management and administration	Management of documentary heritage, human and financial resources, facilities, and tools requires mastery of a complex body of laws and regulations, as well as a wealth of knowledge of administrative and organizational skills to govern institutions or services committed to the preservation of documentary heritage, ensuring the safety of people, property and places. Knowledge of the market and the legislation in force, as well as the ability to write and evaluate projects and contract specifications, is critical in supply and demand for archival services.

Each archival function is articulated in *activities*, as shown in table 8.3.

The triad *knowledge*, *skills*, and *competences* proposed by the European model is implemented at this level onto each of the archival activities identified and coded in table 8.3. Only a couple of such activities are presented here, in order to provide an example of how the archival work can be modeled on the basis of the European model.

Description (activity 4.2) refers to all activities aimed at collecting, analyzing, organizing, and recording information that supports identification, management, location, and illustration of archival material along with its context of creation, use, transmission, and preservation. The creation and maintenance of a records

Table 8.3. Archivist. Functions and Activities

Function	*Activity*
1. Records management	1.1 Designing the records management system 1.2 Recordkeeping
2. Protection	2.1 Monitoring and safeguard 2.2 Inspection
3. Appraisal and disposition	3.1 Appraisal 3.2 Disposition
4. Arrangement and description	4.1 Arrangement 4.2 Description
5. Preservation	5.1 Managing environment 5.2 Curating and preserving archival resources
6. Design and appraisal of information systems and applications	6.1 Design 6.2 Appraisal
7. User services	7.1 Definition of terms for user services 7.2 Reference service 7.3 Distance service 7.4 Reproduction services 7.5 Dissemination of information about archival holdings
8. Promotion, training and education	8.1 Promotion 8.2 Training and education
9. Research	9.1 Scientific research 9.2 Editorial activity
10. Management and administration	10.1 Management of archival holdings 10.2 Management of human resources 10.3 Management of union relations 10.4 Management of financial resources 10.5 Management of facilities and tools 10.6 Management of contracts for supply of archival services

management system or a long-term preservation system requires activities aimed at collecting, organizing, and recording information on records as well as on their context. Therefore, description activities are carried out in the course of records management and preservation processes in a dynamic perspective.

The outcome of the description activities may be a traditional finding aid (e.g., a guide, or an inventory); however, archival information systems implement in the digital environment the functionalities of traditional finding aids, allowing for new and more granular access to records: as a matter of fact, archival information systems are the outcomes of description activities. Description can be carried out at different levels, with different degrees of detail and accuracy, with different purposes (see table 8.4).

Curating and preserving archival resources (activity 5.2) is nested within the *Preservation* function. It denotes the whole of procedures, policies, and strategies aimed at ensuring the curation and preservation of records on whatever media as well as preventing damages and ensuring safety. Preservation is a core mission for archivists, and as such, portrays their identity. However, the complexity of this activity may determine the need for specialization on specific types of records (e.g., photographs, audiovisual material, financial records, health records). Archivists cooperate with other professionals for the management of safety measures and emergency plans, without prejudice to the responsibility of those who run the archival service and the need for training of the personnel on these topics (see table 8.5).

The standard on the librarian's profile has a similar structure, even if less articulated and detailed. There are five points that identify the *mission* of librarians:

- create, organize, and protect library collections through accession, description, preservation, and dissemination of documents;
- accession and manage library information systems;
- provide access to both catalogues and documents and deliver retrieval, loan, and reproduction services for documents; promote the library by selecting and processing information and documents held by the library or accessible through it and presenting them to the general public; deliver educational and cultural services;
- analyze information needs of the community, define objectives, monitor and evaluate outcomes, manage human and financial resources and facilities; and
- research in the LIS domain and related fields.

Such a mission is accomplished by performing specific *activities*, each of which requires a set of *competences*, as depicted in table 8.6—to be specific,

Table 8.4. Archivist. Description

Competence	*Skill*	*Knowledge*
Planning a systematic and comprehensive description of the body of materials Identifying description elements	• Identify objectives and methodology of the description project • Identify criteria to select the materials • Identify articulation and features of the description project • Evaluate objectives of the description project • Evaluate characteristics of documentation • Evaluate relevant national and international standards • Evaluate user needs • Define level and granularity of description • Define description elements • Describe objectives and methodology of the description project • Describe results of the implementation of the methodology • Describe creators and duration of the description project	• Archival theory • Palaeography and diplomatics • Principles, methods and techniques of archival description • National and international standards on archival description • Medieval, modern, and contemporary history • History of medieval, modern, and contemporary institutions • History of ecclesiastic institutions • Foundations of private and public law • Elements of knowledge organization and representation • Elements of data modeling • Relevant requirements of an archival description application

Describing the body of materials	• Describe the body of materials and the related context of creation, use, accumulation, custody, and preservation, on the basis of the archival principles and description elements identified • Describe the body of materials on the basis of their physical location
Reviewing descriptions	• Check completeness, and semantic and syntactic correctness of descriptive data • Supplement descriptive data • Convert descriptive data from a description system to another
Creating auxiliary tools	• Create indexes • Create glossaries • Create calendars • Create lists • Create bibliographies

Table 8.5. Archivist. Curating and Preserving Archival Resources

Competence	*Skill*	*Knowledge*
Managing space	• Plan and monitor space utilization • Plan cleaning and maintenance of spaces	• Archival theory • Principles, methods, and techniques of preservation • Elements of chemistry • Elements of theory and practice of restoration • Elements of informatics • Elements of operational planning • Laws and regulation on archives, preservation, and digital records • Elements of administrative law • Laws and regulations on archives • Laws and regulations on digital records • Laws and regulations on transparency of public action, privacy, classified records, secrecy, copyright
Managing containers	• Plan requirements for diverse typologies of containers • Plan maintenance and monitoring of containers • Plan substitutions of obsolete or damaged containers, along with updating of any attached labels	
Managing preservation processes	• Plan dusting and disinfestation of documentation • Plan restoration of documentation • Plan operations aimed at identifying and cataloging materials needing restoration • Select bids and external operators for restoration activities • Evaluate the restoration activities • Plan and implement copying activities • Identify diverse preservation actions, based on support, format, and typology of documentation, objectives, usage, and other relevant documentation features	

Managing emergency plans	• Plan and implement maintenance and migration of digital records • Create a preservation guidebook where strategies and procedures about preservation are described in a systematic way • Implement the preservation guidebook • Manage moving of rare and ancient materials • Provide directions to technicians when designing the disaster recovery plan • Provide directions to technicians when designing the emergency plans • Plan and organize emergency training courses • Supervise emergency actions • Create disaster reports • Review the disaster recovery and emergency plans	• Laws and regulations on safety in work environments • National and international standards on preservation

Table 8.6. Librarian. Activities and Competences

Activity	*Competence*
1. Planning and development of collections	Plan accession Select resources Manage accession process
2. Handling and organization of documents	Organize documents workflow Organize shelving and storage systems Manage document handling and organization
3. Documents description and indexing, and data production	Define document typologies, description levels, and search criteria for users Evaluate software applications Generate data related to documents Set the metadata structures Monitor data quality
4. Preservation and protection of documents	Prepare plans for dusting, disinfestation, binding, and restoration Establish rules for documents access and use Prepare plans to ensure conformity for premises, furniture, and equipment Prepare plans for long-term preservation Manage preservation and protection
5. Accession and management of equipment, tools, and information systems	Evaluate the need for tools, equipment, and information systems Select purchases Manage hardware, software, and network equipment Manage creation of digital data and documents
6. User services and outreach	Organize reception, assistance, and orientation services for users Create the library service charter Organize resources and tools for users Organize the reference service Manage loan Organize training initiatives for users Promote knowledge of and access to the library Promote reading Evaluate the services in place
7. Design, evaluation, and management of library activities and services	Define objectives and strategies Evaluate the library services and activities Finalize use of human, financial and cultural resources

Activity	Competence
8. Management of human resources, financial resources, and property	Plan human resources requirement Select staff and enterprises Manage the internal organization of the library Evaluate effectiveness and efficiency of human resources Prepare training plans Manage security plan Manage balance Manage property
9. Research in the LIS domain and related fields	Create scientific literature Manage scientific initiatives

activities from 1 to 4 refer to the first bullet above, activity 5 to the second bullet, activity 6 to the third bullet, activities 7 and 8 to the fourth bullet, activity 9 to the last bullet.

Following the EQF model, each competence has skills and knowledge associated. For example, *Document description and indexing, and data production* (activity 3) is at the core of the librarians' work and has five different competences associated, each with its specific skills (see table 8.7).

Apparently—as can be seen from table 8.7—librarians' activities, competences, and skills are quite different from those outlined in the standard for archivists, and this is in line with the need of defining two professional figures with their specific features and peculiarities. Librarians and archivists have developed over a long time their own communities, languages, and disciplines—in other words, they have shaped their professional figures, seeking an autonomous space in the realm of the LIS domain. However, it is also true that new technology has somehow determined an inversion of this process: books and records are totally different objects, with different nature, functions, and characteristics, but in a digital environment they often need similar treatment. In principle, preserving an electronic resource in a library is not that different from preserving a digital record in an archive. Defining a metadata set is a fundamental activity that must be performed in both the library and the archival domain—the differences are in the content rather than in the methodology. The same is true for the design, management, or evaluation of an information system—not to mention non-core activities, like management of human resources or strategic planning.

The two Italian standards reflect such duplicity: they look different on the surface, but once we scratch it, we can see many elements in common. In order to compare their architectures, it is better to focus on the high levels and—despite the different titles and terminology—consider the deep

Table 8.7. Librarian. Documents Description and Indexing, and Data Production

Competence	*Skill*	*Knowledge*
Define document typologies, description levels and search criteria for users	• Identify the set of rules and the description level for each document typology and/or set, on the basis of the specific goals of the library • Establish the access points and research indexes	• Foundations of Library Science • Cataloguing principles and techniques • Relevant national and international standards
Evaluate software applications	• Identify the functional requirements • Choose the data presentation and user interface	• Descriptive, administrative and management metadata
Generate data related to documents	• Apply cataloguing rules and bibliographic standards • Assign persistent identifiers • Use bibliographic indexes and catalogues • Establish relationships among the data elements created	• Basics of languages, alphabets, scripts, and symbols
Set the metadata structures	• Apply metadata syntax • Apply rules for data elements collections • Validate structural consistency of data	
Monitor data quality	• Create authority files • Review data • Update data	

meaning of the activities outlined, trying to get the gist of them. To this aim, the hierarchical sets of the activities as modeled by the two standards are presented side by side in table 8.8.

First of all, it should be noted that both standards list their high-level activities by trying to follow a sort of chronological order, following resources from creation to the preservation stage. Therefore, in the archival standard, we will find *Records management*, *Appraisal and disposition*, *Arrangement and description*, and *Preservation*, followed by other activities that can be considered as cross activities, since they can be performed at any stage (e.g., *User services*, *Promotion*, *Management and administration*). *Protection* is a very peculiar activity because it refers to monitoring and safeguarding of non-state archives. These institutional functions are carried on through an auditing action performed by Archival Superintendencies, so it seems unlikely that an

Table 8.8. Librarian and Archivist. Activities

Librarian	*Archivist*
L1. Planning and development of collections	A1. Records management
1 Plan accession	1 Designing the records management system
2 Select resources	2 Recordkeeping
3 Manage accession process	
L2. Handling and organization of documents	A2. Protection
1 Organize documents workflow	1 Monitoring and safeguard
2 Organize shelving and storage systems	2 Inspection
3 Manage documents handling and organization	
L3. Documents description and indexing, and data production	A3. Appraisal and disposition
1 Define document typologies, description levels, and search criteria for users	1 Appraisal
2 Evaluate software applications	2 Disposition
3 Generate data related to documents	
4 Set the metadata structures	
5 Monitor data quality	
L4. Preservation and protection of documents	A4. Arrangement and description
1 Prepare plans for dusting, disinfestation, binding, and restoration	1 Arrangement
2 Establish rules for documents access and use	2 Description
3 Prepare plans to ensure conformity for premises, furniture, and equipment	
4 Prepare plans for long-term preservation	
5 Manage preservation and protection	
L5. Accession and management of equipment, tools, and information systems	A5. Preservation
1 Evaluate the need for tools, equipment, and information systems	1 Managing environment
2 Select purchases	2 Curating and preserving archival resources
3 Manage hardware, software, and network equipment	
4 Manage creation of digital data and documents	

(continued)

Table 8.8. *(Continued)*

Librarian	*Archivist*
L6. User services and outreach	A6. Design and appraisal of information systems and applications
1 Organize reception, assistance, and orientation service for users	1 Design
2 Create the library service charter	2 Appraisal
3 Organize the resources and tools for users	
4 Organize the reference service	
5 Manage loan	
6 Organize training initiatives for users	
7 Promote knowledge of and access to the library	
8 Promote reading	
9 Evaluate the services in place	
L7. Design, evaluation, and management of library activities and services	A7. User services
1 Define objectives and strategies	1 Definition of terms for user services
2 Evaluate the library services and activities	2 Reference service
3 Finalize use of human, financial, and cultural resources	3 Distance service
	4 Reproduction services
	5 Dissemination of information on archival holdings

L8. Management of human resources, financial resources, and property	A8. Promotion, training, and education
1 Plan human resources requirement	1 Promotion
2 Select staff and enterprises	2 Training and education
3 Manage the internal organization of the library	
4 Evaluate effectiveness and efficiency of human resources	
5 Prepare training plans	
6 Manage security plan	
7 Manage balance	
8 Manage property	
L9. Research in the LIS domain and related fields	A9. Research
1 Create scientific literature	1 Scientific research
2 Manage scientific initiatives	2 Editorial activity
	A10. Management and administration
	1 Management of archival holdings
	2 Management of human resources
	3 Management of union relations
	4 Management of financial resources
	5 Management of facilities and tools
	6 Management of contracts re archival services

analogous activity can be found in the standard for librarians, even if the term *protection* occurs more than once in it.

The standard for librarians follows a similar approach: there is a *Planning and development* stage (*L1*), then documents are *Handled and organized* (*L2*), *Described, indexed, and associated to their metadata* (*L3*), and eventually *Preserved* (*L4*). Some cross-activities complete the list (*Accession and management of equipment*, *Management of human resources*, etc.).

Seeking convergence between archives and library, such similarity is comforting. A closer look at the schemes suggests that some matches can be easily established:

- *L3 Documents description and indexing, and data production* is essentially about describing resources following a set of given criteria, producing data accordingly, and monitoring the quality of data. This is very much what archivists do in their *Description* activity (*A4.2*);
- *L4 Preservation and protection* is easily matched to *A5 Preservation*;
- *L5 Accession and management of equipment, tools, and information systems* can be matched to *A10.5 Management of facilities and tools*;
- *L6 User services and outreach* merges two archival activities: *A7 User Services*, and *A8 Promotion, training, and education*;
- *L8 Management of human resources, financial resources, and property* matches very well some inner entries of *A10 Management and administration*, in particular, *A10.2 Management of human resources, A10.4 Management of financial resources*, and *A10.5 Management of facilities and tools*; and
- *L9 Research in the LIS domain and related fields* matches *A9 Research.*

The matches for the other first-level entries of the librarians' scheme are a bit more complicated:

- *L1 Planning and development of collections* is a bit problematic. Given its position at the top of the structure, one is tempted to consider it as the first stage of the collection life cycle, and match it to *A1*, since this refers to the management of archival resources. However, *L1.1 Plan accession* refers to a planning activity that may rather be matched to *A10.1 Management of archival holdings*—in fact, in the archival scheme, any strategic planning and development of the holdings has been included within *A10 Management and administration*. On the other hand, *L1.3 Manage accession process* may be considered as a management activity pertaining to the initial stage of the life cycle, so it can be matched to *A1.2 Recordkeeping*. In brief, *L1 Planning and development of collections* is a candidate for matching *A1 Records management*; however the critical issue is to decide whether strategic planning is an activity that should be considered as part of the (very practical) management activity or deserves an autonomous space, within *A10 Management and administration* or elsewhere.

- *L2 Handling and organization of documents* is another example of a composite entry. In fact, *L2.1 Organize documents workflow* can be matched to *A1.1 Designing the records management system*, which embeds a specific skill called *Organizing workflow*. The same is true for *L2.3 Manage documents handling and organization*, that could be matched to *A1.2 Recordkeeping*. The critical issue is *L2.2 Organize shelving and storage systems*, since it poses an interesting problem: in the librarians' scheme, this entry is nested within *L2 Handling and organization of documents*, that is, it refers to the active stage. There is no doubt that resources need to be physically allocated and arranged, in order to be managed. However, there can be found no similar entry within the archival *A1 Records management* because function prevails against time in the archivists' scheme: shelving and storing are about preserving; therefore *A5 Preservation* is the entry dealing with them in the archivists' scheme. It is there that we should look to establish a match. In other words, preservation is a function that needs to be implemented at any stage of the life cycle, and so do most of its activities, including shelving and storing, so they are kept under the *A5 Preservation* umbrella in the archivists' scheme (functional approach), while librarians give more emphasis to the sequence of actions performed to manage library resources (procedural/chronological approach). This is no big problem, since a match can be established anyway, but it is an interesting issue that should be investigated in order to both improve internal consistency of each scheme, and support their convergence.
- A similar issue arises with *L3 Documents description and indexing, and data production*. As we noted above, this entry can be matched to *A4.2 Description*. However, its nested activity *L3.2 Evaluate software applications* cannot be matched to any sub-entry of *A4.2 Description*, and needs to be matched to *A6.2 Appraisal of information systems and applications*. The latter is an autonomous entry in the archivists' scheme, since it is an activity that is related to many functions, like creation, management, description, and preservation—any of them needs some evaluation of software applications. Therefore, for the sake of consistency, such evaluation should be either kept separated from the rest of the functions—like in the archivists' scheme—or repeated within each of them. Like above, this is no big issue, but it is an opportunity to reconsider choices and evaluate whether this space for convergence can be exploited.
- *L7 Design, evaluation and management of library activities and services* may be matched to *A10.1 Management of archival holdings*. Analyzing its

components, we can see that *L7.1 Define objectives and strategies* has its exact counterpart, with the same title, nested deeply within *A10.1 Management of archival holdings*, as a skill of the competence *A10.1.1 Programming*; *L7.2 Evaluate the library services and activities* deals with evaluation, so it can be matched again to *10.1 Management of archival holdings*, since this contains the competence *10.1.1 Evaluation*; *L7.3 Finalize use of human, financial, and cultural resources* is not a very clear entry indeed, but it seems that *A10.1* is still a proper place to establish the match.

Summarizing, the comparison between the two standards (rather, the two schemes) shows that there is a lot of room for designing a convergent model that may be applied to both archivists and librarians. There are some peculiarities that cannot—and must not—be eliminated. Some first-level entries in one scheme match deeper-level entries in the other scheme. Some entries seem to match perfectly, but their nested entries do not match at all. All in all, the road to convergence is not easy, nor short. However, even from this superficial analysis, there emerges a structure that may be adopted as the common framework not only for archivists and librarians but also for those who work in galleries and museums—the set of the fundamental functions that identify any professional working in GLAM institutions (see table 8.9).

Table 8.9 is just a rough scheme and a starting point: we are aware that—if GLAM professionals ever agree on it—issues are going to arise as soon as they try to design a shared set of second-level entries. However, this is an opportunity that should not be wasted. This is not about standardization. Rather than a goal, standards here can be a means or leverage to promote integration. Different actors in the same arena may cooperate in order to create a consistent and integrated framework where different professional figures may act with awareness of one another's competences. Education and training systems, as well as the market, would benefit from such an integrated and consistent approach.

Table 8.9. GLAM Professional. Functions

GLAM Professional. Functions
1. Management of resources
2. Description of resources
3. Preservation of resources
4. User services
5. Design and appraisal of information systems and applications
6. Outreach
7. Training and education
8. Research
9. Management and administration of a GLAM institution

Promoting integration starting from a standardization process has a big advantage: stakeholders must accept the loss of a bit of their specificity in favor of shared and common benefits. This is a fundamental feature of any standardization process (and most cooperative initiatives), a methodological approach that forces stakeholders to clarify what their goals are, and to what limit they can push their expectations. Too often, different actors are not aware that sharing, integrating, and creating a common space has a cost. The standardization action sheds light on these hidden or ambiguous aspects. On the other hand, it must be highlighted that standards are not enough to realize convergence: they should be the outcome of a community action—a participatory effort supported by stakeholders. Therefore, standards should be taken as an opportunity rather than as rigid tools to force integration.

In other words, there is no guarantee that convergence can go beyond the very basic level identified by the common purpose of GLAMs—preserving our cultural heritage. Therefore, there is no guarantee that a common standard can be designed. However, the effort of trying is worthy, because "[s]tandards are indeed valuable as technical tools *per se*, but their fundamental value lies rather in their capacity to raise awareness and issues, and bring the community to discussion. Standards are a way by which a community [. . .] identifies itself" (Michetti, 2014, p. 35). Convergence may or may not be the correct interpretation of diverse emerging phenomena. Standards on professional profiles are a practical opportunity to test such interpretation—whatever the result, the standardization process will help GLAM professional redefine their role and identity.

REFERENCES

Cencetti, G. (1939). Il fondamento teorico della dottrina archivistica. *Archivi*, *VI*, 7–13.

European Commission. (2008, April 23). *The European Qualifications Framework: A new tool to translate qualifications.* IP/08/631. Retrieved from http://europa.eu/rapid/press-release_IP-08-631_en.htm?locale=en

European Parliament and Council (2008, April 23). *Recommendation of the European Parliament and of the Council of 23 April 2008 on the establishment of the European Qualifications Framework for lifelong learning.*

Klieme, E., Avenarius, H., Blum, W., Döbrich, P., Gruber, H., Prenzel, M., . . . Vollmer, H. J. (2004). *The development of National Educational Standards. An expertise*. Berlin: Federal Ministry of Education and Research (BMBF).

Michetti, G. (2014). Knowledge, skills and competences: An Italian standard to design the archivist's profile within the European Qualifications Framework. In *Innovation and Engagement in Archival Education. 3rd Asia Pacific Conference on Archival Education. Renmin University, China. 23–24 October 2013.* International Council on Archives (ICA). Section on Archival education and Training (SAE), *1*(1),

19–37. Retrieved from http://www.ica-sae.org/proceedings/beijing2013/Proceedings_Beijing.pdf.

Pearce-Moses, R., and Davis, S. E. (Eds.). (2008). New skills for a digital era. *A Colloquium sponsored by National Archives and Records Administration, Society of American Archivists, Arizona State Library, Archives and Public Records. 31 May–2 June 2006. Washington, DC. Proceedings.* Chicago: Society of American Archivists.

Winterton, J., Delamaire-Le Deist, F., and Stringfellow, E. (2006). *Typology of knowledge, skills and competences: Clarification of the concept and prototype*. Luxembourg: Office for Official Publications of the European Communities.

Chapter Nine

Managing Cultural Heritage beyond Professional Boundaries

Problem or Opportunity?

Maria Luisa Russo and Timoty Leonardi

ABSTRACT

Multifaceted collections preserved in memory institutions show that a more comprehensive approach to the description, management, and access of collections is necessary. The traditional distinction between books, documents, and works of art falls short when a true image of certain types of collections is required (such as personal fonds or mixed collections) and also when enabling the user to find various sources that are typologically different, yet related to one another. This chapter addresses the issue of professional boundaries, both concerning the characteristics of objects and collections and providing access to them.

INTRODUCTION

The management, care, and preservation of the various types of cultural artifacts (books, documents, and works of art) have been historically marked by boundaries that have become delimitations among the professionals of various fields. Most of these boundaries have been outlined by different ways of describing the characteristics of the items, on the one hand, and the access by users to those items on the other. A more comprehensive approach to cultural artifacts in their complexity and historical life, and to the role they play in memory institutions, shows that collections can be managed more effectively through the collaboration of various professionals.

LIBRARY, ARCHIVE, MUSEUM: WHICH KIND OF ARTIFACTS?

Libraries and archives preserve artifacts that can be grouped under the definition of written cultural heritage. It is a well-known fact that the presence of the component "text" has marked the path of access, use, and preservation of books and documents. The aspect of "readability" has influenced preservation and conservation policies in archives and libraries, paying much more attention to content access and mechanical functionality than to the preservation of physical integrity of items in their original characteristics. The negative aspect involved in an approach of this kind is quite evident: a number of books have been repaired with the main (or only) aim of rebinding them in a resistant and practical way in order to make them once again accessible and readable for users, yet destroying the historical and archaeological values of the books at the same time. Unbound and rebound books whose original covers have been discarded and have therefore lost all traces of their historical stratification, are mere examples of the consequences of this typc of approach. On the other hand, museum artifacts, not intended for use, have been preserved in a different manner, with much more attention paid to the material aspects.

Even if libraries and archives have an important element in common, another professional boundary appears at a more in-depth view: the difference between *book* and *document*. In the traditional theory, the concept of "archival bond" has traced a very sharp delimitation between archives, which preserve documents that are connected to one another and to their creator, and libraries, to which this bond has traditionally been denied by affirming that each item in a library is autonomous and is the product of the will of collecting (while spontaneity is the other characteristic of archival aggregation).[1]

AN INTERESTING VIEWPOINT: PERSONAL FONDS

Recent research is critically revising the distinction between library and archive because curators have to deal more and more often with "hybrid" collections. In order to show this aspect, it is necessary to consider unconventional fonds: we have to analyze the issues and challenges created by what is not traditionally taken into consideration in theoretical elaborations. Personal fonds are one of these issues (Crocetti, 1999). These fonds, or documentary complexes, normally include documents, books, and objects owned by an individual: they therefore represent a useful viewpoint. Management and preservation policies must take into account the fact that in the mentality of the individual (the creator), there was probably no will for keeping a neat distinction between library and archive, and that if we adopt such a rigid categorization today, we certainly risk depriving our collections of one of their most important characteristics: their being documentary complexes in their whole.

Contemporary fonds put many of our professional axioms and practices to the test. On the one hand, we can see how hard it is to adapt the traditional way of rearranging archives into a hierarchical structure, made of series and subseries, to certain fonds that are not institutionally born, that is, fonds in which documentary production comes from an individual's life and/or professional activity. The archivists' attempt at rearranging documents into a hierarchical structure is certainly a hard task and is dictated by the need of organizing information by creating paths of research that go from general to particular and vice versa.[2] Whenever books are preserved in this type of fond, more serious issues arise and the limits of professional boundaries appear evident. In many cases, the library has been artificially separated from the archive. Items have been processed in different ways, according to respective theoretical rules: books have been catalogued as normal library collections, while documents have been rearranged following archival rules. On close examination, the outcome of the arrangement does not appear to be totally satisfactory. The main reason is that if we are dealing, as often occurs, with the fonds of an intellectual who has produced books and documents at the same time, and whose book production has been fed by other books and supported by documentary production, we already have the first obstacle to rigid categorizations. By only focusing on books published by the author himself, we first find various stages of book publication (drafts, blueprints) that cannot be separated from the final product if we want to maintain the integrity of the intellectual itinerary; moreover, we often see traces of an intellectual elaboration after publication, which stratifies the published book with notes and corrections covering a relevant time span. Therefore, using rigid theoretical structures implies cutting the documentary bond (not just the archival bond) that links a document to a book and to an object in this type of fonds.

Nowadays the need for a more flexible approach to our artifacts is made easier by the availability of enhanced information-technology tools that enable curators to reconstruct, at least virtually, what has been historically separated. There is a widespread diffusion of software that is useful for cataloging the various types of documentary sources and, more importantly, allowing for the establishment of links among different items. This means that even if the cataloguer needs to catalogue an item as "book," he will be able to point out to the user that the book is closely linked to a file in the archive, or to other books; moreover, this virtually enables us to highlight the presence of an archival value in a printed book, for example, in the frequent cases of annotated books.[3]

THE BOOK AS TEXT AND AS MATERIAL OBJECT: OLD DEBATE, NEW PERSPECTIVES

Concerning books, besides the above-mentioned area of potential overlapping with archival theory and practice, we also see the overlapping with museum artifacts due to the presence of material characteristics whose interest certainly goes beyond the textual relevance of the books' contents. The debate regarding the duality of book as text and material object is dated and has led to relevant changes in the approach to book preservation and conservation; nevertheless, it is difficult to reach an equilibrium due to the predominant function given to books as tools for study and research. Regarding their material characteristics (and in order to enhance their preservation), books would certainly benefit if they were managed in the same way as museum objects. A contribution by Pickwoad (2011, p. 122) is quite meaningful in this regard: "There will need to be a radical change in attitude towards books, a move away from the library, where they are seen as tools to be read, towards the museum, where they are seen as historic artefacts whose preservation must include the materials from which they are made." This should not be interpreted as a way of building new boundaries instead of the previous ones, but as a need of synergic management, deeply aware of issues posed by written cultural heritage.

As for the legislative framework in which heritage professionals act, collaboration is theoretically being encouraged, and in this regard an important step was undertaken with the creation of MAB (Musei Archivi Biblioteche), a result of the cooperation among the three main professional associations[4]: at an international level, a meaningful example is the UNESCO project *Memory of the World*. In 2002, the guidelines of the project proposed a cross-disciplinary view on cultural heritage and expressed the will of pursuing objectives without being delimited by institution typologies or professions (UNESCO, 2002, pp. 5, 9, 10).

The need of convergence in what we can call "memory institutions" has been highlighted for several years now, indicating that, from the user's point of view, the type of institution in which a certain source is kept is irrelevant as long as he can find it (Hedegaard, 2003, p. 2). We could add to this statement: as long as it is correctly preserved in that institution. Current technologies have allowed for the digital convergence of various memory institutions: the most famous initiative of this kind is certainly *Europeana*, but there are also some interesting solutions at a national level, such as the *BAM*, the joint portal for libraries, archives, and museums of the Bibliotheksservice-Zentrum Baden-Württemberg (BAM, n.d.), also discussed in Kirchhoff, Schweibenz, and Sieglerschmidt (2008), and experiences in the framework of the so-called case-museo at a more specific level. Once again, these experiences demonstrate how knowledge can be improved and facilitated by linking sources together—a sort of "Google" way of searching documentary sources.

CASE STUDIES

Some institutions and projects in the Piedmont region of Italy can be observed that show a progressive convergence among libraries, archives, and museums.

As for the above-mentioned overlapping of documentary typologies in archives and libraries, certainly the Paul Kahle Fonds, which is preserved in the University of Turin, has been a real challenge for the personnel in charge of the description and rearrangement of the archive. The fonds were the scientific archive and library of the German orientalist Paul Ernst Kahle (1875–1964), acquired by the University of Turin for its relevance in the field of oriental studies. The fonds appear to be the true laboratory of the intellectual: papers, books, notes, and loose leaves represent a whole documentary complex, which was used by the individual for study and research. Thanks to a project specifically devoted to the fonds, co-funded by Regione Piemonte (Directorate for Innovation, Research, University and Sustainable Energy Development),[5] it has been possible to describe, inventory, and rearrange the archive; a special section is dedicated to noted books and to documents preserved inside books, highlighting the relationships among the various items.[6] In this way, if various sources are linked to the same topic, or to the same name (author, correspondent, etc.), the user can see them by following the links indicated in the database.

A different approach to the overlapping of documentary typologies can be observed in the items kept in the Fondazione Museo del Tesoro del Duomo e Archivio Capitolare in Vercelli.[7] Its specific aim is to preserve, protect, and valorize the great heritage of the Cathedral Chapter of Vercelli, which includes medieval works of art, manuscripts, early printed books, and documentary evidence of the chapter life of Vercelli. Since its establishment in 2005, the Foundation has been involved in national and international research projects, exhibitions, educational discussions, and activities aimed at promoting its items. A field of research is dedicated to the collection of reliquaries, one of the most important collections of sacred goldsmith's art in northern Italy, belonging to the period between the seventh and the eighteenth centuries and made in various shapes and materials: bag-shaped, box-shaped, in wood or ivory or gold and silver plated, Limoges style, and also true-cross reliquaries, statuette reliquaries, monstrance-reliquaries, and bust reliquaries (Minelli, 2014). Research on these items takes advantage of literary sources (documents, manuscripts) preserved in the Capitulary Library and Archives, thus highlighting the usefulness of a cross-disciplinary approach to the various types of cultural heritage, which are linked to one another. In this case, the various sources can be connected and made accessible to scholars and researchers by means of the cross-disciplinary skills of the Foundation's staff, who are always ready to assist researchers with catalogs and inventories of documentary heritage.

Just to mention a couple of significant examples of this link among the various items with historical roots: the first census of the works of art preserved in the Cathedral was carried out during the first half of the twentieth century, while a scientific analysis dates back to 1965 and was conducted by Vittorio Viale, thanks to the advice provided by Giuseppe Ferraris, the librarian of the Capitulary Library of Vercelli (Viale, 1967; 1973). Today, due to the lack of material evidence, it is essential to study this census: scholars have thoroughly investigated Viale's catalogues, correcting and integrating the information according to the available documents and manuscripts. Another example concerns the architectonic structure of the medieval Cathedral of Vercelli before its renovation in 1571. The Capitulary Library preserves a manuscript (ms. LIII), *Liber continens usum psallendi secundum consuetudinem ecclesiae vercellensis,* signed and dating back to 1372 (Brusa 2009). The book is a guide for the holy celebrations of the canons, but it is also very important for reconstructing the internal architecture of the cathedral: thanks to the manuscript, we learn that there were thirteen altars dedicated to several saints in the aisles of the church that were used during ordinary and extraordinary solemnities. There is an inventory that is strictly connected to the manuscript, which is dated 1426. It is preserved in the Capitulary Archives and contains a list of the manuscripts, documents, and works of art owned by the canons (List no. 25, *Inventarium scripturarum existentium in Archivio Sancti Eusebii Vercellensis confectum de anno 1426* by G. De Guidalardis). Besides giving us an overall view of the canons' possessions by describing their richness and variety, this manuscript provides us with important data for a more in-depth study of the reliquaries, which are mentioned in the inventory in great detail.[8] More specifically, this 1426 inventory supplies the scholar with important information regarding two objects that are today a single metalwork: the architectural reliquary of the Holy Virgin, St. Catherine, St. Barnabas, and a coral that was donated to the Cathedral by Martino de Bulgaro. This coral, dating back to 1350, was reported in manuscript number V of the library in a partially deleted inscription. The coral, with a silver foot and pendant stones, is also included in the list dated 1426. The same list also mentions the architectural structure in which the coral is located today—which means that the objects were joined together after 1426.

This may represent practical proof of the links among the various items preserved in the same institutional framework, which can take mutual advantage of cross-linked management and access, yet there is also a recent project on the census of historical bookbindings in the Piedmont Region that gives interesting information concerning another approach to cultural heritage in a cross-disciplinary perspective. Conceptually, the binding can be associated to a work of art: this does not mean underestimating the textual content of the book but giving the bookbinding its due value in relation to the material and historical data that are widely analyzed by book historians. Relevant projects can be observed at an international level that focus on the bookbinding as a material object and are aimed at reconstructing a wider panorama on bookbindings regarding their materials and historical development.[9]

The commitment of the Piedmont region in preservation and valorization of historical bookbindings had already given rise in the past to a series of books dedicated to this subject (Malaguzzi 1995–2013) and in more recent years another project, funded by Regione Piemonte, Settore Promozione dei Beni Librari ed Archivistici, Editoria ed Istituti Culturali, and Centro Studi Piemontesi, has been undertaken in this purpose. The aim of the new project was to create a database of bookbindings, by both uploading the entries of the previous project (revised and with a greater quantity and variety of information), and widening the study to include bookbindings that have not yet been taken into consideration.

The software used for the cataloguing is SIGECWeb,[10] which had been created and mainly used, up to now, for cataloguing works of art. For the bookbinding project, the model form for works of art (OA) was adapted and used to catalogue bookbindings. In this way, the survey has been enlarged, data have been organized into a uniform standard description, and photographic documentation has been added for each bookbinding (in the printed books, there were only pictures of some of the bindings described). The Piedmont region is the first region that, over the last year, has begun to catalog bookbindings with this software; the database currently contains descriptions of about 1,500 bookbindings owned by public and ecclesiastical libraries from different parts of the Piedmont. The records are classed as "pre-catalog," a mid-step between the "inventory" and the "catalog" stages.[11]

CONCLUSION

Multifaceted collections cannot be interpreted and accessed at one level only; one-sided perspectives, or excessively rigid structures, show their limitations regarding both the description and access of the collections. A more flexible consideration of professional boundaries is necessary in order to effectively achieve the integrated management that multifaceted collections require today. This does not mean giving up professional specificities; it just means that a closer interaction and a more flexible way of caring for artifacts is necessary—and in this sense, it represents much more an opportunity, not to be missed, than a problem.

Examples of personal fonds and of mixed collections, where objects and works of art are closely related to books and documents, show that a critical rethinking is required concerning professional boundaries, and that the interaction and integration of various competences and skills is a concrete need in cultural heritage management. The fact that it is necessary to organize the information following professional rules, for practical reasons, should not become an obstacle for users, and the case studies show examples of preserving cultural heritage while providing access to it, thus acting in the respect of the characteristics of the items and of users' needs.

NOTES

1. Archival theory stresses this point. International Standard Archival Description (ISAD) rules define the creator as "The corporate body, family or person that created, accumulated and/or maintained records in the conduct of personal or corporate activity. Not be confused with collector." (ICA, 2000, p. 10).
2. On this subject see also Del Vivo (2012).
3. In this way, the mere entry about the printed book is enriched by the presence of annotations, or documents preserved inside the same book, so that both the user interested in the solely printed book and the user interested in the author's annotations, can find the entry. The simultaneous presence, in the same documentary source, of a serial item (the printed book) and unique, owner-linked information (annotations and documents) poses other kinds of problems from the preservation point of view. It is just worthwhile reminding how the care and management of such collections should undergo careful evaluation because the concept of serial items, replaceable by definition, is not applicable.
4. AIB (Associazione Italiana Biblioteche), ANAI (Associazione Nazionale Archivistica Italiana), ICOM Italia (International Council of Museum–Italian National Committee).
5. Co-funded in the frame of the "Bando Scienze Umane e Sociali 2008." For further information see the website of the Paul Kahle Fonds (UNITO, 2013).
6. Archival issues have been described in recent contributions (Russo, 2013). A similar procedure has been used in Giuseppe Ferraris's archive, preserved as a fond of the Capitulary Archives of Vercelli (Negro, 2010).
7. The Foundation is a nonprofit cultural institution with the aim of preserving, researching, and studying the history and cultural heritage of the Archdiocese of Vercelli, in particular related to the Capitulary Library and Archives, and the Cathedral

Treasure Museum. Fondazione Museo del Tesoro del Duomo e Archivio Capitolare, piazza A. D'Angennes 5, 13100 Vercelli (Italy), www.tesorodelduomovc.it, info@tesorodelduomovc.it.

8. Among the items mentioned in the inventory, we find the zoomorphic reliquary of St. James, St. Demetrius, and St. Theodore; the latter includes the SS. Innocents relics that were celebrated, as stated in ms LIII, on one of the altars in the cathedral with a particular ritual.

9. See the websites devoted to bookbindings: Husby, n.d.; British Library, n.d.; BSB, n.d.; RBPRM, n.d.; Folger Shakespeare Library, n.d.; Uppsala and Lund, n.d.; BNF, n.d.; BSG, n.d.

10. Software developed by the Ministero dei Beni e delle Attività Culturali e del Turismo through the Istituto Centrale per il Catalogo e la Documentazione (ICCD).

11. The database can be seen on the webpage www.catalogo.beniculturali.it.

REFERENCES

Bayerische Staatsbibliothek München (BSB). (n.d.). *Einbandnatenbank*. Retrieved from http://www.hist-einband.de/

Bibliotheksservice-Zentrum Baden-Württemberg. (n.d.). *Portal zu Bibliotheken, Archiven, Museen (BAM)*. Retrieved from http://www.bam-portal.de/

Bibliothèque de Sainte-Geneviève (BSG). (n.d.). *Reliures estampées à froid 12th–18th siècles de la Bibliotèque Sainte-Geneviève, Paris*. Retrieved from http://bsg-reliures.univ-paris1.fr/fr/accueil/

Bibliothèque Nationale de France (BNF). (n.d.). *Base des reliures numérisées*. Retrieved from http://reliures.bnf.fr/

British Library. (n.d). *Database of bookbindings*. Retrieved from http://www.bl.uk/catalogues/bookbindings/

Brusa, G. (2009). *Usus psallendi ecclesiae vercellensis (Vercelli, Biblioteca Capitolare, Cod. LIII)*. Roma: Centro Liturgico Vincenziano.

Crocetti, L. (2009). Memorie generali e memorie specifiche. *Biblioteche oggi*, *4*, 24–27.

Del Vivo, C. (2012). Accostarsi a un archivio di persona: ordinamento e condizionamento. In F. Ghersetti and L. Paro (Eds.), *Archivi di persona del Novecento. Guida alla sopravvivenza di autori, documenti e addetti ai lavori* (pp. 15–38). Treviso: Antiga Edizioni.

Folger Shakespeare Library. (n.d). *Bindings image collection (LUNA)*. Retrieved from http://luna.folger.edu/luna/servlet/BINDINGS~1~1

Hedegaard, R. (2003). *Benefits of archives, libraries and museums working together*. 69th IFLA General Conference and Council. Retrieved from http://archive.ifla.org/IV/ifla69/papers/051e-Hedegaard.pdf

Husby, S. (n.d.). *Bookbindings on incunables in American library collections*. Retrieved from http://www.bibsocamer.org/BibSite/Husby/

International Council of Archives (ICA). (2000). *ISAD(G): General international standard archival description* (2nd ed.). Retrieved from http://www.icacds.org.uk/eng/ISAD(G).pdf

Kirchhoff, T., Schweibenz, W., and Sieglerschmidt, J. (2008). Archives, libraries and museums and the spell of ubiquitous knowledge. *Archival Science*, *8*(4), 251–66.
Malaguzzi, F. (1995–2013). *De libris compactis. legature di pregio in Piemonte* (9 vols.). Torino: Centro Studi Piemontesi.
Minelli, S. (2014). Silver in celebration: Speaking reliquaries. Paper presented at the 49th International Congress on Medieval Studies, Kalamazoo, MI, May 10.
Negro, F. (2010). Il laboratorio dello storico: gli apparati di note. In T. Leonardi (Ed.), *Mons. Giuseppe Ferraris. . . a 10 anni dalla morte. Un sacerdote vercellese tra storia e pastorale. Atti della Giornata di Studio. Seminario Arcivescovile di Vercelli, 7 novembre 2009* (pp. 119–45). Vercelli: VercelliViva.
Pickwoad, N. (2011). Library or museum? The future of rare book collections and its consequences for conservation and access. In P. Engel, J. Schirò, R, Larsen, E. Moussakova, and I. Kecskeméti (Eds.), *New approaches to book and paper conservation-restoration* (pp. 113–30). Verlag Berger: Horn/Wien.
Real Biblioteca del Palacio Real de Madrid (RBPRM). (n.d.). Base de datos de encuadernaciones. Retrieved from http://encuadernacion.realbiblioteca.es/index.php
Russo, M. L. (2013). Il fondo Paul Kahle nell'Università di Torino: Da fondo privato a fondo speciale in biblioteca. *Culture del testo e del documento*, *14*(42), 133–54.
United Nations Educational, Scientific and Cultural Organization (UNESCO). (2002). *Memory of the world. General guidelines to preserve documentary heritage.* Retrieved from http://unesdoc.unesco.org/images/0012/001256/125637e.pdf
Università degli Studi di Torino (UNITO). (2013). *Paul Kahle Fonds, Turin*. Retrieved from www.paulkahle.unito.it
Uppsala and Lund University Libraries (n.d.). *Probok*. Retrieved from http://probok.alvin-portal.org/alvin/
Viale, V. (1967). *Opere d'arte preromanica e romanica del duomo di Vercelli.* Cassa di Risparmio di Vercelli, Vercelli.
Viale, V. (1973). *Il duomo di Vercelli*, Cassa di Risparmio di Vercelli, Vercelli.

Part III

INFORMATICS—BIG DATA

Chapter Ten

Big Data

Opportunities and Barriers across the Cultural Heritage Sectors

Bob Pymm, Mary Carroll,
Sigrid McCausland, and Mary Anne Kennan

ABSTRACT

This chapter considers the explosion of data occurring across all sectors of society, from that generated by individual and government activities and by scientists and other researchers to major digitization projects being undertaken by cultural institutions worldwide. Given the overarching term "big data," these large datasets require a high level of expertise and knowledge in their management to ensure accessibility and preservation over the long term. This raises the issue of education in managing big data and how this can be undertaken, given limited resources but a growing need. Cooperation across sectors is considered and formal education programs are reviewed in order to better understand the current situation and how it may evolve in the future.

INTRODUCTION

Large datasets have been around for a long time; national census data could be seen as an early example. The last two decades, however, have seen an explosion in data generated across the entire spectrum of society—government, business, research, social, and individual. Much of this data remains in the hands of its creators, but, increasingly, institutions concerned with capturing the cultural record of a society are becoming involved. The Library of Congress is archiving half a billion tweets a day (and after three years, the Twitter archive comprised 85 terabytes of data [Luckerson, 2013]); national libraries in a number of countries have been capturing the entirety of the sites in their Web domains (for example, the National Library of Australia expects to acquire one billion unique files from their 2014 crawl [National Library of Australia,

2014]); audiovisual archives around the world are now acquiring digital cinema packages comprising hundreds of gigabytes of data; government departments are generating massive datasets (Lexology, 2014), which will eventually be deposited in archives around the world that are now moving toward accepting only digital materials; and researchers and others are filling university or discipline-specific repositories with the digital results of their research.

In addition, physical collections are being digitized on a large scale (for example the recently launched 1914–1918 Europeana site including over 400,000 digitized items [Europeana, n.d]); the JFK Library and Museum will have 300 terabytes of data by 2016 (Roth and Bordreau, 2011); the London Metropolitan Archives report digitization of over twenty million parish records (City of London, 2014) and the secretary of the Smithsonian Institution recently outlined plans on how to tackle the challenge of creating digital copies of fourteen million objects (Stromberg, 2013).

Such huge collections create a digital resource of immense size, complexity, and value. Developing the necessary infrastructure, including the standards, policies, practices, and the technology required to store, manage, and make accessible such huge volumes of data has considerable resource implications. *The Cost of Digitising Europe's Cultural Heritage*, the 2010 report that looked at libraries, archives, and museums, estimated around $100 billion dollars would be required to digitize existing physical collections, with ongoing maintenance costs over ten years estimated at 50 to 100 percent of initial outlay, imposing a long-term, large-scale economic obligation on the institutions involved (Poole, 2010, p. 3).

Yet governments around the world are generally seeking to cut expenditure and save money. For most countries, this means that government-funded institutions such as libraries, archives, and museums face a bleak future of trying to do more with less direct government support. Joint ventures that cross traditional boundaries may be the only viable way for large-scale projects to be successfully undertaken. Given the lack of boundaries in the digital world—a digital file is a digital file regardless of its contents—some have taken the approach that management of digital collections requires similar knowledge and infrastructure regardless of the institution that created or acquired the original digital object. Others point to the importance of context and different areas of expertise and focus, and in research data, specifically, disciplinary differences (Borgman, 2007). This also flows on to education for the profession, where new professionals across the cultural heritage sectors (considered here to comprise galleries, libraries, archives, and museums) require some of the same knowledge and skills in digital curation. Cooperation in education and in managing and curating large datasets is critical.

Given this commonality, it would seem that the need to manage large digital collections can be viewed as an opportunity, or a driver, for cooperation across the cultural heritage field, and perhaps even more broadly, in order to achieve the best outcomes for digital collections, wherever they happen to be hosted.

BIG DATA

The situation for memory institutions is not, of course, unique. In recent years, governments and organizations around the world have been grappling with the explosion in data being created and both the opportunities and challenges that this offers.

Commonly referred to as "big data," this has been defined as "high-volume, high-velocity and high-variety information assets that demand cost-effective, innovative forms of information processing for enhanced insight and decision making" (Gartner, n.d.). Big data is differentiated from other forms of information by its sheer magnitude and by the need for innovative solutions to deliver benefits that have the potential to change how societies function (Mayer-Schönberger and Cukier, 2013). It presents particular challenges for institutions in the cultural heritage sector that have traditionally performed the role of custodians of discrete collections of information. Big data analytics rely on the availability of data that usually originate from a variety of sources, rather than from a single creator or custodian, and are often not well described, raising the issues of access to a wide range of discrete datasets and impediments to reuse.

It is not only its volume that presents a significant challenge for those involved in creating and managing big data, it is also that much big data generated by government, industry, and social networks is unstructured (Davenport and Patil, 2012). One Australian estimate is that 80 percent of big data is now unstructured (AGIMO, 2013a). This means that new technologies and new paradigms are needed if the promise of the value of big data is to be met, with Davenport and Patil (2012) suggesting that the data management techniques and skills that have been effective during the last few decades in dealing with structured data may be inappropriate for dealing with unstructured data (p. 74).

In Australia over the last few years, big data has become a focus of strategic planning by the Australian Government Information Office (AGIMO). Reports from this agency emphasize the implications of big data for governments in developing policy and in delivering services to citizens. They also emphasize the critical role of collaboration within a government and between government and industry, and to a lesser extent, collaboration between government, industry, and the education sector, in meeting the need to develop the skills required now and into the future in order to better manage and exploit the affordances offered by the unprecedented volume of information being made available (AGIMO, 2013a; 2013b).

While most heritage institutions are unlikely to face the challenge of large volumes of unstructured data, they will need to engage with new forms of automated gathering or harvesting of online resources and their associated metadata. However, organizations such as legislated archives may well end up being the repository for large volumes of relatively unstructured data gathered by government agencies, data that will then need to be managed in order to ensure future accessibility in a meaningful way.

Similarly, university repositories, usually linked in some way to the library, may be dealing with large amounts of data as they acquire the research outputs of their faculty, but it is likely to be structured (possibly with help from repository staff) rather than unorganized data. Witt (2008) talks of librarians, as repository managers, curating data and working in a "bottom up" approach with researchers who "lacked time to organize their datasets" (p. 198).

Acknowledging the complexities associated with big data, the University of Minnesota has recently established the Informatics Institute (UMII), working closely with the digital library services, focusing on "harnessing the power of big data," exploring its impact, and fostering data-intensive research (University of Minnesota, 2014). Such initiatives would seem to offer real opportunities for shared learning and skills development, relevant across the entire spectrum of industries working with big data. At the same time, they would help enhance and cement the role of the library, archive, or repository as the place with the skills and knowledge to effectively manage this research output.

COOPERATION

Cooperation across the digital heritage and related sectors already has a well-established tradition. Organizations such as JISC (Joint Information Systems Committee) in the United Kingdom have been around twenty years, and while their focus has evolved over that time, they are still very much involved with developing and supporting education around digitization, digital literacy, preservation, repositories, and network capabilities (see their current training program at http://www.jiscdigitalmedia.ac.uk/training).

The more recently established Europeana Foundation, seen by the European Union (EU) as one of Europe's most ambitious cultural projects, has a very clear vision that states:

> We believe in making cultural heritage openly accessible in a digital way, to promote the exchange of ideas and information. This helps us all to understand our cultural diversity better and contributes to a thriving knowledge economy.

This vision includes virtually all the countries of Europe involved in creating and sharing data, providing local expertise for training and education in managing digital collections at the grassroots level, and linking with governments and big data through supporting Hackathons and other data-use initiatives (Europeana Professional, 2014).

Smaller, more specialized cooperatives also exist. The PrestoCentre Foundation, based in the Netherlands, is a nonprofit organization focusing on audiovisual digitization and digital preservation that provides assistance and training at the institution level as well as playing an advocacy role in order to "to forge closer ties with government, industry, and academia" (PrestoCentre Foundation, 2014). Many of the major players, institutions, and professional associations also provide (or organize the provision of) education and training in the fields of digitization and digital preservation in particular, focused on the needs of their membership. With a number of these events recorded in some way and made available in the form of podcasts, vodcasts, or interactive webinars to a worldwide audience. Examples include a series of podcasts from the State Records Authority of New South Wales (Australia), including "Implementing Effective Social Media Record Keeping and State Records Digital Archives Migration Methodology"; the National Information Standards Organization (NISO) in the US series of webinars including "Metadata for Preservation and Research Data Curation"; and the Yale University preservation lecture series, including "But Storage Is Cheap: Digital Preservation in the Age of Abundance."

This wealth of support and education already available, in some case at no cost (other than staff or the interested individual's time), suggests that in this field, the cultural heritage sector, and others, have recognized the urgent need to raise skill levels and awareness to address what is, as everyone would agree, a pressing problem that needs urgent attention—now. But exactly what is needed? Is there a core of education useful to anyone involved in the digital cultural heritage, including the management of big data?

EDUCATION

Education is focused on providing students with the ability to acquire new skills, flexibility in times of change, and a commitment to lifelong learning (Kennan, Corrall, and Afzal, 2014). But as students become new professionals, they also need specific skill sets to get work (Ferreira et al., 2007). Trying to balance the big-picture perspective expected of a university education—"Graduate education is about why . . . not 'how to' in any operational sense" (Nesmith, 2009, p.10), together with the complaints of most students and future employers "that their graduates do not arrive in the workplace able to just step in and start work" (Anderson, 2007, p. 99)—is a challenging balancing act.

In order to work with big data, or data of any sort, some of the knowledge and skills required already come as a part of traditional courses in the cultural heritage sector. For example, information management, provenance, knowledge description, and organization are just as important in the management of big data as of information (Lynch, 2008). However, there are knowledge and skill areas required for working with big data that are less a part of the current cultural heritage-sector education. These include the requirements for a high level of expertise in handling, manipulating, and using often-quantitative data and also deep knowledge and understanding of computing and IT in the areas of large-scale storage, continuing access, and preservation of data (Swan and Brown, 2008). In the use of big data in business, while there are larger strategic issues to be considered, there is still a need for expertise in data management, governance, and quality and also for the development and use of the technological tools to manage and interrogate data usefully (LaValle, Lesser, Shockley, Hopkins, and Kruschwitz, 2011). In a recent survey of university libraries about their research data management, respondents identified a requirement for data curation skills, technical and ICT (information and computer technology) skills, and knowledge of research methods, particularly quantitative methods and statistics (Kennan, Corrall, and Afzal, 2014). These broader skills, relevant beyond just university repositories, can be seen as highly relevant to the wider cultural heritage sector.

These generic skill sets, which also include management skills, combine with profession-specific learning focused on the student's future career as a librarian, archivist, curator, or information manager. The changing nature of these professions and the overwhelming impact of information technology (IT) on all aspects of work (and life generally) suggest that a greater focus on IT as integral to the learning program in these fields is inevitable. Hu (2013), indeed, suggests that between one-third and one-half of all subjects taught in an LIS master's degree program should be IT focused, and relevant IT-related aspects should be embedded in existing subjects. In addition, in the research data domain, surveys conducted by JISC and RIN (the Research Information Network), reported researchers perceive that in order to properly manage data, data managers/librarians require a substantial level of disciplinary and research process knowledge (Pryor, 2012), as well as information management and IT knowledge, suggesting a further broadening of the syllabus for academic librarians.

Hu's (2013) research indicated that of the top fourteen LIS schools in the United States, thirteen belonged to the iSchools consortia, and all delivered a substantial IT component to their degrees, with many changing the name of their degrees to reflect this influence—from master of library and information science to master of science in information (University of Michigan, p. 6). Such a focus may be less relevant to the archival and museum professions, but it is certainly indicative of the general move toward acknowledging the central role IT plays, even in the cultural heritage arena.

Yet fitting more into an already crowded curriculum is always a challenge and hard decisions will have to be made—in concert with relevant professional associations—as to what can be taught differently or removed from the curriculum if this focus on IT and other skills and knowledge related to data curation and management is to be implemented. At the same time, for research data management, the curriculum will also require a focus on research and discipline knowledge. The impact on staffing and resources generally also needs careful consideration—reengineering of courses is no simple matter.

Having faculty available, with the appropriate knowledge base, to develop and administer IT-focused subjects relevant to the cultural heritage and data management fields may also be challenging. Perhaps this is an area where cooperation across the professional disciplines, and across institutions, offers possibilities. The model of the WISE consortium, comprising a group of fifteen LIS schools from the United States, Australia, and New Zealand that collaborate in making available to students from any participating university the possibility of undertaking one or two subjects offered online by any of the schools involved, may work in providing opportunities for smaller schools, with fewer resources, to offer access to these IT-focused subjects.

Other initiatives include those where a number of universities have entered into joint initiatives to deliver both face-to-face and online courses on digital libraries, data curation, and digital preservation, rather than offering subjects individually. An example is digital library learning (DILL), which brings together Oslo and Akershus University College of Applied Sciences (Norway), Tallinn University (Estonia), and the University of Parma (Italy). Students spend time at each university experiencing a mix of face-to-face and online delivery.

Generally, however, the move to provide intensive IT subjects, focused strongly on big data and its management, is only slowly gaining momentum. Nonetheless, in the United States and elsewhere, there are LIS schools offering various subjects, courses, and specializations in research data management (RDM), including courses open to students from other disciplines (Corrall, 2012; Harris-Pierce and Liu, 2012). There are even stand-alone courses in data science, such as that offered by the Sheffield iSchool (http://www.sheffield.ac.uk/is/pgt/courses/data_science). There has also been a growth in privately developed courses and subjects, much of it available free, online. Thus, the Big Data University is essentially run by enthusiasts keen to build on the potential value offered by exploiting large datasets for social good, as well as profit. Their short courses are focused on software and programming languages used to effectively interrogate large datasets, providing students with the basic knowledge and skill set necessary to "explore data that can lead to important discoveries in the health industry, the environment, and any other area you can think of!" (Big Data University, 2014). It may be that more formal university-offered courses and subjects can learn from the success of these more modular, bite-sized offerings, readily available on the Web.

Gartner forecast that by 2015, 4.4 million professionals with experience in data analysis will be needed worldwide (quoted in AGIMO, 2013b, p.17). Collaboration and engagement within a government and between governments and the private sector are seen as central to approaching the issue of skill development, suggesting the likelihood of further growth in the private sector as a training provider in this field. Yet there is no mention of the data management or curation that will be necessary to ensure that these datasets are available for interrogation not only this year but, in many cases, for decades to come. This critical aspect of preserving big data does not receive the same level of attention as the excitement offered by its potential exploitation.

If we think roles in the management of big data create opportunities for information professions and the cultural heritage sector, then we need to think of how we collectively advance these roles. One aspect of this is to consider how, and whether, our graduates go into the working world equipped for roles in big data. Do we provide subjects or modules within our traditional larger courses or programs? What role do professional organizations have to play in the redesign of programs? Are we to offer specializations within those courses or programs? Or are the differences so great that entire new courses need to be offered? Much of the discussion has addressed what is new and should be taken up, but also needing to be addressed is what should be dropped to "make space" (Kennan, Corrall, and Afzal, 2014), both in our practice and in education and training. What can go from the curriculum to "make space" for more advanced education in big data, data management, and the appropriate IT skills? Or will big data become a separate path with separate education and training (Swan and Brown, 2008)? This question has implications for accreditation-granting bodies, practitioners, and for the academics who teach in the cultural heritage sectors. Another question for the information professions and the cultural heritage sector to consider is the need to establish connections with educators in the business and IT disciplines who are addressing the drivers of big data education coming from their sectors. If this challenge is not taken up, then the role of "data scientist" as big data expert, but without the perspective of the information professions, may come to dominate employment in this new field.

CONCLUSION

This chapter has sought to draw attention to the opportunities and potential problems for the information professions in meeting the challenges of big data. It has characterized big data as a new and powerful type of information that requires a change in thinking about curatorial practice. The chapter also explores education for information professionals, acknowledging the gaps in skills and knowledge that have been identified in the literature and asking how educators across the cultural heritage sectors can begin to address the need to add big data to the curriculum. Changes to our existing education programs will be essential if we are to succeed in embracing the opportunities and in minimizing the barriers presented by big data now and into the future.

REFERENCES

AGIMO (2013a.). *Big data strategy—Issues paper*. Australian Government Information Management Office. Retrieved from http://www.finance.gov.au/files/2013/03/Big-Data-Strategy-Issues-Paper1.pdf

AGIMO (2013b). *The Australian public service big data strategy*. Australian Government Information Management Office. Retrieved from http://www.finance.gov.au/sites/default/files/Big-Data- Strategy_0.pdf

Anderson, K. (2007). Education and training for records professionals. *Records Management Journal*, *17*(2), 94–106.

Big Data University. (2014). *Our mission*. Retrieved from http://bigdatauniversity.com/

City of London. (2014). *Digitisation*. Retrieved from http://www.cityoflondon.gov.uk/things-to-do/visiting-the-city/archives-and-city-history/london-metropolitan-archives/family-history/Pages/Digitisation.aspx

Corrall, S. (2012). Roles and responsibilities: Libraries, librarians and data. In G. Pryor (Ed.), *Managing research data* (pp. 105–33). London: Facet.

Corrall, S., Kennan, M. A., and Afzal, W. (2013). Bibliometrics and research data management services: Emerging trends in library support for research. *Library Trends*, *61*(3), 636–74.

Davenport, T. H., and Patil, D. J. (2012). Data scientist: The sexiest job of the 21st century. *Harvard Business Review*, *90*(10), 70–76.

Europeana. (n.d.). *Europeana 1914–1918*. Retrieved from http://www.europeana1914-1918.eu/en

Europeana Professional. (2014). *Who we are*. Retrieved from http://pro.europeana.eu/about

Ferreira, F., Santos, J. N., Nascimento, L., Andrade, R. S., Barros, S., and Borges, J. (2007). Information professionals in Brazil: Core competencies and professional development. *Information Research*, *12*(2). Retrieved from http://InformationR.net/ir/12-2/paper299.html

Gartner (n.d.) *Gartner IT Glossary "big data."* Retrieved from http://www.gartner.com/it-glossary/big-data/

Harris-Pierce, R. L., and Liu, Y. Q. (2012). Is data curation education at library and information science schools in North America adequate? *New Library World*, *113*(11/12), 598–613.

Hu, S. (2013). *Technology impacts on curriculum of Library and Information Science (LIS)–A United States (US) perspective.* Retrieved from http://libres.curtin.edu.au/libres23n2/Sharon%20Hu%20Paper%20for%20LIBRES_%20Final.pdf

Kennan, M. A., Corrall, S., and Afzal, W. (2014). "Making space" in practice and education: Research support services in academic libraries. *Library Management, 35*(8/9). doi:10.1108/LM-03-2014-0037

LaValle, S., Lesser, E., Shockley, R., Hopkins, M. S., and Kruschwitz, N. (2011) Big data, analytics and the path from insights to value. *MIT Sloan Management Review, 52*(2), 21–31.

Lexology (2014). *Big data and the public sector*. Retrieved from http://www.lexology.com/library/detail.aspx?g=4ea46df7-fd1d-490a-b0a1-df17594babe9

Luckerson, V. (2013). What the Library of Congress plans to do with all your tweets. *Time.com*. Retrieved from http://business.time.com/2013/02/25/what-the-library-of-congress-plans-to-do- with-all-your-tweets/

Lynch, C. (2008). Big data: How do your data grow? *Nature, 455*(7209), 28–29.

Mayer-Schönberger, V., and Cukier, K. (2013). *Big data: A revolution that will transform how we live, work and think*. London: John Murray.

National Library of Australia. (2014). *The National Library's whole Australian domain harvest project–2014*. Retrieved from http://pandora.nla.gov.au/crawl.html

Nesmith, T. (2009). What is an archival education? *Journal of the Society of Archivists, 28*(1), 14–23.

Poole, P. N. (2010). The cost of digitizing Europe's cultural heritage: A report for the Comité des Sages of the European Commission. Retrieved from http://ec.europa.eu/information_society/activities/digital_libraries/doc/refgroup/annexes/digiti_report.pdf

The PrestoCentre Foundation. (2014). *Who we are and what we do*. Retrieved from https://www.prestocentre.org/about-us

Pryor, G. (Ed.). (2012). *Managing research data.* London: Facet.

Roth, J., and Bordreau, E. (2011). Managing large (digitisation) collections, digital commonwealth. Retrieved from http://www.masshist.org/pub/digicomm/digicomm_2011conf_roth_boudreau.pdf

Stromberg, J. (2013). *What digitization will do for the future of museums*. Retrieved from http://www.smithsonianmag.com/smithsonian-institution/what-digitization-will-do-for-the-future-of-museums-2454655/?no-ist

Swan, A., and Brown, S. (2008). *The skills, role and career structure of data scientists and curators: An assessment of current practice and future needs: A report to the Joint Information Systems Committee (JISC)*. Key Perspectives for JISC, Truro. Retrieved from http://www.jisc.ac.uk/publications/reports/2008/dataskills careersfinalreport.aspx

University of Minnesota. (2014). *Informatics Institute*. Retrieved from https://sites.google.com/a/umn.edu/informatics-institute/infrastructure/library

Witt, M. (2008). Institutional repositories and research data curation in a distributed environment. *Library Trends, 57*(2), 191–201. Retrieved from http://docs.lib.purdue.edu/lib_research/104/

Chapter Eleven

Characteristics of Tweets about African Cultural Heritage

Abebe Rorissa, Shimelis Assefa, and Daniel Gelaw Alemneh

ABSTRACT

Tourism has the potential to be the engine of a country's economic development. Some developing countries, especially those in Africa, rely on tourism for their citizens' employment. Consequently, the rise and fall of their unemployment rates are closely associated with that of tourist numbers. Hence, they need to constantly find ways to promote their cultural heritage in order to attract more tourists. One of the key promotion tools is Twitter, and an investigation to understand the nature of tweets about cultural heritage institutions is an important undertaking. However, investigations into the nature of tweets about African cultural heritage are nonexistent. Our research aims to shed some light on the broad characteristics of tweets about African cultural heritage. We also identify possible implications for marketing by cultural heritage administrators and other stakeholders in their use of social media in general and Twitter in particular.

INTRODUCTION

Tourism has the potential to be the economic engine and contribute to a country's economic development due to its power to generate billions in income for businesses, governments (at all levels: local, state, national), institutions, and other sectors of society. It is estimated that, globally, tourism accounts for over 5 percent of gross domestic product (GDP) (United Nations Conference on Trade and Development, 2010). Some developing countries, especially those in Africa, partially rely on tourism for their citizens' employment. As a result, the rise and fall of their unemployment rates are closely associated with that of tourist numbers. Consequently, they need to constantly find ways to promote their cultural heritage sites and institutions in order to attract more tourists.

What is more, cultural heritage institutions and their resources are big draws for tourists, and marketing campaigns require a significant amount of investments. While traditional methods still exist to promote a country's cultural heritage and conduct effective marketing campaigns, it is very difficult to gauge their effectiveness in terms of attracting more visitors. The Internet and social media have opened new avenues for institutions to market any products and services practically for free, in part because users/clients generate some of the publicity and promote the products and services by sharing information as well as their experiences. One of the key tools for promoting a service, product, or anything for that matter, is social media such as Twitter. Twitter offers countries and their cultural heritage institutions new platforms for connecting their resources with potential users, customers, and/or visitors.

Characteristics of tourists' or visitors' tweets (e.g., how, what, when, where, how often, etc.) about their experiences at a cultural heritage institution and/or visits to a country could affect the countries' future reputation and ability to attract more visitors. Hence, an investigation to understand the nature and broad characteristics of tweets about cultural heritage institutions and experiences by tourists is an important undertaking because the findings of such investigations could assist not just the cultural heritage institutions but also the countries to devise appropriate strategies and policies. However, investigations into the nature of African cultural heritage institutions in general, and tweets about them in particular, are nonexistent. Hence, we set out to conduct a study that addresses the broad research question: What are the characteristics/nature of tweets about African cultural heritage with respect to their sources, influential Twitter users, the information flow network of those users, topics and subjects of the tweets, and the sentiments of the tweets? More specifically, the study attempts to:

- identify the source and location of tweets about African cultural heritage;
- determine the most influential twitter users with respect to African cultural heritage;
- characterize visitors who tweet about African cultural heritage and their information flow network;
- identify trending topics and most popular subjects discussed with respect to African cultural heritage; and
- identify sentiments of tweets about African cultural heritage.

Recognizing the value of social amplification or promotion tools like Twitter, this research aims to shed some light on the broad characteristics or nature of tweets about African cultural heritage. Content analysis, social network analysis, and visualization tools will be used to analyze data obtained through a number of Twitter APIs (application program interface). Based on our findings, we identify possible implications and suggest potential strategies for cultural heritage administrators and other stakeholders in their use of social media in general and Twitter in particular.

BACKGROUND

Tourism and the Continent of Africa

Tourism, in all its forms (be it cultural, social, business, environmental, etc.), has existed since time immemorial. To look beyond one's surroundings and be inquisitive about what lies elsewhere, or the curiosity to discover, is an innate human nature. By its very nature, tourism is associated with travel or the movement of people from one locale or country or region or continent to another, often far away. Africa has long been at the center of early human migration. One of the prevailing theories of the early origin and movement of modern humans is often referred to as the "out-of-Africa" theory (Armitage et al., 2011), which posits that the modern human evolved mainly in Africa until a branch of *Homo sapiens* trekked elsewhere sometime between 125,000 and 60,000 years ago, eventually replacing the Neanderthals and *Homo erectus* (Meredith, 2011). While the early humans' main reason for migration may not have been for tourism purposes, one of the main reasons why people travel to faraway places and among the often-mentioned attractions for tourists are the cultural heritage of a place and/or country.

In Africa, a continent with nearly a billion people and a place where little is known when it comes to its history and cultures, storytelling is and always has been a way of life. Stories and storytelling are, in a way, the only tools that were available to a variety of African communities in their quest for knowledge transfer and preservation. Hence, when one talks of cultural heritage in Africa, it is not necessarily about things such as printed materials, although one can find those in some of the countries where ancient manuscripts have been preserved and passed down through the generations.

Unlike Europe, North America, and Asia, African cultural heritage lies in the historical and other physical structures and artifacts that one can see, touch, smell, and feel, as well as in the customs and ceremonies that existed and had been practiced literally for millennia. Not in spite of this very fact, but rather because of it, Africa presents a unique experience to tourists from around the globe, particularly from regions of the world where the same experience cannot be offered.

Economic Benefits of Tourism

Although it is not a panacea for a country's economic woes, tourism has always been an integral part of economic activity for some countries. With increased globalization and international travel, countries in every corner of the world are benefiting from tourism, especially where there is relative peace and stability. In Africa alone, according to the World Bank's 2013 report on tourism, the number of tourists traveling to sub-Saharan African countries grew over 300 percent since 1990, and in 2012 the highest number of tourists, 33.8 million, visited the region (World Bank, 2013). However, African countries still need to effectively integrate tourism into their economies in order to compete with places such as Asia. During the twenty years at the tail end of the last millennium (1980 to 2000), the Asia-Pacific region saw an increase from 8 percent to 22 percent of global tourist numbers, leading to tremendous economic growth and improved livelihoods. In the thirty years since 1980, Africa's share of global tourism was between 3 percent (1980) and 5 percent (2010).

As a result of this increase in the number of tourists, albeit modest, more and more African countries are beginning to compete with other regions of the world for tourist dollars. Ethiopia, for example, aims to triple its number of foreign visitors (from the current 750,000) to more than 2.5 million by 2020 (Maasho, 2015). In comparison to that of Egypt, where 9.9 million tourists visited in 2014–2015, the threefold target in five years is still modest. In terms of tourist dollars, in 2012, the continent generated income totaling over US $36 billion from tourism-related activities and sectors such as hotels, tours, and various kinds of attractions. This figure amounted to a little over 2.8 percent of the continent's GDP (World Bank, 2013). Some (see, for instance, Rogerson, 2007; Sharpley, 2015; Srinivasan, 2015) argue that while the growth in the GDP as a result of tourism is relatively small, it is steadily growing, and the impact on the region's economy is significant.

African Cultural Heritage

There are no shortages of World Heritage Sites in Africa recognized by UNESCO and potentially attractive to tourists from both inside and outside the continent. They range from the Royal Palaces of Abomey in Benin and the ruins of the ancient Aksumite Civilization in Ethiopia to the Great Pyramid of Giza in Egypt and the Great Zimbabwe National Monument, to mention a few. However, challenges remain when it comes to attracting tourists to Africa. These include: lack of security/safety, underdeveloped infrastructure, poor or nonexistent publicity, and lack of proper marketing strategies. Many popular tourist spots in Africa were rocked by terror attacks in recent years. In Egypt, Kenya, and Tanzania's island of Zanzibar, for example, various terrorist groups systematically targeted the countries' tourism industry. Some of these countries were removed from international tour operators' programs, resulting in a drop of more than 22 percent in international tourism.

In addition to lack of security and safety as well as high crime rates, according to the World Bank (2013), other constraints such as access to finance for investors, taxes on tourism investments, low levels of tourism skills among Africa's population, and bureaucratic processes are present in varying degrees in sub-Saharan African countries. Many countries took significant measures to overcome most of the above-mentioned obstacles through increased security, infrastructure development, aggressive marketing, and promotion efforts.

African countries with a successful track record in terms of tourism and those with thriving tourism-based economies have a variety of factors in their favor. For instance, tourists flock to places such as Egypt because of its rich and ancient history, sites such as the pyramids, and other artifacts. Other African countries such as South Africa, Kenya, Botswana, and Tanzania are able to attract tourists due to their game parks and safari expeditions, while others such as Morocco and Tunisia are reaping benefits from their attractive beaches as well as their relative proximity to Europe.

Other African countries, while they have not been as attractive to tourists as those mentioned above, should be as attractive, if not more attractive, because they also possess rich cultural heritage. For instance, countries such as Ethiopia are some of the few places in the world where tourists can experience centuries-old rock-hewn churches as well as exclusive cultural and religious celebrations such as the UNESCO-honored Meskel festival (Finding of the True Cross of Christ) (Sahle, 2015), which has survived for thousands of years. Ethiopia's rich cultural heritage also consists of ancient architecture that shows the high level of skill and civilization of ancient African societies and kingdoms such as the Axum Kingdom (UNESCO, 2015), which is comparable to the world's great empires of China, Persia, and Rome.

Despite breathtaking, tangible, and intangible heritage, among the main reasons why countries such as Ethiopia have not been one of the top tourist destinations until recently is that they have not invested in promotion and marketing, taken steps to enhance their image, and provided incentives to investors in the tourism and other sectors. In addition, countries working to deepen their success need to diversify their tourism offerings, address seasonality, and manage growth strategically (World Bank, 2013).

What is more, tourists learn about the existence of a cultural heritage, and whether it is worth their effort and money to visit and travel sometimes tens of thousands of miles (or kilometers), through a source of information about the cultural heritage. These days, such sources of information are postings on social media sites/outlets such as Twitter.

The Promise and Power of Social Media

As more and more people around the world get connected to the Internet, and with the explosive proliferation of mobile devices in the workplace and personal and social lives of even those in the remote parts of the globe, the number of social media users is increasing astronomically. The scale of the growth in the number of social media users is particularly evident on Twitter where about a billion tweets are posted by close to 650 million registered users in less than a week (Bhattacharya, Yang, Srinivasan, and Boynton, 2015). With this increase, come greater opportunities for interactions and information sharing, not to mention the power to influence and effect action.

Social media have been used to, among other things, organize protests, create and maintain a community, rally support for a cause, encourage and publicize participation in events and activities, keep in contact/touch with friends and family, exchange ideas and share information, influence public policy, advertise products, and promote services. Over the past few years, social media tools such as Twitter have opened new avenues for individuals, businesses, governments, and others to conduct marketing campaigns practically for free, dramatically changing the media landscape. According to Hirschhorn (2015), by the end of the decade, many traditional networks will be shocked to find that they have been supplanted in the minds of many millennials and generation Zs. In the end, it should come as no surprise that there have been threats that have gone unseen or under-addressed by the major and minor media networks.

The United Nations World Tourism Organization (UNWTO), in its 2014 report (http://www.e-unwto.org/doi/pdf/10.18111/9789284416899), predicts that tourism arrivals in Africa will reach 134 million by 2030. In this regard, the importance of infrastructure to tourism development and growth in the continent cannot be overemphasized. African governments recognize the potential contribution of tourism to the transformation of the continent, given that Africa is endowed with rich and diverse cultures and landscapes. What is more, tourism is one of the strategic areas for the New Partnership for Africa's Development (NEPAD). To foster the development of tourism on the continent, the NEPAD Tourism Action Plan (TAP) was formulated under the guidance of African ministers of tourism, who convene annually under the auspices of the World Tourism Organization (WTO) Commission for Africa (African Development Bank Group, 2014).

If they are to bolster their tourism sectors, African countries need to constantly find ways to promote their cultural heritage sites using, among other tools, social media. Although existing cultural heritage and unique resources can be a big draw for tourists, Africa is also a continent with a long, rich, fascinating, and mysterious history known only to the locals or curious wanderers. However, several African historical sites remain hidden from the outside world.

Tools such as Twitter offer countries and their cultural heritage institutions new platforms for connecting their resources with potential users, customers, and/or visitors in a more personal way. Tourists' or visitors' tweets about their experiences at a hotel, a cultural heritage institution and/or site visits could positively or negatively affect the host countries' or institutions' images, future reputations, and abilities to attract more visitors. With the help of the power of social media such as Twitter and tourists who share their experiences about African cultural heritage, the cultural heritage could be brought to the attention of not just other tourists, but also organizations such as UNESCO that have the authority to designate them World Heritage Sites, thereby preserving them for the future.

METHODS

The purpose of this study is to understand the characteristics of tweet messages in connection with African cultural heritage and visitors' experiences as expressed in the tweeter universe. Who is tweeting about African cultural heritage, what is the nature of the tweet content, and what is the information flow network are some of the questions this study set out to answer. In view of the goal of the study, it is important to collect all tweets that are posted on the Twitter platform. Tweets were acquired via twitter API (https://dev.twitter.com/rest/tools/console) and Apigee (https://apigee.com/console) services using combinations of broad search terms such as *Africa and cultural heritage*, *Africa and museum*, *Africa and safari*, *Africa and tourism*, and *Africa and holiday destinations*. Also included in the search are combinations of hashtags such as: #VisitAfrica, #MuseumAfrica, #TravelAfrica, #AfricaTravel, #Africatourism, #AfricaSafari, #SafariAfrica. The tweet datasets were prepared and organized into categorical variables to reflect the actual tweet messages, tweet usernames, hashtags, retweet counts, location, and user mentions. Without any cutoff date, a little over twenty thousand tweet messages were downloaded and saved as textual documents.

Using statistical and linguistic text-analysis software called T-LAB (http://tlab.it/en), the textual document is transformed into corpus files for processing. The corpus files are then converted into lexical units (words and multi-words) that are organized in data tables (matrices) for further analysis. This study heavily relied on sequence and thematic analysis tools; key analytic tools in T-LAB used to characterize, explore, and measure the occurrences and relationships between key terms; understanding emerging themes; and performing sequence analysis of key terms. These tools are suitable to characterize the nature of tweets and their relationships in the domain of African cultural heritage and tourism (in general), and of course help answer the research questions.

RESULTS AND DISCUSSION

1. Identify the Source and Location of Tweets about African Cultural Heritage

In very few countries, such as South Africa, Kenya, Tanzania, Egypt, Tunisia, Namibia, and the Seychelles, tourism ministries, tourism boards, and sport, art, and culture departments tweet promotional content regarding events and celebrations having to do with their respective country's cultural heritage sites and artifacts. However, the bulk of the sources of tweet messages comes from international media outlets such as CNN, the BBC, Bloomberg Media, the *New York Times*, and international organizations such as UNESCO and UNwebcast (UN Web TV), GermanForeignOffice, and local tour operators. The tweets from international media sources and international organizations are dominated by current events that endanger the destruction of cultural heritage sites due to conflict and war. Considering the fact that UNESCO is the world-leading institution with a mission to protect and support world heritage sites, and the word "UNESCO" appearing as the most frequently occurring term across the tweet documents, the word-association diagram in figure 11.1 presents the results to illustrate what other words are associated with it. In addition, there are extensive tweet message and images being cross-posted on Facebook and Instagram.

True to its mission, UNESCO is communicating via its tweet feed about African countries and world heritage sites, and about the protection, looting, and safeguard measures around cultural heritage sites. Also shown in the word association diagrams are places of cultural heritage sites such as Mali, Timbuktu, Egypt, Ethiopia, Libya, and Nigeria.

2. Determine the Most Influential Twitter Users with Respect to African Cultural Heritage

One of the categorical variables used to prepare the tweet corpus is the @ username. Travel enthusiasts, explorers, bloggers, writers, photographers, adventurers, cultural heritage advocates, local tour operators, and culture,

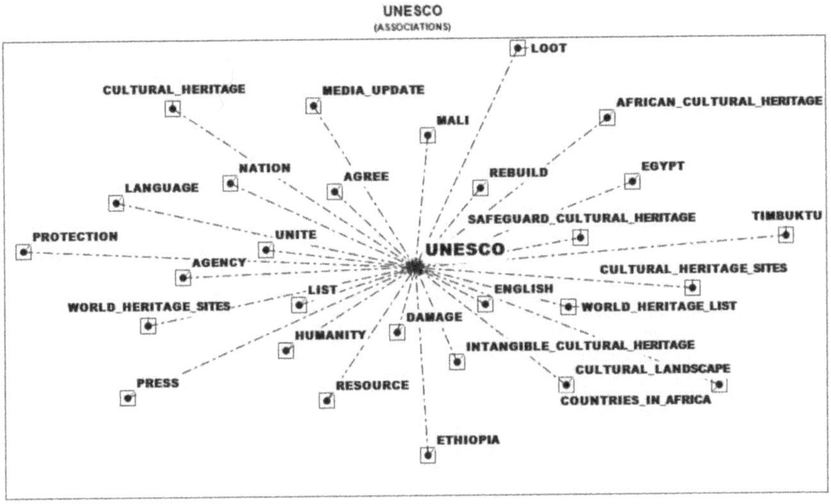

Figure 11.1. Word Association, UNESCO, as Source of Tweet Messages

tourism, and art ministries and departments are the most influential twitter users in the tweet landscape surrounding the topic of "African cultural heritage," and "African tourism" in general. Based on the number of tweets they periodically post and the number of followers they have, table 11.1 presents the top fifteen influential twitter users.

As can be seen from table 11.1, the most influential twitter users come from South Africa. Given the country's enormous potential in tourism and the level of infrastructure development in South Africa, this could be an obvious finding. The lesson, however, is that other African countries can emulate what South Africa is doing due to the ubiquity of smartphones and popularity of social media.

3. Characterize Visitors Who Tweet about African Cultural Heritage and Their Information Flow Network

To better understand the characteristics of tweets and the information flow network, we needed to generate a network graph. In T-LAB, the appropriate tool available to achieve a network graph is through sequence analysis where, based on selected key terms, graphs will be generated that present other related key terms that succeed and precede the selected key terms. The sequence analysis graphs are then exported as graph markup XML (GraphML) files, which are then opened with and external graph editor. In our case, we used a tool called yEd (http://www.yworks.com/en/products/yfiles/yed/) to create a fully interconnected graph between and among the selected key terms.

Table 11.1. Most Influential Twitter Users, Selected List

Account Name	*Username*	*Bio, Profile*
AWHF	@African_WH_Fund	The African World Heritage Fund—a Category II Centre under the auspices of UNESCO that works with protection of Africa's natural and cultural heritage
Velma Corcoran	VelCorcoran	Head of Marketing @capetowntourism. People-watcher, traveler, runner & mom who believes life is best when accompanied by bubbles
Sasibai Kimis	@sasibai	Founder of @earthheir—global nomad—sustainability—faith at work—triple bottom line—Africa enthusiast—cultural heritage advocate
SANParks	@SANParks	SANParks manages a system of parks which represents the indigenous fauna, flora, landscapes and associated cultural heritage of South Africa
Moja Heritage	@mojaheritage	Awesome natural, historical, and cultural places to visit around South Africa, local food, amazing people doing amazing creative things, and inspiring SA design
Bella Bride Africa	@Bella_Bride	Preserving African Heritage in the form of Weddings, Fashion, Culture! Wedding Planning, Inspiration & Wedding Vendors! follow on IG @bellabrideafrica
Radio Mbao	@radiombao	Official Twitter for Radio Mbao-The Africa Online radio station. We celebrate Africa Music, heritage and Culture. Email: Radiombao@gmail.com
Christine Lundy	@ChristineLundy	French in South Africa—Passionate about stories and design—columnist @AMACUCULTURE focus on #culture #Art #Wines #Food #Design. . . .
Laura Kate Gibson	@DigitisationSA	PhD candidate at KCL doing research in democratizing cultural heritage collections in South Africa. Former Digitization & Collections Manager. . . .
Wanderluster vacation.co.za	@VacationZA	Online Tourism and Destination Marketing Portal for Southern Africa and surrounds—we promote the beauty, natural heritage and products of. . . .
Max Magazine	@magazinemax1	Max Magazine promotes African culture & heritage, celebrity, Music, Fashion, Art Awards, we give publicity to artistes IG: maxmagng / maxmagng@gmail.com
SouthAfrican Tourism	@GoToSouthAfrica	The official Twitter account for South African Tourism
Visit South Africa	@SouthAfrica	This is the Official Twitter page of South African Tourism for North America. Leave Ordinary Behind and join the adventure! #visitsouthafrica
Atta Africa	@atta_tourism	The Voice of African Tourism. Atta promotes tourism to Africa from all corners of the world through membership of elite buyers and suppliers of tourism product
Hon. Phyllis Kandie	@Kandie_Phyllis	Cabinet Secretary Ministry of East African Affairs, Commerce and Tourism. Official handle for East African Affairs Commerce and Tourism of Kenya

Related to the research question, we chose to generate a sequence analysis around "cultural heritage" and "Africa." The key terms in the corpus text sorted by number of occurrences reveal the fact that "Cultural_Heritage" and "Africa" are the top two most frequently occurring lexical units (keywords). For the purpose of selecting the other key terms to add to the network graph, we chose a threshold of forty, the minimum number of occurrences, as criteria for adding to the graph. This is done so as not to clutter the graph so much that reading would be difficult. This method resulted in 140 nodes and 232 edges. In the network graph, the nodes are the most significant key terms, and the edges establish the level of association between succeeding and preceding key terms surrounding the selected nodes.

As stated above, to find a plausible answer to this research question, we chose to investigate the measure of association through a network graph by selecting "cultural heritage" and "Africa." Figure 11.2 presents the network graph for 'Cultural Heritage." As shown in the graph (figure 11.2), a reasonable interpretation can be made that the network graph is dominated by a flow network that represents the celebration and promotion of rich cultural and natural heritage in the African continent, with South Africa and major cities in South Africa such as Johannesburg, Durban, and the KwaZulu-Natal province cited as destinations for tourists, as well as celebrating national heritage days. The second major observation in the graph pertains to the other

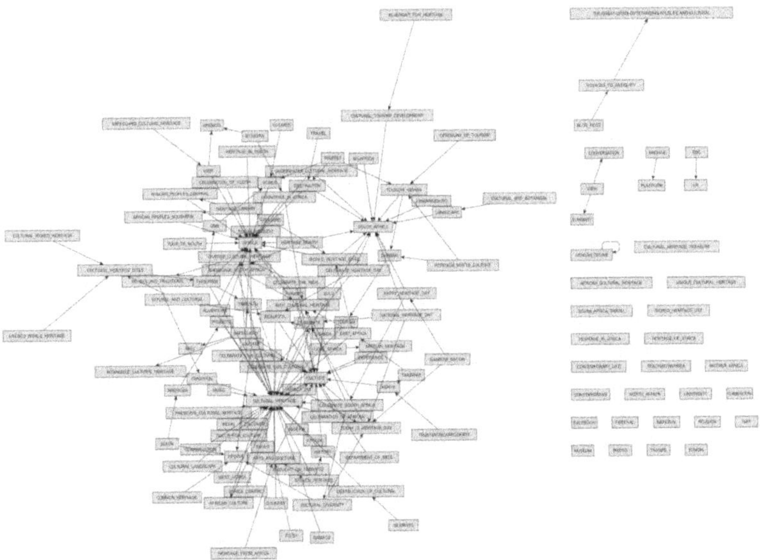

Figure 11.2. Network Graph around the First Most Occurring Key Term, "Cultural Heritage"

African countries visibly shown in connection with cultural heritage and tourism sites, including Kenya, Mali/Timbuktu, Tanzania, Egypt, Benin, Nigeria, and Uganda. Third, we also observe from the graph that media outlets such as CNN world, the BBC, and the *New York Times* are tweeting about the risk African cultural heritage faces from conflict and looting.

In figure 11.3, because "Africa" is the second most frequently occurring key term after to "cultural heritage," the graph presents a more or less similar result with a similar information flow network as in figure 11.2. Again, we observe "Africa" closely related to travel destinations, attractions, adventure, and cultural heritage sites and treasures.

4. Identify Trending Topics, Most Popular Subjects, and Places Discussed with Respect to African Cultural Heritage

Word association, concept mapping, and thematic analysis are available tools in T-LAB that provide adequate explanations to identify trending topics and subjects. Again focusing on the key terms relevant to this study (i.e., "cultural heritage," "adventure travel," "museum," "UNESCO," and 'tourism"), we ran word-association analyses. Therefore, by selecting one of these key terms, we were able to determine the relationships and local meaning or context within which these selected words occur. Figures 11.4 and 11.5 present results of the word-association analysis for the most frequently occurring

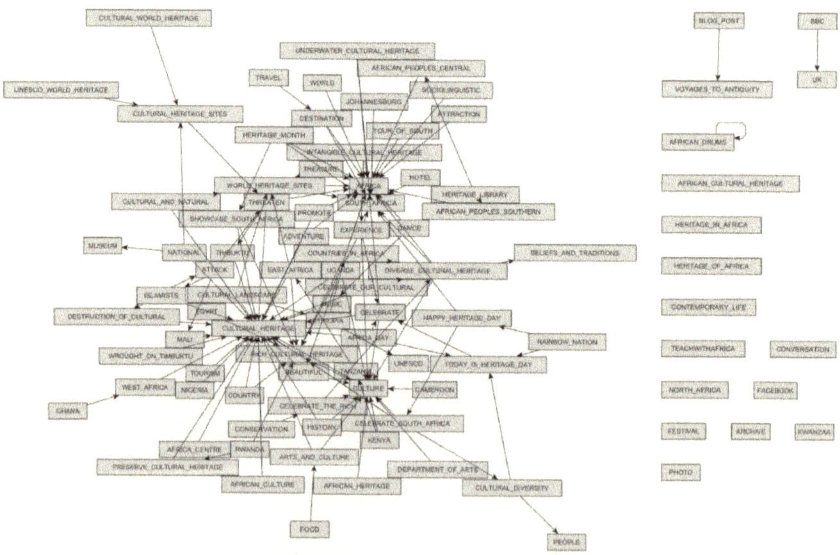

Figure 11.3. Network Graph around the Second Most Occurring Key Term, "Africa"

lexical unit/keyword, "adventure_travel" (figure 11.4), and co-occurrence graph for Tourism (figure 11.5). In figure 11.4, we can see that the central theme, adventure_travel, occurs within the local context of travel, wildlife, park, beach, getaway, honeymoon, and culture, largely in the context of South African tourism.

In figure 11.5, the co-occurrence analysis reveals what other key terms occur when the word "tourism" is mentioned in the African context. Taking 60 percent as the cutoff point for the co-occurrence threshold, the following key themes and topics emerge alongside "Tourism": African countries' tourism ministries agree to promote the sector; the downturn in tourism, and often the sector defying the slump; tourism industry as a source of revenue; the threat on the sector due to export of elephant tusks; and how war and conflict threatens the tourism industry.

Also shown in figure 11.4, is that there are some indications either (1) of where the travelers are from or (2) that those tweeting about adventure travel and related activities in Africa have some connection in America, Asia, Latin America, and South America.

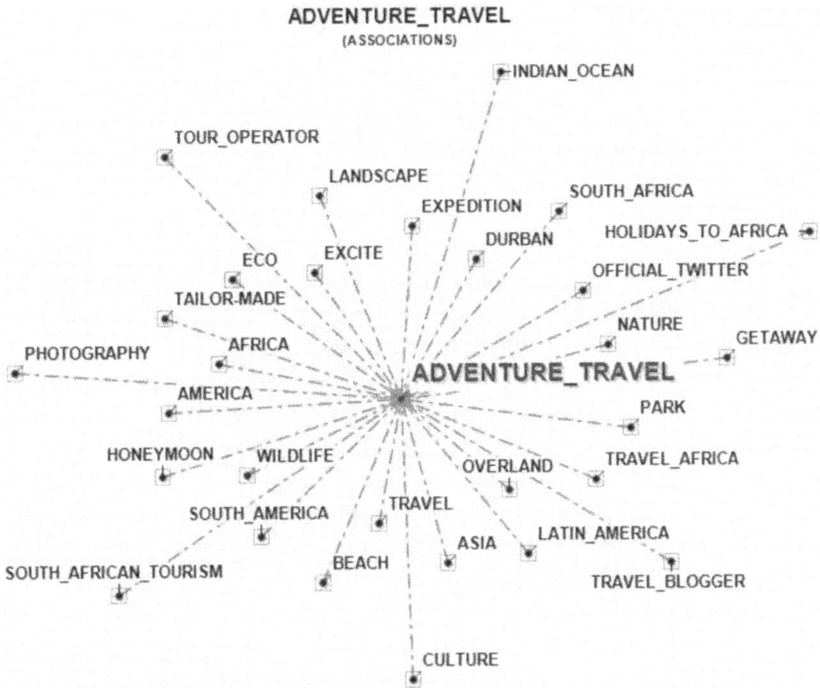

Figure 11.4. Word Association around "Adventure Travel," as One Trending Topic in the Tweet Corpus

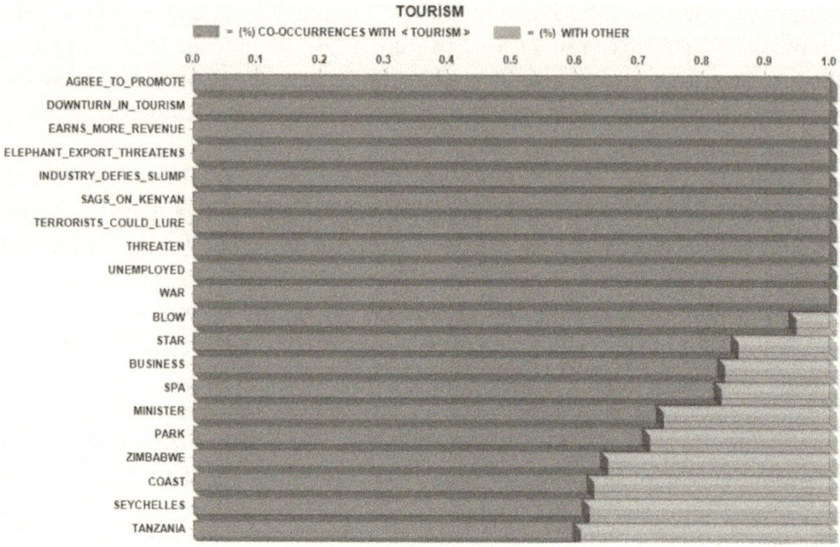

Figure 11.5. Sequence of Keywords around Adventure_Africa

In figure 11.5, selecting tourism as one trending word, the co-occurrence analysis graph shows what other key terms are mentioned in 60 percent to 100 percent of the cases. The co-occurrence analysis clearly shows which other themes and topics emerge across the tweet corpus related to African tourism.

5. Identify Sentiments of Tweets about African Cultural Heritage

Sentiments in the Twitter corpus can be detected by keywords that convey negative or positive messages and/or experiences as a result of visits and travels by those who tweet about African cultural heritage. In T-LAB, each tweet message is recorded as a document with its own record ID. One of the tools used to understand the sentiment of the tweet message is the application called "modeling emerging themes" in the thematic analysis category of tools. This application is used to discover, examine, and model the themes that emerge from the tweet corpus/text. Using the naïve Bayes classifier algorithm, we classified the elementary contexts of the documents (tweet messages). The maximum number of themes the application allows to be selected is fifty. To reproduce the fifty themes with all of their context requires much more space. We only chose pertinent themes, such as African_Cultural_Heritage, UNESCO, Timbuktu, Rich_Cultural_Heritage, and Preserve_Cultural_Heritage. Table 11.2 presents samples of positive and negative sentiments that are present in the tweet corpus for the themes—"rich cultural heritage" and one famous heritage site, Timbuktu.

Table 11.2. Select Positive and Negative Sentiments Expressed about African Cultural Heritage

Theme	*Score*	*Context, Positive*	*Theme*	*Score*	*Context, Negative*
RICH_ CULTURAL_ HERITAGE	0.444	Full of scenic_beauty & rich in culture_and_ heritage, #Cape Town, #Africa is an ideal place_to_plan a pleasant_vacation_	TIMBUKTU	0.86	Jihadis On March in Africa—Pt 6: Mali Urges UN Action After Timbuktu Attacks - - Islamists Attack cultural_heritage
RICH_ CULTURAL_ HERITAGE	0.422	On a rich American's party, Peru and the Bangwa Queen	TIMBUKTU	0.713	Mali: Experts at UN Forum Adopt Plan to Safeguard Mali's cultural_heritage : [UN News] International exper .
RICH_ CULTURAL_ HERITAGE	0.422	> Africa's stolen art heritage. On a rich American's party, Peru and the Bangwa Queen	TIMBUKTU	0.713	BBC_News—Timbuktu's Sidi Yahia mosque attacked by Mali militants
RICH_ CULTURAL_ HERITAGE	0.415	As mentioned before, South_Africa has a rich and very diverse_cultural_heritage	TIMBUKTU	0.69	Sad. http:// nation. co.ke/News/africa/Mali+ Islamists + bulldoze + independence + monument + in + Timbuktu /- /1066/1605210/-/7shh0j/-/index.
RICH_ CULTURAL_ HERITAGE	0.415	The Drakensberg Is Rich In cultural_heritage. It Is Home To 35% Of South_Africa's San Rock Art Sites	TIMBUKTU	0.69	Timbuktu's Destruction: Why Islamists Are Wrecking Mali's cultural_heritage
RICH_ CULTURAL_ HERITAGE	0.415	Never known a beautiful continent like #Africa? What a rich cultural musical_ heritage?	TIMBUKTU	0.69	Mali Islamists Destroy More Holy Timbuktu sites—http ://nyti.
RICH_ CULTURAL_ HERITAGE	0.415	Celebrate_South_Africa's rich and diverse_ cultural_heritage	TIMBUKTU	0.69	Truly a sad week for humanity: Mali Islamists destroy Timbuktu shrines
RICH_ CULTURAL_ HERITAGE	0.415	Divas are back to Celebrate_South_Africa's rich cultural_heritage_	TIMBUKTU	0.628	Mali: UN, European Union team up to restore Timbuktu's cultural_heritage: The United Nations and the E.
RICH_ CULTURAL_ HERITAGE	0.415	The state_is_1of Africa's richest stores_of_ artworks	TIMBUKTU	0.628	More centuries-old cultural_heritage smashed as conflict continues in Mali- BBC_News: Timbuktu mausoleums destroyed
RICH_ CULTURAL_ HERITAGE	0.415	A great event that raised awareness towards the rich cultural #heritage of West #Africa: the Griot Summit	TIMBUKTU	0.628	RT @ajenglish : Fighter in Mali destroy more Timbuktu tombs

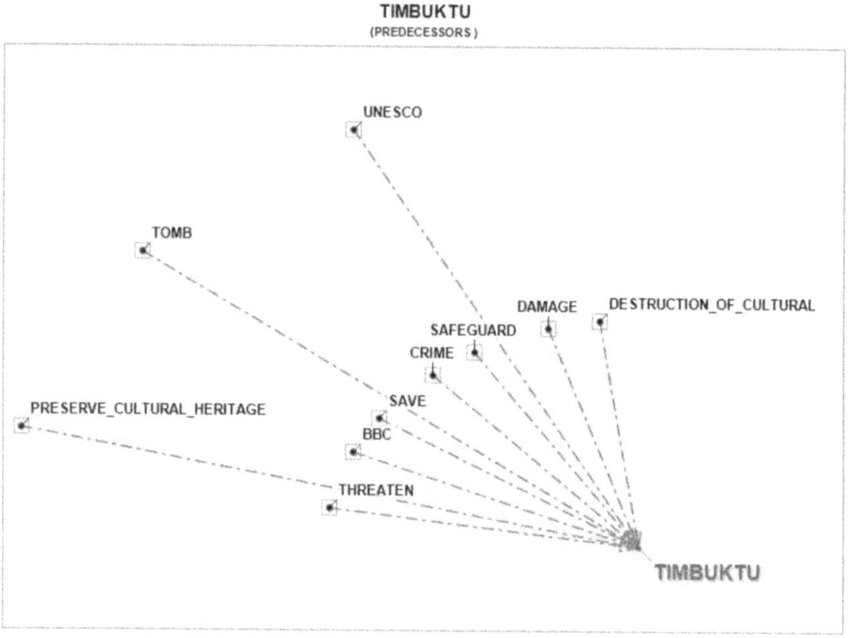

Figure 11.6. Sequence Analysis, Predecessors, for Timbuktu

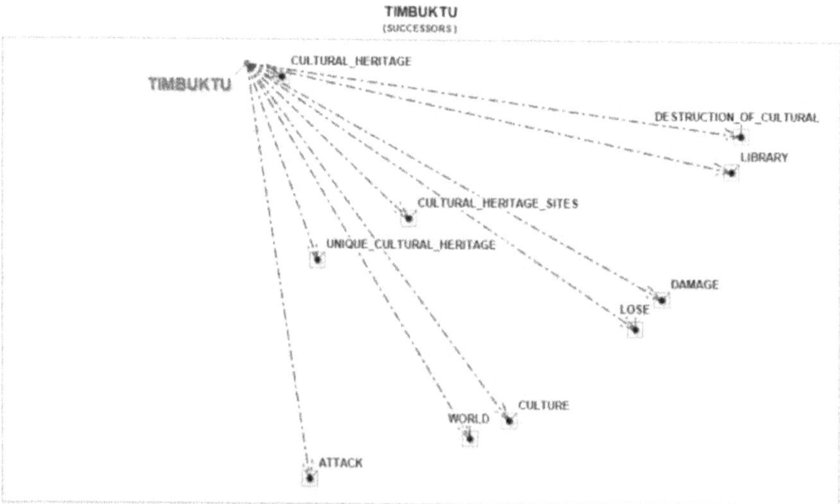

Figure 11.7. Sequence Analysis, Successors, for Timbuktu

Table 11.2 presents a partial view of only the top ten document classifications via thematic analysis. As can be seen from table 11.2, on one side, we have positive sentiments about the riches and celebrations of African cultural heritage, and on the other, we have negative sentiments that dominated the situation in Mali, especially the damage and destruction of Timbuktu shrines caused by Islamists in 2012 and 2013. Looking at the sequence of themes surrounding Timbuktu, we can also get a better view of the analysis, as shown in figures 11.6 and 11.7. The two figures show the result of the sequence analysis (figure 11.6 for predecessors, and figure 11.7 for successors).

CONCLUSION AND RECOMMENDATIONS FOR FUTURE WORK

Countries around the world have benefited from tourism as international global arrivals have grown. Visitor numbers in Africa have risen (up to 10 percent a year) for the past decade, albeit from a very low base. Considering the global middle-income population increases, progress is still needed to promote greater regional integration. About two-thirds of African countries still demand visas from Africans traveling outside their native lands. Greater cooperation is needed between governments to facilitate the intra-African or trans-border movement of persons within Africa. With the right policies and strategies, African countries can make tourism a pillar of their growing economies (African Development Bank Group, 2014).

There is a clear indication that Twitter has proven to be a strong platform for individuals and institutions both inside and outside Africa to disseminate information about African cultural heritage and the tourism industry in general. Tweets are posted from government tourism ministries, art and culture departments, tour operators, and travel enthusiasts, as well as international organizations such as UNESCO and media outlets. The most influential Twitter users are from South Africa or have some connection with South Africa. Trending topics and subjects include: the rich cultural heritages of Africa, the preservation of African cultural heritage, adventure travel and getaways, promotion of the tourism industry, a downturn in the tourism sector, tourism as a source of revenue and as an economic engine, and, most importantly, conflict and war that has brought destruction to cultural heritage sites, as well as the export of elephant tusks threatening the tourism industry. Looking at the information flow network and generating a network graph around African cultural heritage, we observe characteristics that visitors and Twitter users express around the same topics and themes. Oftentimes, the tweet centers around individual African countries such as Mali, Egypt, South Africa, Ethiopia, Kenya, and the

Seychelles. Other relevant nodes in the network graph relate to cultural artifacts such as art, food, music, and museum.

We also looked at the sentiments expressed via the Twitter universe revolving around African cultural heritage. Looking at the positive and negative messages expressed via the Twitter platform, we see on the positive side tweets and messages exalting the riches of African cultural heritage and natural beauty. On the negative side, we observe war, conflict, and destruction causing incalculable damage to African cultural heritage, especially cultural heritage in Mali and Timbuktu.

As we have outlined from the outset, one of the main challenges faced by African countries to attract more tourists and thus benefit economically from tourism is lack of marketing. Those countries that are able to use both traditional and social media tools such as Twitter are able to brand not only their cultural heritage as well as other attractions but also improve their own perceptions and images. Therefore, in order to create an overall awareness of their cultural heritage and build a positive image, African countries need to embark on marketing campaigns using twenty-first-century tools. After all, communications channels such as Twitter are ideal for individuals, companies, governments, and others on the continent because Twitter users and users of social media have a multiplier effect when it comes to publicity for a brand or service or product or, in this case, cultural heritage site.

Tourists' tweets are indeed the most influential words and powerful marketing tools in the tourism industry because it is the customers themselves who rate or endorse tourist destinations based on their overall experience. With the growing presence of world-class airlines, international chain hotels, and global groups operating in Sub-Saharan Africa, some individual countries have already provided successes (in terms of addressing existing infrastructure constraints, ranging from improved air transport facilities to decent accommodations) that have created positive experiences for their visitors.

Finally, we acknowledge that we can gain further understanding of the nature of tweets about African cultural heritage through methods and approaches other than ours. We also do not claim our work to be the definitive and final work on the topic. Additional research, using longitudinal data, needs to be conducted in order to have a continued and fuller picture of the characteristics of social media posts in general, and tweets in particular, about African cultural heritage—the bedrock of tourism on the continent. Moreover, one can look beyond simply the nature of the text in the tweets and information flow network of the users and analyze the hyperlinks in the tweets to see what they reveal about, among others things, the topic or subject of the tweet as well as the target audience of the tweets.

With full recognition of the complexities of the tourism sector in today's globalized market, the authors would like to reiterate that tourism is a powerful engine for economic growth. By creating job opportunities, generating foreign direct investments and foreign currency, and contributing to image building, the tourism sector can indeed energize the economy and lead the African Renaissance in the twenty-first century.

REFERENCES

African Development Bank Group (2014, *November*). *Africa Tourism Monitor*, *2*(1). Retrieved from http://www.afdb.org/fileadmin/uploads/afdb/Documents/Publications/Africa_Tourism_NOV_2014.pdf

Armitage, S. J, Jasim, S. A., Marks, A. E., Parker, A. G., Usik, V. I., and Uerpmann, H-P. (2011, January). The southern route "out of Africa": Evidence for an early expansion of modern humans into Arabia. *Science*, *331*(6016), 453–56. Retrieved from http://www.sciencemag.org/content/331/6016/453.full.pdf

Bhattacharya, S., Yang, C., Srinivasan, P., and Boynton, B. (2015). Perceptions of presidential candidates' personalities in Twitter. *Journal of the Association for Information Science and Technology*. doi: 10.1002/asi.23377

Hirschhorn, J. (2015). *7 deadly sins: Where Hollywood is wrong about the future of TV*. Retrieved from https://www.linkedin.com/pulse/7-deadly-sins-where-hollywood-wrong-future-tv-jason-hirschhorn

Maasho, A. (2015, October 4). Ethiopia aims to grow tourism threefold in five years: Minister. Retrieved from http://www.reuters.com/article/2015/10/04/ethiopia-tourism-idUSL5N12235F20151004

Meredith, M. (2011). *Born in Africa: The quest for the origins of human life*. New York: Public Affairs.

Rogerson, C. (2007). Reviewing Africa in the global tourism economy. *Development Southern Africa*, *24*(3), 361–79.

Sahle, E. (2015, September 27). Meskel Ethiopian fabulous carnival. *The Ethiopian Herald*. Retrieved from http://www.ethpress.gov.et/herald/index.php/environment/item/2281-meskel-ethiopian-fabulous-carnival

Sharpley, R. (2015). Tourism: A vehicle for development? In R. Sharpley and D. Telfer (Eds.), *Tourism and development: Concepts and issues* (2nd ed.) (pp. 3–30). Clevedon, UK: Channel View Publications.

Srinivasan, S. (2015). Ethiopia: 'Ger'alta', Ethiopian sacred homeland of Christian heritage—A tourism viewpoint. In *All Africa global media*. Retrieved from http://allafrica.com/stories/201506151078.html

UNESCO (2015). *Rock-hewn churches*. Retrieved from http://whc.unesco.org/en/list/18

United Nations Conference on Trade and Development. (2010). *The contribution of tourism to trade and development*. Retrieved from http://unctad.org/en/docs/cid8_en.pdf

United Nations World Tourism Organization (2014). *UNWTO tourism highlights: 2015 edition*. Retrieved from http://www.e-unwto.org/doi/pdf/10.18111/9789284416899

World Bank (2013). *Tourism in Africa: Harnessing tourism for growth and improved livelihoods*. Retrieved from http://www.worldbank.org/afr/tourism

Part IV

INFORMATICS IN THE ARCHIVE

Chapter Twelve

Challenges for Web Archivists

Issues in the Preservation of Digital Cultural Heritage

Brenda Reyes Ayala

ABSTRACT

In recent years, web archiving has become increasingly common for many cultural heritage institutions around the world. Archives, museums, universities, and national libraries seek to build and manage their own collections of websites. Many of these institutions employ the Internet Archive's Archive-It service, a subscription-based web archiving service that helps organizations build and manage their own web archives. Archive-It is currently the most popular web archiving service, with over three hundred clients (called "partners") consisting of universities, state libraries and archives, museums, and national libraries in several countries. This chapter presents a qualitative study conducted during a stay at the Internet Archive, where the author worked with the Archive-It team to analyze and categorize their support tickets. These tickets are submitted by Archive-It partners who need help creating or managing their web archives. They are a reliable source of information that sheds light on which aspects of the web archiving process are most challenging for institutions. This chapter identifies and analyzes the challenges that web archivists face most often and presents a theoretical, platform-independent typology of web archiving issues.

INTRODUCTION

Web archiving is the process of storing and maintaining websites to preserve them as a historical, informational, legal, or evidential record. A *web archive* is a system that contains archived websites. In recent years, web archiving has become increasingly common for many cultural heritage institutions around the world. Archives, museums, universities, and national libraries seek to build and manage their own collections of websites. As demand has grown, the creation of software to create web archives, along with services to manage them, has accelerated.

This chapter is an attempt at identifying the challenges that web archivists face most often, with a special focus on the issue of quality in a web archive. The goal is to begin to make a theoretical contribution to the field by answering the following question:

> What are the most important issues that web archivists are faced with as they build and manage a web archive?

Most of the research presented here took place during a summer internship with the Internet Archive in 2014, during which I worked with their Archive-It team to analyze and categorize their support tickets.

Background

A Brief History of Web Archiving

Web archiving as a field is only a few years older than the Web itself, and can be said to have arisen due to fears that digital information would not withstand the passage of time, and thus important pieces of the historical record would eventually be lost. In a conference for the International Federation of Library Associations and Institutions, Terry Kuny referred to the future as a "Digital Dark Age," an "era where much of what we know today, much of what is coded and written electronically, will be lost forever" (Kuny, 1997, p. 1). She warned that enormous amounts of digital information had already been lost and that "Digital history [could not] be recreated by individuals and organizations [could not] recreate a digital history" (p. 2).

Kuny's notion of a Digital Dark Age proved popular, though efforts had already begun to address the problem. A year earlier, in 1996, Brewster Kahle founded the Internet Archive with the mission of creating a universally accessible digital library. As stated on its website, the Internet Archive works "to prevent the Internet—a new medium with major historical significance—and other 'born-digital' materials from disappearing into the past" (Internet Archive, 2012). To achieve this goal, the Internet Archive periodically takes snapshots of the entire World Wide Web and stores copies of the captured resources in massive storage warehouses. Users can then access these resources using the Wayback Machine, a special piece of software developed by the Internet Archive (https://archive.org/web/). An example of an archived website is shown in figure 12.1. Due to its size and scope, the Internet Archive has remained the largest and most ambitious web archiving project to date.

Figure 12.1. Screen Shot from Internet Archive Wayback Machine

In 1996, the National Library of Australia inaugurated the first-ever web archiving program by a national library—an effort to capture portions of Australia's national domain (.au) as well as other web resources deemed significant to Australia's history and culture. In 2000, the Library of Congress began its Minerva Project (now the Library of Congress Web Archives), a web archiving effort aimed at creating topical collections of materials relevant to American history and culture. Many national libraries soon followed suit, for example the British Library, which began its UK Web Archive in 2004, and the National Library of France in 2006. Over the years, many universities have also begun web archiving projects (Wikipedia, n.d.).

In 2003, the International Internet Preservation Consortium (IIPC) was founded with the mission of "improving the tools, standards and best practices of web archiving while promoting international collaboration and the broad access and use of web archives for research and cultural heritage" (International Internet Preservation Consortium, n.d.). It has remained the only organization addressing the needs of the web archiving field. The founding of the IIPC also coincided with a greater awareness of the importance of digital content and its relationship to cultural heritage. That same year, the United National Educational Scientific and Cultural Organization (UNESCO) established its Charter on the Preservation of the Digital Heritage. In it, UNESCO recognized that "[cultural] resources of information and creative expression are increasingly produced, distributed, accessed and maintained in digital form, creating a new legacy—the digital heritage" (United National Educational Scientific and Cultural Organization, 2003). UNESCO acknowledged that the world's digital heritage was at risk of being lost and noted that "its preservation for the benefit of present and future generations is an urgent issue of worldwide concern" (United National Educational Scientific and Cultural Organization, 2003). It postulated that efforts should be undertaken to prevent the loss of the digital cultural heritage:

> Member States may wish to cooperate with relevant organizations and institutions in encouraging a legal and practical environment which will maximize accessibility of the digital heritage. (United National Educational Scientific and Cultural Organization, 2003).

The process of web archiving usually occurs in the following order:

1. Selection: During this phase, web archivists select the websites they are most interested in preserving.
2. Acquisition/Capture/Harvest: A piece of software known as a "crawler" accesses every resource to be captured, makes a copy of it, and stores it on a files system. In the web archiving community, the most popular crawler is called Heritrix (https://webarchive.jira.com/wiki/display/Heritrix/Heritrix).
3. Access: Access to the captured content is provided, either by the organization responsible for the selection process or the organization involved in harvesting it. These are sometimes separate organizations; other times they are one and the same. Some organizations implement the entire web archiving process, while others simply select the sites they wish to preserve and let a separate entity capture and provide access to them. Most archived websites are viewed using the Internet Archive's Wayback Machine.

THE ARCHIVE-IT SUBSCRIPTION SERVICE

The Internet Archive's Archive-It service is a subscription-based web archiving service that helps organizations build and manage their own web archives. Archive-It is very popular, with over three hundred clients (called "partners") consisting of universities, state libraries and archives, museums, and national libraries in several countries (Archive-It, 2014). The accounts of Archive-It partners are managed by a team of partner specialists. When a partner encounters a problem with the Archive-It service, they first open a support ticket using Zendesk, a popular customer-service platform (https://www.zendesk.com/beautifully-simple/). The ticket is received by the partner specialists, who are then responsible for addressing the issue. These initial tickets are part of the "Level 1" support. If the partner specialist determines that a problem is more serious or highly technical in nature, the issue becomes a "Level 2," and a ticket is opened in JIRA, another issue-tracking platform. A support engineer is responsible for addressing Level 2 tickets. If he determines that the problem requires more extensive technical efforts, he will convert it to a "Level 3" ticket, which is then addressed by the engineers at the Internet Archive.

PREVIOUS WORK IN QUALITY IN WEB ARCHIVING

The topic of quality in web archives is not new, and it was first addressed formally in 2006. In *Web Archiving*, the concept of quality in a web archive can be defined using the following two aspects (Masanès, 2006):

- the completeness of material (linked files) archived within a target perimeter, and
- the ability to render the original form of the site, particularly regarding navigation and interaction with the user.

Quality has also been addressed during the general assemblies of the International Internet Preservation Consortium. At the 2010 General Assembly for the IIPC, Voorburg (2010, May) described the approach taken by the National Library of the Netherlands (KB) regarding quality assurance, a process undertaken to assure all archives meet a certain standard of quality. According to Voorburg, the KB would capture websites of interest, which would then be checked for quality by web archiving analysts. The analysts would then decide to archive a site if its quality was sufficient, or choose to reject it if serious quality problems existed. Quality problems were recorded by the analysts using annotations within the Web Curator Tool, an archiving tool originally developed by the National Library of New Zealand and the British Library (http://webcurator.sourceforge.net/).

In a second presentation in Vienna, Voorburg (2010, September) explained some of the most important issues pertaining to quality assurance in the field of web archiving. Some of these were:

- The large amounts of data involved in web archiving pointed to a need for automation;
- The quality assurance process was complex, requiring special tools, procedures, and experts with specialized knowledge—it did not scale well; and
- The issue of quality itself was confusing; it was difficult to define a "good enough" level of quality for a captured resource.

In order to gain a broader perspective, the KB surveyed six institutions, most of them national libraries, as to their quality assurance practices. Based on the results, Voorburg presented the following list of the top ten quality issues most often seen in web archiving (2010, September):

1. URIs could not be discovered by crawler (~ 20 %)
2. Access restrictions (~ 15 %)
3. Multi-media missing in harvest (~ 12 %)
4. Display problematic; rewrites fail (~ 10 %)
5. Speculative links cause crawler traps (~ 6 %)
6. Sites have a near endless URI-space (~ 6 %)
7. Seeds missed during selection (~ 4 %)
8. Selection was too broad (~ 2 %)
9. Redirects broaden crawl scope too much (~ 2 %)
10. The "agnostos daemon": the (yet) unknown problem . . .

The results indicated that there was room for better and more efficient quality assurance of harvested websites. In order to achieve this, tools and processes for automating quality assurance were needed as an alternative to the expensive and time-consuming manual process. To achieve this goal, Voorburgh recommended starting an IIPC work group on quality assurance so that members would be able to share knowledge and create a common classification and technology.

In 2014, Reyes Ayala, Phillips, and Ko (2014) presented the results of a survey of quality assurance practices among institutions that engaged in web archiving. The authors received fifty-four responses to the survey, which included respondents who worked at large national libraries, universities, and various other institutions. Many of them did not have a custom, in-house system to carry out their web archiving activities, but relied on pre-built, "off the shelf" web archiving tools such as the Internet Archive's Archive-It service.

The results of the survey identified quality assurance as a process that almost all web archiving institutions undertake with their archives. Most institutions conducted quality assurance after the capture phase and employed various prebuilt tools from the Internet Archive, usually the Archive-It platform and the Heritrix web crawler. Though most institutions surveyed kept records of any quality problems they encountered, only a minority used the information to recrawl the site or attempted to manually patch the crawled content.

One important finding was that quality assurance is currently undertaken manually at most places, necessitating a significant time commitment from web archivists, as well as specialized training, knowledge, and skills. The authors concluded that the scope of many captures, as well as the small size of most web-archiving teams made manual quality assurance impractical. Reyes Ayala, Phillips, and Ko (2014) stressed the need for the development of tools to automate the quality assurance process.

METHOD

The work described here was meant to build on the prior efforts of Reyes Ayala, Phillips, and Ko (2014). Most of this took place during a summer internship with the Internet Archive in 2014. Before I began the internship, I met with a partner specialist and the head of the Archive-It service. They were particularly interested in two goals: gathering statistics about the tickets in the Archive-It support system and creating a system of classification that would allow them to see the amount and type of issues they dealt with most often.

To this end, I began by examining the many tickets submitted since the system began in 2011. The Zendesk system had over 600 tickets, while the JIRA system had over 400. At the time, they were not categorized. I was also given an analysis that had been conducted by an Archive-It intern several years prior. In it, she had created a typology of ticket issues and labeled a large number of them using her categorization system. Despite its usefulness, this typology was never implemented.

After examining the tickets and the prior work on them, I began to create a brand-new hierarchical classification system for Archive-It issues using qualitative content analysis. Qualitative content analysis is a method that seeks to "examine meanings, themes and patterns that may be manifest or latent in a particular text" (Zhang and Wildemuth, 2009, p. 1). It is an inductive process whereby the researcher's inferences and conclusions are strongly grounded in the data. The process of qualitative content analysis usually leads to creating thick descriptions or typologies about the data (p. 2). An individual support ticket served as my primary unit of analysis.

To increase the credibility of my findings, I also employed *member checks*, which is one of several methods of "'taking findings back to the field and determining whether the participants recognize them as true or accurate'" (Tracy, 2010, p. 844, quoting Lindlof and Taylor, 2002, p. 242). During these member checks, I distributed a draft of my classification system to the Archive-It partner specialists, who provided feedback on the accuracy and correctness of my categories. I created a second draft, which I then tested by classifying about 190 Zendesk tickets dating from 2013 through 2014. This led me to change some categories, add new ones, and merge others to arrive at a final classification system, which I present here. I then made several important modifications to the ticket system in both Zendesk and JIRA,

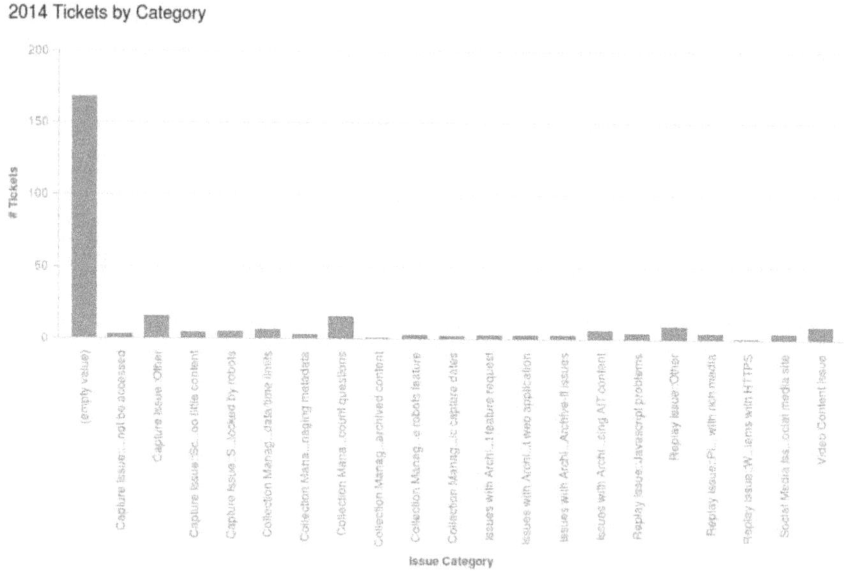

Figure 12.2. 2014 Issue Categories

allowing partner specialists to categorize their tickets using the typology. I also used Zendesk Insights, an advanced reporting tool, to create automated reports that would supply statistics on the number of issues in each category over time (see figure 12.2).

It is important to note that, due to time constraints, most tickets were not classified. Zendesk does not allow users to edit tickets that have been closed, thus restricting the number of tickets I could classify. However, partner specialists decided to use the system to classify future tickets. In the future, this would contribute important data that would illuminate what types of issues are most critical and need most attention from the Internet Archive.

FINDINGS

The following is a typology of issues that web archivists encounter when building and managing web archives. The focus of these categories is on identifying the *root cause* of a problem, rather than how the problem is addressed. Though these categories are specific to Archive-It, they could be applied to any other web archiving tools or system, with some small modifications.

I. *Capture Issues*: refers to content that was not captured and is not present in the web archive due to any number of reasons.
   A. Site blocked by robots: site was not captured because it was blocked by a robots.txt file. A robots.txt file is a set of instructions used by a website to communicate with a crawler. If desired, a website administrator can block certain parts of a website from being captured, or even the entire site.
   B. Content cannot be accessed: content was not captured because the site requires a password or an account to be accessed. This is most common with password-protected sites, for example, newspapers that require a username and password to view their articles, or forums that require an account to view or post comments.
   C. Site contains a crawler trap: a crawler trap is a set of websites that confuse a crawler by generating an infinite number of URLs for it to capture, intentionally or unintentionally. When this occurs, a crawl will stall. As a result, a bottleneck is created, whereupon many relevant sites are not captured because the crawler never got to them.
   D. Too much or too little content due to scoping issues: scope rules determine the amount of content that a crawler will capture, such as how many levels deep it can go within a site or whether it will be able to capture subdomains. Incorrect scoping causes a crawl to capture too much or too little content.
   E. Stylesheets are missing and site displays incorrectly as a result: this occurs when the site's stylesheet was not captured and now the site displays incorrectly. This can result in an archived site that looks very different from the original and has a degraded appearance and functionality, such as missing images and drop-down menus.
   F. Other: refers to problems that do not fit into the above categories but still result in missing content.

II. *Replay Issues*: occur when the appearance or functionality of a captured site does not resemble the original. This occurs when the software used to replay the archived site (usually the Wayback Machine) cannot do so accurately.
   A. Wayback has problems with HTTPS protocol: URLs that contain or redirect to an "https" address cannot be displayed. It causes many sites, such as Twitter, to display incorrectly in Wayback.
   B. Playback problems with rich media: elements such as video and audio have been captured, but do not function in the archived site.
   C. Javascript problems: the Wayback Machine often has problems executing JavasScript elements, and this causes an archived site to look different or lose its functionality.

D. Archived site does not display well because site has changed how it serves up content: occurs when a site with dynamic content, such as Twitter or YouTube, changes how it embeds or displays its content. Many sites with rich media encode their content using a variety of methods, which they change every few months. If a crawler is not optimized to deal with these changes, the site can display incorrectly.
E. Other: refers to other issues that do not fit into the above categories but still result in replay problems.

III. *Collection Management Issues*: questions that deal with the more general aspects of managing a web archive. These are specific to the Archive-It service.
A. Managing metadata for a collection: The Archive-It service offers its partners the ability to create and edit metadata for individual archive websites or for their entire web archive.
B. Dealing with data limits: questions about an account's data storage limits. Upon signing up for the service, a partner is assigned a limit on how much data it can store with Archive-It, with more expensive accounts allowing for greater data storage. Some partners may worry that they have exceeded or will exceed their data limit.
C. Request to remove access to specific capture dates. Sometimes a partner institution requests that Archive-It remove or limit access to some archived content for a number of reasons, such as wishing to increase the amount of data storage left on their account or if a particular capture has low quality. During this process, a partner usually specifies the specific date of the capture to be removed.
D. Questions about the privacy or public access of archived content. Some partners, wishing to maintain privacy, are interested in keeping their collections private, or perhaps limiting access to a specific range of IP addresses (such as those from a particular institution). Others are confused about the accessibility of their online web archives.
E. Questions about Archive-It search functionality: this refers to issues with search in the public site (archive-it.org) or in the private Archive-It web application. Oftentimes these questions are submitted when a partner cannot find a specific archived website or content.
F. Request to enable "ignore robots feature": partner asks to be able to ignore robots.txt settings for crawls. Partners usually request this when their institutional collecting goals require them to capture a certain site or content as completely as possible.
G. Other account questions.

IV. *Issues with the Archive-It service*: refers to problems with the Archive-It web application not working as it should.
A. Bugs in the Archive-It web application.

   B. Access problems: user cannot access the Archive-It web application because the site is down or for other reasons.
   C. Archive-It feature requests: a suggestion for future improvement of the Archive-It software.
   D. Other Archive-It issues: refers to other problems with the Archive-It service that are not covered in any of the above categories.
V. *Social Media*: problems that arise specifically with social media sites.
   A. Problems archiving password-protected content: occurs when user needs to enter account information in order to be able to crawl password-protected content.
   B. Video content: problems with any embedded video content, such as YouTube, Vimeo, and other formats.
   C. Other problems with social media sites: refers to other problems with social media sites that are not covered in any of the above categories.

DISCUSSION

When developing this model, some issues arose regarding the different ways researchers and practitioners view web archives. The Archive-It partner specialists were interested in having special categories for issues relating to social media and video, regardless of whether partners were experiencing capture or replay issues with these elements. Having separate categories helped them to better understand the nature of these issues and to prioritize the way in which the tickets would be handled. However, conceptually, a capture or display issue can occur with any site, whether it is social media, a blog, or an institutional website.

Furthermore, some issues in the original typology are specific to the Archive-It service or to current crawling and display technologies and can be abstracted further. If we eliminate these special categories, we arrive at a more compact typology that describes the more important issues web archivists face when building and managing a web archive. These categories are further discussed below:

I. Quality Issues
   A. Capture quality (completeness)
   B. Replay quality (correspondence)
II. Collection Management Issues
   A. Managing metadata for a collection
   B. Managing storage: how a web archive is stored and issues of storage limits
   C. The privacy/public access of archived content
   D. Search and retrieval in a web archive

Quality Issues

Upon further examination of my original classification system, it was clear that collection management issues stood apart from capture and replay issues, which were based upon the notion of quality. The quality of a web archive is intrinsic, dependent on the mechanisms used to capture and replay its content and independent of how it is managed by an institution, where it is stored on a server, or whether or not it is available to the public. Partners were always concerned with the quality, or goodness, of their web archives, in particular whether they *had captured the right content and were able to replay it in the right way*.

The notion of capture quality can also be referred to as the *completeness* of a web archive. Partners worried about capturing too much or too little content, whether or not relevant content was being blocked by a site's robots.txt file, or about not being able to capture content behind a paywall. They wanted web archives that had all their constituent elements—archives that were, in essence, complete.

Partners were also concerned about being able to accurately replay the website once it had been captured. They wanted the archived website to have the same look and feel as the original one, with the same drop-down menus, videos, and search forms as the original. For example, websites containing videos and other rich media were a particular source of concern for partners, who wanted the archived website to be able to replay these elements. This constant comparison between the original site and the archived site can be expressed using the notion of *correspondence*. Correspondence requires equivalence, or at least a close resemblance, between the original resource and the archived resource. A site with high correspondence is necessarily one with high replay quality, and vice versa.

Collection Management Issues

Collection management issues deal with the more general aspects of managing a web archive and are often determined by the policy of the partner institution. The decisions and questions that web archivists face are the same as those faced by digital preservation professionals elsewhere. They grapple with questions about how to create and manage the metadata for their web archives, how to harness limited computational and financial resources for their collections, and whether or not archived content should be made public or private. They also concern themselves with usability. Search and retrieval issues, those issues concerned with the ability to search the web archives and find relevant content, were particularly important to them.

CONCLUSION

This chapter is an attempt at identifying and categorizing important issues that web archivists face in their day-to-day jobs. After creating a system specific to Archive-It, I refined and abstracted it once again in order to make it broader and applicable to many different types of institutions and services. The typology singles out the issues of quality and collection management as being the most important to web archivists. In the future, this typology of issues can be expanded and refined through further empirical research. For example, once enough tickets are labeled and classified at the Internet Archive, a study could be conducted identifying the most pressing issues faced by web archivists. Armed with this information, web archivists could attempt to drive the development of tools and software to address these issues.

REFERENCES

Archive-It. (2014). *Learn more*. Retrieved from https://archive-it.org/learn-more

International Internet Preservation Consortium. (n.d.). *About IIPC*. Retrieved December 12, 2012, from http://netpreserve.org/about-us

Internet Archive. (2012). *About IA*. Retrieved November 30, 2012, from http://archive.org/about/

Kuny, T. (1997, September). *A digital dark ages? Challenges in the preservation of electronic information*. Presented at the 63rd International Federation of Library Associations and Institutions (IFLA) Council and General Conference, Copenhagen, Denmark. Retrieved from http://archive.ifla.org/IV/ifla63/63kuny1.pdf

Lindlof, T. R., and Taylor, B.C. (2002). *Qualitative communication research methods* (2nd ed.). Thousand Oaks, CA: Sage.

Masanès, J. (2006). *Web archiving*. Berlin, Germany: Springer.

Reyes Ayala, B., Phillips, M. E, and Ko, L. (2014, May). *Current Quality Assurance Practices in Web Archiving*. Presented at the International Internet Preservation Consortium (IIPC) General Assembly, Paris, France. Retrieved from http://digital.library.unt.edu/ark:/67531/metadc287034/

Tracy, J. (2010). Qualitative quality: Eight "big-tent" criteria for excellent qualitative research. *Qualitative Inquiry*, *16*(10), 837–51.

United National Educational Scientific and Cultural Organization. (2003, October 15). *Charter on the preservation of the digital heritage*. Retrieved from http://portal.unesco.org/en/ev.php-URL_ID=17721&URL_DO=DO_TOPIC&URL_SECTION=201.html

Voorburg, R. (2010, May). *QA of webharvests @ KB.nl*. Presented at the IIPC General Assembly, Singapore.

Voorburg, R. (2010, September). *Improving quality assurance for selective harvesting*. Presented at the IIPC Access Working Group Meeting, Vienna, Austria.

Wikipedia. (n.d.). *List of web archiving initiatives*. Retrieved December 4, 2012, from http://en.wikipedia.org/wiki/List_of_Web_archiving_initiatives

Zhang, Y., and Wildemuth, B. M. (2009). Qualitative analysis of content. In B. Wildemuth (Ed.), *Applications of Social Research Methods to Questions in Information and Library Science* (pp. 308–19). Westport, CT: Libraries Unlimited.

Chapter Thirteen

Expanding Engagement with Public Library Archives and Special Collections through Public Programming and Social Media

A Literature Review

Diantha Dow Schull

ABSTRACT

Public library archives and special collections are increasingly engaging members of the general public with primary sources through participatory activities ranging from traditional in-library programs to online exhibitions and crowdsourcing initiatives. The literature on these activities is uneven, reflecting a paucity of research on public library archives and special collections and even less scholarly attention to archival programming in the public library setting. To gain a better understanding of current trends in archival programming, the author conducted a study of public libraries across the United States, resulting in the recent publication *Archives Alive: Expanding Engagement with Public Library Archives and Special Collections* (Schull, 2015). This chapter discusses the literature that provided context for that study and raises questions about the lack of scholarship on public libraries' efforts to connect public users with archival sources.

INTRODUCTION

All across the United States, public library archivists and special collections librarians are experimenting with programs that raise awareness of and promote engagement with special collections. Through outreach to new communities, residencies for artists, workshops for educators, oral and video documentation, and varied uses of social media, archivists and librarians are developing new approaches to connecting patrons with rare, fragile, and historically or culturally significant collections. The programs take multiple forms, engage diverse audiences, sometimes involve organizational partners, and, more and more often, use digital technologies and new software to extend their visibility and enable remote participation. Programs range from Chicago Public Library's photovoice projects involving recent refugees and Providence Public Library's exhibitions of contemporary art featuring local artists inspired by archival collections to San Francisco Public Library's involvement of citizens in crowdsourcing historical photographs.

These programs are among the more than one hundred programs, projects, and archival departments profiled in *Archives Alive: Expanding Engagement with Public Library Archives and Special Collections* (Schull, 2015), the result of a two-year study by the author to examine the scope and character of contemporary public library archival programming. That study confirmed that archivists, special collections librarians, and reference librarians with responsibilities for primary sources are moving beyond traditional exhibitions and scholarly lectures to offer programs that have the potential to reframe public and professional consciousness about public libraries' archival collections. The programs are significant as vehicles for access that complement cataloging, scholar services, and digitization. And, they are especially significant in the context of professional discussions regarding the meaning of access, the value of special collections, and the evolving roles of archivists in the twenty-first century. Despite the extent and the significance of these new activities, they do not generally show up in the professional literature. With the exception of exhibitions and tours, there are few studies of or guides to archival programming in the library and information science literature or the literature of the archival profession. Relevant sources are widely scattered, derive from multiple organizational sources, represent diverse disciplinary perspectives, and do not provide a cohesive intellectual framework through which to examine current or future archival programming by public libraries.

The following discussion reflects the author's efforts to identify key sources and other complementary materials that, together, offer a framework for considering public libraries' current efforts to engage the public with special collections. It also explores some reasons for the lack of rigorous scholarship on public library archives and archival programming and how that lack undermines institutions and professionals. The discussion is organized around four primary themes that each offer a window into the larger picture of archival programming:

1. Archives and Special Collections in Public Libraries
2. Changing Theories on Access to Archival and Special Collections
3. Web 2.0, Social Media, Digitization, and Digital Humanities Projects
4. Archival Programming Practices in Public Libraries

PUBLIC LIBRARY ARCHIVES AND SPECIAL COLLECTIONS

Public libraries in the United States have a special place on the spectrum of cultural heritage institutions as repositories of public memory and primary sources unique to specific communities. Dating back to the founding of the Boston Public Library in the mid-nineteenth century, when its "collections of distinction" were cited as the library's fundamental asset, library and archival leaders have acknowledged special collections as core components of public libraries. Yet they have been overshadowed in professional literature by research on academic and special libraries. In fact, it was not until 2010 that the Society of American Archivists formally approved the formation of a Public Library Archives and Special Collections Roundtable.

The relative lack of research on public library archives and special collections may derive from several factors. Archives and special collections have suffered from general cutbacks experienced by municipal and other public libraries in the past decades, resulting in a smaller pool of professional archivists on staff who might document, analyze, and publish observations about their work. In addition, academic and special libraries have missions more obviously aligned with special collections. They have built-in constituencies in the form of faculty and students, with the result that documentation and analysis of professional practices is more often encouraged in those settings.

Whatever the reason, there is relatively little literature, other than case studies, on public library archives and special collections, and even less concerning collections-based programming. Four key sources provide exceptions to this observation. Laura Linard's 1987 article "Special Collections in Public Libraries" (Linard, Summer 1987) provides a foundation for looking at trends today. It is based on a survey of twenty-four public libraries, only nine of which, at the time, had full-time staff. As the curator of the Chicago Public Library's Special Collections Department, Linard uses that library to examine her core questions: the types of special collections held in libraries, the history of the departments, the audiences they serve, how the departments perceived their institutional roles, and whether or not there were characteristics common to special collections departments in public libraries.

As part of her survey Linard asked, "Do you have an active exhibition program or other public outreach programs?" She discovered that "an important feature of all special collections departments surveyed was the emphasis on outreach programs" (p. 187), and she cited the Atlanta Public Library's history workshops and San Francisco Public Library's lectures on book arts. She also noted that "all of the libraries indicated that they mount exhibits" (p. 184). The Chicago Public Library's Special Collections Department, for instance, regularly mounted at least four exhibits annually. Linard (p. 186) argued for the value of such programs in helping special collections departments to maintain "a high profile with the institution and the community":

> Our outreach programs garner community support and show the administration the important role these programs play in educating and providing services to the community.

Deirdre Stam's article "Bridge That Gap! Education and Special Collections" is another key source on archives and special collections and related programs. The article, based on Stam's keynote address at the 2005 Rare Books, Manuscripts and Cultural Heritage (RBM) preconference on education and special collections, appeared in the spring 2006 inaugural edition of *RBM, A Journal of Rare Books, Manuscripts and Cultural Heritage*. Although it is not focused on public libraries, the discussion is as relevant to public library archivists and special collections professionals as it is to others in the archival profession. Within a general discussion of two aspects of "education," the education of users and the education of librarians, Stam discusses methods for attracting and instructing users of special collections, including "planned and structured exhibitions," "informal displays," and lectures. She also discusses the potential for special collections librarians to adopt "discovery" methods of instruction, through which teachers, students, and other learners have access to primary or digital materials relevant to their particular inquiry.

Stam's article is important in that it reflects an increasingly important theme in special collections librarians' discourse: the value of special collections for education in the broadest sense, including teachers, youth, and adults who are not scholars or collectors. This theme has particular relevance for public library archives.

Eric Linderman's article, "Archives in Public Libraries," which appeared in the January-February 2009 issue of *Public Libraries*, has a different focus. While Stam argues for archivists and special collections librarians, themselves, to understand their powerful pedagogical role in society, Linderman is concerned about the role of archives and special collections within the institutional context. He examines the reasons for misperceptions of archives as separate or marginal from other parts of the library and argues for their value as "asset[s] to the local community" (p. 46). While he does not address the issue of archives and special collections-based programming per se, he argues that these departments must demonstrate "their usefulness to the general public" and must promote "the value of archival resources within some of the mainstream priorities of the library" (p. 48). Linderman also notes the importance of electronic website collections, virtual archives, and the potential to use new technologies to link archives to general collections—all of which are issues for consideration by archivists and special collections librarians considering increasing their public programming and working more closely with colleagues in other departments.

Departmental blogs and websites are another source of documentation on special collections and their programs. These often contain statements by special collections librarians about their department's missions, programs, and projects. In the absence of more formal documentation or analysis, these blogs and websites constitute a type of "literature"; they are windows into the current state of archival programming. As one example, Hartford Public Library's Hartford History Center maintains a website and blog that includes a discussion of its Digital Repository, reports on current exhibitions and events, and descriptions of key collections or projects underway (hhc.hplct.org). Another example is the San Francisco Public Library's San Francisco History Center/Book Arts and Special Collections Blog, *What's on the 6th Floor?*, at sfhcbasc.blogspot.com. The Queens (New York) Memory Project at www.queensmemory.org is designed to encourage browsing of its digital collections and provides information on its outreach and oral history programming, its Historypin activities, and the Queens Library Archives Collection. The Memphis Library and Information Center's Memphis and Shelby County Room maintains a blog at https://memphisroom.wordpress.com/ with a variety of offerings including a recent series of podcasts, "Musical Memphis," and access to its *Dig Memphis* Digital Archive. There are numerous other similar points of access to the programming and communications taking place in public library special collections. They merit study in and of themselves.

The meeting minutes of the Society of American Archivists' Public Library Archives/Special Collections Roundtable are another source of information on public library archivists' current concerns and projects (see http://www2.archivists.org/groups/public-library-archivesspecial-collections/public-library-archivesspecial-collections-forum). Beyond these sources, there are other background materials that help round out a picture of public library special collections—speeches by public library leaders that reference special collections, blogs by archivists and their patrons, mentions of archives and special collections in books and manifestos about the value of the public library, and articles on reference services that bear some relation to new service approaches in special collections.

CHANGING THEORIES OF ACCESS TO ARCHIVES AND SPECIAL COLLECTIONS

There is considerable theoretical literature on archives and special collections; however, for the reasons alluded to above, the scholarship is more often targeted to research libraries than to public libraries. Because of the impact of academic theory on the overall profession, this literature is directly relevant to special collections professionals in public libraries. This is especially true in relation to access, a topic that has generated much discussion in the library and archival worlds in recent years.

Four core sources help frame the current discourse on access, archives, and special collections. The first is Daniel Traister's (2000) *Is there a Future for Special Collections? And Should There Be?—A Polemical Essay,* which appeared, along with Stam's essay (see above) in the inaugural issue of *RBM* titled *What's So Special About Special Collections*. Traister explains his conversion to a point of view that preservation of "precious books, manuscripts and other special materials" should not take precedence over making these materials accessible. He proposes that "reconsideration of some of the essential assumptions our field operates with are long overdue" (p. 55), and he states that "our priorities may be misplaced" (p. 67). He acknowledges that some of his colleagues may view a less restrictive environment as an "opening of the floodgates" (p. 71), but he argues that rigid restrictions on special collections "simply does no one any good" and discourages teachers, students, and other learners from being able to use archives "as expeditiously as possible" (p. 75). His vision involves "aggressive pursuit and encouragement" of visits to special collections, provision of noncredit seminars, and "collaboration with students, faculty and special collections staff" to ensure wider access to material relevant for study (p. 72). While his comments are aimed at academic librarians, they are applicable to public libraries as well. Traister concludes with the following statement:

> America's special collections have a future—at least insofar as our colleges, universities, public libraries, and reading and writing have a future. The world in which these collections exist and persist, however, is changing radically, not in the direction of increased restrictions but toward expanded access and openness. Every study of the impact of the Internet suggests that, even despite efforts to privatize intellectual capital, this is one of its most important outcomes—certainly in libraries. (p. 76)

Traister's polemical essay anticipates subsequent and even more vehement calls for change from his colleagues in special collections, carrying through to today's arguments that Web 2.0 and social media provide tools for entirely new forms of openness and access and, indeed, collaboration and coproduction with users.

Mark A. Greene, as incoming president of the Society of American Archivists, raised a similar call for change in his 2007 inaugural address titled "Strengthening Our Identity, Fighting our Foibles." He argued for a "serious dialogue" about the profession's "resistance to change," and the need to "put users first," over processing, over preservation, and over item-by-item intellectual control. Greene called for processing and digitizing collections more quickly and for a more "user-centered" profession (pp. 4–6).

There are other sources that illuminate the ongoing debate within the profession about the position and functions of archives and special collections, going back to Elizabeth Yakel's (2000) *Archivaria* article, "Thinking Inside and Outside the Boxes: Archival Reference Services at the Turn of the Century." That debate has, to a large extent, been reframed by the adoption of new communications technologies such as Web 2.0 and tools for mass digitization of collections or creation of online exhibitions. Arguments for openness and new strategies for access are now bolstered by the technologies at hand.

Lisa Carter, in her February 11, 2009 essay "It's the Collections That Are Special," which appeared in the online journal *In the Library with the Lead Pipe*, picks up Traister's theme and takes it several steps further:

> The collections themselves are special in that they are rare, unique, fantastic and archaic and they do need special handling and care. However, our regard for these materials has enabled us to treat them so differently that they are not accessible. We have locked these materials up in our processes and our delivery systems, which has kept them out of the mainstream of information available to knowledge seekers.

Further, Carter argues that librarians and archivists must "redefine" themselves and "embrace their special collections and archives as a locus of distinction, experimentation and core value."

Carter's recommendations for change include integration of special collections "into the flow in every aspect of our work," using special collections to improve teaching and learning (an echo of Stam's call for a more pedagogical outlook) and streamlining access through use of new models for mass digitization of special collections materials and adoption of other new tools for "enhanced discoverability."

From Traister, Stam, and Greene to Carter, it is clear that new theories of special collections librarianship are emerging. These theories are relevant to the position and use of special collections in public libraries, including public programming as a form of enhanced access.

As a final indication of a shift in professional thinking on the part of archival leaders, the National Archives and Records Administration (NARA) has been in the process of revising its mission statement for the past several years. In 2009, the mission was articulated as follows:

> The National Archives and Records Administration serves American democracy by safeguarding and preserving the records of our Government, ensuring that the people can discover, use, and learn from this documentary heritage.

> We ensure continuing access to the essential documentation of the rights of American citizens and the actions of their government. We support democracy, promote civic education, and facilitate historical understanding of our national experience. (NARA, 2009, p. viii)

In March 2014, the new mission statement read:

> We [NARA] drive openness, cultivate public participation, and strengthen our nation's democracy through public access to high-value government records. (NARA, 2014, p. 4)

It is clear from this revision that there is a change in thinking at the highest levels of archival leadership, from an emphasis on stewardship to an emphasis on action and participation. This change is reflected in the new programs emerging in public library archives and, especially, in the statements made by many of the special collections librarians interviewed for *Archives Alive*.

WEB 2.0. SOCIAL MEDIA, ONLINE EXHIBITIONS AND DIGITAL HUMANITIES

As can be inferred from the foregoing discussion, there is a surge in contemporary discussions about special collections librarianship and new access strategies, specifically in relation to new technologies and online environments. While there is considerable literature about digitization, digital catalogs, and handling of born digital materials, there are also case studies and discussions of social media in the professional literature that indicate archivists' recognition of the opportunities for increased access and increased user-archive interaction.

The integration of digital technologies into their public communications and programming correlates with the trend for archival departments to adopt one or another social media platform, or several different platforms, as a means of communicating with current patrons and building new constituencies. Adam Kreisberg's article in the fall/winter 2014 issue of *American Archivist* is a case in point: "Increasing Access in 140 Characters or Less: Or, What Are Archival Institutions Doing on Twitter?" reports on a survey of archival institutions regarding their uses of Twitter. Although none of the thirty-four institutions surveyed are public libraries, the findings corroborate this author's less formal observation, during research for *Archives Alive*, that many public library special collections have added Twitter to their roster of Facebook, Pinterest, and other social media sites.

Some of the literature on new applications of digital technologies addresses the practical challenges and relative merits of one platform over another, while there are other reports on uses of different software with implications for public programming, such as mobile apps, social archives, and crowdsourcing to build community-based archives. The literature on crowdsourcing, for instance, is large and growing. Several sources stand out, one being a series of posts by Trevor Owens (2012) of the Institute of Museum and Library Services titled *The Crowd and the Library*. Four subsequent posts discussed what crowdsourcing is, and is not, and reviewed several project examples, including New York Public Library's "What's On the Menu" project. Rose Holley's article "Crowdsourcing: How and Why Should Libraries Do It?" in *D-Lib Magazine* (2010) provides an excellent overview of the issues that would help to inform an archivist in any type of library.

One aspect of the discourse about archival uses of digital technologies reflects change in how some archivists, including public library archivists, are interacting with their peers in the humanities. It is clear from the literature that the interdisciplinary nature of digital humanities work brings archivists, historians and other humanities scholars, and digital media specialists together to collaborate in creating online educational enterprises. While such efforts are intended to increase access to primary sources, they may also fundamentally reshape heretofore separate professions.

A key participant in all these discussions is Kate Theimer, whose publications and blog (*ArchivesNext* at http://www.archivesnext.com/) reveal a commitment to traditional archival concepts but also a deep conviction that archivists and special collections librarians must harness the power of new technology to more deeply engage users and to help strengthen the position of archives within the profession and the larger community of users. Her two most recent works, *Web 2.0: Tools and Strategies for Archives and Local History Collections* (2010) and *A Different Kind of Web: New Connections between Archives and Our Users* (2011) are basic texts for special collections professionals with public services responsibilities in public libraries. In addition, *ArchivesNext* is an excellent resource on the issues being discussed by archivists and professionals in related professions.

Some participants in the *ArchivesNext* discussions are public historians or individuals involved with digital humanities projects—major stakeholders in new initiatives to expand engagement with archives and special collections. On January 24, 2012, Theimer quoted Peter Wosh, who participated with her in the session "Archivists, Historians and the Future of Authority in the Archives" at the American Historical Association's annual 2012 conference, regarding what he sees as a growing overlap between the archival and historian professions, particularly as a result of increased access to primary sources. As the chair of the Society of American Archivists' publication board and the director of New York University's program Archives and Public History, his comments are relevant to archivists in public libraries, many of which have historical archives and local history rooms. In building new connections with users of these collections, especially historians and history teachers and their students, public library archivists may find them to be helpful partners in collections documentation and interpretation.

PUBLIC LIBRARY ARCHIVES AND SPECIAL COLLECTIONS PROGRAMS

There could hardly be a greater contrast between the general discourse(s) about the roles of archives and special collections and their integration of new technologies with the limited discourse on public programs based on public library archives and special collections. While the former is wide ranging, including both theory and practice, the latter is limited and primarily practical. For the reasons cited at the outset of this analysis, public library-based archivists may simply be too few or too stretched to reflect on their roles or to report on their experiments with education and outreach. And yet, paradoxically, some of the most interesting public programs in the field of archives and special collections are emanating from public institutions. Beyond exhibitions, and beyond curriculum development, public library archivists are engaging with diverse publics in diverse ways. Performance interpretations of collections, yearlong festivals related to collections, programs for teachers and high school students, national conferences—despite their variety and positive local reception, these kinds of programs fall under the radar of formal scholars and graduate students who might help to develop scholarship on public library programs.

Even the literature on adult programming in public libraries fails to reflect trends in archival programming. Just as some professionals regard special collections as "hidden," so, too, are the public program models emerging from libraries large and small.

For an understanding of professional thinking about public programming in public libraries from a historical perspective, several texts set the stage for today's trends: William S. Learned's *The Public Library and the Diffusion of Knowledge* (1924) and John Cotton Dana's *Thoughts on the Library and Adult Education* in *Library Journal* (1928). Dana, who led several major urban libraries, was influential in shaping the thinking of some library leaders regarding the importance of collection-based public programming. Lynne E. Birge's *Serving Adult Learners: A Public Library Tradition* (1981) provides some useful subsequent arguments for the concept of public library–based "adult education."

For more contemporary thinking, there are David Carr's *Open Conversations: Public Libraries* (2011) and Anne Prentice's *Public Libraries in the 21st Century* (2011). For practical "how-to" information on adult programming and humanities programming, there are several useful texts: Brett Lear's *Adult Programs in The Library* (2013) and Deborah Robertson's *Cultural Programming for Libraries: Linking Libraries, Communities, and Culture* (2005). Even more specifically, there are several sources that focus on exhibitions, including *Organizing Exhibitions: A Handbook for Libraries, Archives and Museums* by Freda Matassa (Facet, 2014). None of these works focus on archives and special collections per se, but they offer insights regarding the evolution of programming concepts—insights that could be helpful to archivists and special collections librarians considering why and how to carry out programming in a public library setting.

The best overall source of information on current public programming in public libraries is the ALA Public Programs Office (PPO), which has a clearinghouse of information for "programming librarians," including a blog, program examples, and lists of resources. It is an excellent resource for public library archivists who are considering whether and how to design collection-based programs. The case studies presented on the recently revamped website (http://www.ala.org/offices/ppo) are particularly useful for special collections programmers.

Traveling exhibitions with complementary public programs have been a hallmark of PPO services, as have reading and discussion programs. Many PPO exhibitions have been supported by the National Endowment for the Humanities and have involved scholars and even archivists as curators or consultants. It is ironic that these exhibitions—which have often drawn on public library special collections, using primary materials or facsimiles of rare items from major institutions—are in high demand, yet there is little professional or public recognition of the importance of public library archives as sources for exhibition themes and artifacts with wide public appeal.

Together, the core texts discussed above, and other complementary sources listed in the appendix at the end of this chapter, can provide multiple points of inquiry regarding public library archival programming. They are not comprehensive—the field is too dynamic. No work, to date, synthesizes the literature and case studies into a cohesive whole that could be used for teaching and practice. More professional attention and rigorous scholarship are long overdue.

CONCLUSION

To conclude this literature review, it is important to repeat that the literature on archival and special collections programming in public libraries is diffuse, uneven, and inadequate in relation to the speed with which institutions and practices are changing. The paucity of rigorous scholarship on special collections programming poses problems at multiple levels. Librarians and archivists charged with developing and implementing programs are handicapped by a lack of guidelines or recognized criteria for excellence, both of which would only result from systematic research and analysis. Even the most sophisticated and creative programming librarians do not have the time to seek out all the pieces of the research puzzle that presently exists. For departmental and institutional leaders, the lack of scholarship makes it impossible to judge the effectiveness of programming and/or make decisions on investments to start or sustain programs. Without more research and analysis, in fact, there can be no consensus regarding best practices or assessment criteria, nor can the scattered literature be translated easily into a curriculum for archival studies and library and information science. Perhaps most importantly, without rigorous surveys, informed analysis, and dissemination of results, the excellent public programs that are occurring are lost assets to the archival and library professions. Isolated, and undocumented, potential models are not, ironically, part of any archival record.

The fact that new programming is occurring, in the absence of a guide to new practices or clear sources for professional development or library education, is a reflection of the spirited commitment to public service and experimentation on the part of many special collections librarians in public libraries. Better documentation of their work is overdue and would fill an important gap in archival and library literature.

APPENDIX: SOURCES

The following sources are grouped into four thematic categories that collectively offer a conceptual approach to the topic at hand. Within those, key sources are distinguished from contextual sources.

1. SPECIAL COLLECTIONS IN PUBLIC LIBRARIES

A. Key Sources

Linard, L. (1987, Summer). Special collections in public libraries. *Library Trends*, *36*(1), 179–88.

Linderman, E. (2009, January/February). Archives in public libraries. *Public Libraries*, *48*(1), 46–51.

Schwartz, M. (2012, September 10). Something old, something new: Dicing data at NYPL labs. *Library Journal*. Retrieved from http://www.thedigitalshift

.com/2012/09/digital-libraries/something-old-something-new-dicing-data-at-nypl-labs-cover-story/

Stam, D. (2006, Spring). Bridge that gap! Education and special collections. *RBM: A Journal of Rare Books, Manuscripts, & Cultural Heritage*, 7(1), 16–30 (this article, appearing in the "What's So Special About Special Collections?" inaugural issue of *RBM, A Journal of Rare Books, Manuscripts and Cultural Heritage* is based on Stam's keynote address at the 2005 RBM preconference on education and special collections).

B. Contextual Sources

Cronenwett, P., Osborn, K., and Streit, S. A. (Eds.). (2007). *Celebrating research: Rare and special collections from the membership of the Association of Research Libraries*. Washington, DC: Association of Research Libraries (with an Introduction by Nicholas Barker; this guide to special collections cites only a limited number of public libraries, such as the Boston Public Library).

Dearstyne, B. W. (2001). *Leadership and administration of successful archival programs.* Westport, CT: Greenwood Press.

Eberhart, G. (2013, January 22). Public library users want both books and technology. *American Libraries.* Retrieved from http://www.americanlibrariesmagazine.org/article/public-library-users-want-both-books-and-technology

Edwards, J. B., Rauseo, M. S., and Unger, K. R. (2011, September/October). Community-centered: 23 reasons why your library is the most important place in town. *Public Libraries Online*. Retrieved from publiclibrariesonline.org/2013/04/community-centered-23-reasons-why-your-library-is-the-most-important-place-in-town_

Finch, E. F. (1994). *Advocating archives: An introduction to public relations for archivists*. Metuchen, NJ: The Society of American Archivists and Scarecrow Press.

Kreneck, T. H. (1985, Summer). Documenting a Mexican-American community: The Houston example. *American Archivist*, *48*, 272–76, 278–85.

Ohlson, K. (2009, March 1). *Libraries' surprising special collections*. Smithsonian.com. Retrieved from http://www.smithsonianmag.com/arts-culture/libraries-surprising-special-collections-54792335/

Marx, A. (2013, August 9). *From the collections to the classroom.* Retrieved from http://www.nypl.org/blog/2013/08/09/collections-classroom (speech by New York Public Library president).

Public Library Archives/Special Collections Roundtable. (2010, 2011, 2012). *Meeting minutes*. Society of American Archivists. Retrieved from http://www2.archivists.org/groups/public-library-archivesspecial-collections/public-library-archives-special-collections-forum

Robotham, J. S., and LaFleur, L. (1981). *Library programs: How to select, plan, and produce them* (2nd ed.). Metuchen, NJ: Scarecrow Press.

Treacy, M. (2011, July 14). *What's so SPECIAL about special collections: A patron's perspective* [Web log comment]. Retrieved from https://marytreacy.wordpress.com/2011/07/14/whats-so-special-about-special-collections-a-patrons-perspective/

Waggener, L., and Markowiz, K. (forthcoming). *Starting a local history collection in your public library*. Chicago: American Library Association.

Zabel, D. (Ed.). (2011). *Reference reborn: Breathing new life into public services librarianship*. Santa Barbara, CA: Libraries Unlimited.

2. THEORIES OF ARCHIVAL AND SPECIAL COLLECTIONS, ESPECIALLY IN RELATION TO PUBLIC SERVICES AND PROGRAMS

A. Key Sources

Carter, L. (2009, February 11). It's the collections that are special [Web log comment]. *In The Library With the Lead Pipe*. Retrieved from www.inthelibrarywith theleadpipe.org/2009/its-the-collections-that-are-special/

Greene, M. (2007, September 1). *Strengthening our identity, fighting our foibles*. Inaugural Presidential Address, Society of American Archivists. Retrieved from http://www.archivists.org/governance/presidential/ma-green2007.pdf

(NARA) National Archives and Records Administration. (2014, March). U.S. National Archives and Records Administration fiscal year 2014–2018 strategic plan. Washington, DC: National Archives and Records Administration. Retrieved from http://www.archives.gov/about/plans-reports/strategic-plan/2014/nara-strategic-plan-2014-2018.pdf (the draft includes a major revision of the NARA's mission statement, emphasizing public participation and public access).

Traister, D. (2000). Is there a future for special collections? And should there be? A polemical essay. *RBM: A Journal of Rare Books, Manuscripts and Cultural Heritage*, *1*(1), 54–76 (appeared in *What's So Special about Special Collections*?, the inaugural issue of *RBM*).

Yakel, E. (2000, Spring). Thinking inside and outside the boxes: Archival reference services at the turn of the century. *Archivaria*, *49*, 140–60.

B. Contextual Sources

Allan, S. M. (1999). Rare books and the college library: Current practices in marrying undergraduates to special collections. *Rare Books and Manuscript Librarianship*, *13*(2), 110–19.

Calhoun, K. (2006, March 17). *The changing nature of the catalog and its integration with other discovery tools: Final Report*. Prepared for the Library of Congress. Retrieved from www.loc.gov/catdir/calhoun-report-final.pdf (this report was a landmark in the debate about the shifting nature of bibliographic access; key points are discussed in The "Changing Nature" of Cataloging: Report on 21st Century Bibliographic Control in the *Library of Congress Information Bulletin* [May 2006], retrieved from http://www.loc.gov/loc/lcib/0605/catalog.html; see also a critique of this paper, and its emphasis on digital access and new forms of intellectual control over traditional services to scholars, by Thomas Mann, cited below).

Carini, P. (2009). Archivists as educators: Integrating primary sources into the curriculum. *Journal of Archival Organization*, 7(1–2), 45–46.

Cook, T. (2011, Fall/Winter). The archive(s) is a foreign country: Historians, archivists, and the changing archival landscape. *American Archivist*, 74, 600–632.

Cullingford, A. (2011). *The special collections handbook*. London: Facet Publishing.

Dachs, K. (1993, Summer). Is there a future in library exhibitions? *Harvard Library Bulletin*, *4*(1), 63–66 (in special issue, R. Wendorf (Ed.), *Rare books and manuscript libraries in the twenty-first century: An international symposium, part one*).

Dearstyne, B. (1987, Winter). What is the USE of archives? A challenge for the profession. *American Archivist*, *50*, 76–87.

Dooley, J. M., and Luce, K. (2010.) *Taking our pulse: The OCLC research survey of special collections and archives*. Dublin, OH: OCLC Research. Retrieved from http://www.oclc.org/research/publications/library/2010/2010-11.pdf

Greene, M. A. (2009, October 15). *Existential archives: Looking to the value propositions of archives and special collections.* Retrieved from http://www.arl.org/storage/documents/publications/ff09-greene-remarks.pdf (remarks presented at the CNI Forum "An Age of Discovery: Distinctive Collections in the Digital Age").

Eastwood, T., and MacNeil, H. (Eds.). (2010). *Currents of archival thinking.* Santa Barbara, CA: Libraries Unlimited.

Evans, M. J. (2004, January). The archival time machine: A closet engineer looks at our profession. *NEA Newsletter* 31:1, 4–9. Retrieved from http://www.newenglandarchivists.org/Resources/Documents/Newsletter/NEA_Newsletter_January2004.pdf

Evans, M. J. (2007, Fall/Winter). Archives of the people, by the people, for the people. *American Archivist*, 70, 287–400. Retrieved from http://yalearchivalreadinggroup.pbworks.com/f/max_evans_article.pdf

Galbraith, S. K., and Smith, G. D. (2012). *Rare book librarianship: An introduction and guide.* Santa Barbara, CA: Libraries Unlimited.

Greene, M. A., and Meissner, D. (2005, Fall/Winter). More product, less process: Revamping traditional archival processing. *American Archivist*, *68*, 208–63.

Hendry, J. (2007, Spring/Summer). Primary sources in K–12 education: Opportunities for archivists. *American Archivist*, *70*, 114–29.

Jones, B. M. (2003, June). *Hidden collections, scholarly barriers: Creating access to unprocessed special collections materials in America's research libraries*. A White Paper for the Association of Research Libraries Task Force on Special Collections. Retrieved from http://www.arl.org/storage/documents/publications/hidden-colls-white-paper-jun03.pdf

Mann, T. (2006, April 3). *The changing nature of the catalog and its integration with other discovery tools. Final report. March 17, 2006.* Prepared for the Library of Congress by Karen Calhoun. *A critical review.* Retrieved from http://www.guild2910.org/AFSCMECalhounReviewREV.pdf (prepared by AFSCME 2910, The Library of Congress Professional Guild).

Mitchell, E., Seiden, P., and Taraba, S. (Eds.). (2012). *Past or portal: Enhancing undergraduate learning through special collections and archives*. Chicago: Association of College and Research Libraries.

Rare Books and Manuscripts Section, ACRL/ALA Task Force on Core Competencies for Special Collections Professionals. (2008, July). *Guidelines: Competencies for special collections professionals.* Retrieved from http://www.ala.org/acrl/standards/comp4specollect (guidelines were approved July 1, 2008).

Schreyer, A. (2006). What's so special about special collections librarians? RBM: *A Journal of Rare Books, Manuscripts and Cultural Heritage*, *1*(1), 49–54 (inaugural issue).

Traister, D. (1983, October). Rare book collections: The need for interpretation. *Wilson Library Bulletin*, *58*, 96–119.

Traister, D. (2003, Summer). Public services and outreach in rare book, manuscript, and special collections libraries. *Library Trends*, *52*(1), 87–108.

3. WEB 2.0, SOCIAL MEDIA, ONLINE EXHIBITIONS AND DIGITAL HUMANITIES

A. Key Sources

Bridges, K. (2012). *Beyond the browser: Web 2.0 and librarianship*. Santa Barbara, CA: Libraries Unlimited.

Holley, R. (2010, March/April). Crowdsourcing: How and why should libraries do it? *D-Lib Magazine*, *16*(3/4). Retrieved from http://www.dlib.org/dlib/march10/holley/03holley.html

Theimer, K. (n.d.). *ArchivesNext* [Web log comment]. Retrieved from http://www.archivesnext.com/

Theimer, K. (2010). *Web 2.0: Tools and strategies for archives and local history collections*. New York: Neal-Schuman, 2010.

Theimer, K. (2011). *A different kind of web: New connections between archives and our users*. Chicago: Society of American Archivists.

B. Contextual Sources

Association of Research Libraries. (n.d.) *Special collections.* Retrieved from http://www.arl.org/focus-areas/research-collections/special-collections (the ARL site includes a "Focus Area" on Special Collections at http://www.arl.org/focus-areas/research-collections#.Vc-wVvlViko that offers multiple resources such as webinars, toolkits, working group reports, and guidelines that are relevant to public library archivists carrying out public programs).

Association of Research Libraries, Special Collections Working Group. (2010). *Transforming special collections in the digital age*. Retrieved from http://www.arl.org/publications-resources/1111#.Vczd1flViko (see also *Statements, Principles, and other Reports* by the Working Group, http://www.arl.org/focus-areas/research-collections/special-collections/2482-statements-principles-and-reports-of-arl-special-collections-working-groups).

Crymble, A. (2010). An analysis of Twitter and Facebook use by the archival community. *Archivaria, 70*, 125–51.

Erway, R. (2008). Supply and demand: Special collections and digitization. *Liber Quarterly, 18*, 324–36.

Erway, R., and Schaffner, J. (2007). *Shifting gears: Gearing up to get into the flow*. OCLC Programs and Research. Retrieved from http://www.oclc.org/research/publications/library/2007/2007-02.pdf

Hirtle, P. (2002, Winter). The impact of digitization on special collections in libraries. *Libraries and Culture, 37*(1), 42–52.

Kreisberg, A. (2014, Fall/Winter). Increasing access in 140 characters or less: Or, what are archival institutions doing on Twitter? *American Archivist, 77*, 534–57.

LaLonde, K., Sanagan, C., and Smith, S. (2014, Fall/Winter). The War of 1812 in 140 characters or less: "Supercool or super un-Tweet worthy?" *American Archivist, 77*, 558–68.

Lankes, D. R., Silverstein, J., and Nicholson, S. (2007). *Participatory networks: The library as conversation: A technology brief of the Information Institute of Syracuse*. Retrieved from http://quartz.syr.edu/rdlankes/Publications/Others/ParticiaptoryNetworks.pdf

Lietzau, Z., and Helgren, J. (2011, April). *U.S. public libraries and the use of web technologies, 2010*. Denver: Colorado State Library, Library Research Service. Retrieved from http://www.lrs.org/documents/web20/WebTech2010_CloserLookReport_Final.pdf

Mayer, P. H. (2013, Spring/Summer). Like a box of chocolates: A case study of user-contributed content at footnote. *American Archivist, 76*, 19–46.

New York Public Library. (2015). *NYPL Labs*. Retrieved from http://www.nypl.org/collections/labs (website for NYPL Labs, a special unit of the New York Public Library, dedicated to helping curators and archivists develop innovative methods for using new technologies to expand public access to and engagement with the library's special collections).

OEDb (2013, March 25). *250+ killer digital libraries and archives*. Retrieved from http://oedb.org/ilibrarian/250-plus-killer-digital-libraries-and-archives/ (prepared by OEDb, an online education directory for free and for-credit learning).

Ridge, M. (2013, October). From tagging to theorizing: Deepening engagement with cultural heritage through crowdsourcing. *Curator: The Museum Journal, 56*, 435–50.

Roy Rosenzeigh Center for History and New Media. (2015). *Digital Humanities Now*. Retrieved from http://digitalhumanitiesnow.org/ (an online publication; see also *The Journal of Digital Humanities*, available at http://journalofdigitalhumanities.org/).

Smithsonian Libraries (n.d.). *Library and archival exhibitions on the web*. Retrieved from http://www.sil.si.edu/SILPublications/Online-Exhibitions/ (an international guide to online exhibitions from museums and libraries maintained by Diane Shaw, special collections librarian at the Smithsonian Institution Libraries).

Snavely, L. (Ed.). (2012). *Student engagement and the academic library*. Santa Barbara, CA: Libraries Unlimited.

Springer, M., Dulabahn, B., Michel, P., Natanson, B., Reser, D., Woodward, D., and Zinkham, H. (2008, October). *For the common good: The Library of Congress Flickr pilot project report.* Retrieved from http://www.loc.gov/rr/print/flickr_report_final.pdf

Tarulli, L. (2012). *The library catalogue as social space promoting patron driven collections, online enhanced reference and readers' services*. Santa Barbara, CA: Libraries Unlimited.

Theimer, K. (2012, January 24). Peter Wosh's thoughts on the "archival divide": Remarks delivered at AHA [Web log comment]. Retrieved from http://www.archivesnext.com/?p=2475 (report by Kate Theimer on Peter Wosh's remarks at the session "Archivists, Historians and the Future of Authority in the Archives" at the 2012 conference of the American Historical Association).

Thiel, S. G. (2007). *Build it once: A basic primer for the creation of online exhibitions*. Lanham, MD: Scarecrow Press.

Washburn, B., Eckert, E., and Proffitt, M. (2013). *Social media and archives: A survey of archive users*. Dublin, OH: OCLC Research. Retrieved from http://www.oclc.org/content/dam/research/publications/library/2013/2013-06.pdf

Whittacker, B., and Thomas, L. M. (2009). *Special collections 2.0: New technologies for rare books, manuscripts, and archives*. Santa Barbara, CA: Libraries Unlimited.

Zastrow, J. (2014, October). The digital archivist. Crowdsourcing digital heritage: Citizen archivists of the future. *Computers in Libraries*, *34*(8), 21.

Zazzau, V. (2007, December). Transforming archives through information technologies: A bibliography. *Journal of the Association for the History of Computing, 10*. Retrieved from http://quod.lib.umich.edu/j/jahc/3310410.0010.303?rgn=main;view=fulltext

4. PROGRAMMING PRACTICES IN PUBLIC LIBRARIES

A. Key Sources

American Library Association. (2015). *Public Programs Office*. Retrieved from http://www.ala.org/offices/ppo (offers a variety of professional development materials to enhance libraries' capacities to present, communicate and fund cultural programs, including Programming Librarian, an online information clearinghouse, forum, and blog on library programming).

Birge, L. E. (1981). *Serving adult learners: A public library tradition*. Chicago: American Library Association.

Dana, J. C. (1928, November 15). Thoughts on the library and adult education. *Library Journal*, *53*, 945.

Learned, W. S. (1924). *The public library and the diffusion of knowledge*. New York: Harcourt, Brace and Company.

Prentice, A. E. (2011). *Public libraries in the 21st century*. Santa Barbara, CA: Libraries Unlimited.

Robertson, D. A. (2005). *Cultural programming for libraries: Linking libraries, communities, and culture.* Chicago: American Library Association.

B. Contextual Sources

Berelson, B., and Asheim, L. (1949). *The library's public: A report of the public library inquiry.* New York: Columbia University Press.

Carr, D. (2011). *Open conversations: Public learning in libraries and museums.* Santa Barbara, CA: Libraries Unlimited.

Lacher-Feldman, J. (2013). *Exhibits in archives and special collections libraries.* Chicago: Society of American Archivists.

Lear, B. (2013). *Adult Programs in the Library* (2nd Ed.). Chicago: American Library Association.

Matassa, F. (2014). *Organizing exhibitions: A handbook for libraries, archives and museums.* London: Facet Publishing.

Matthews, J. R. (2009). *The customer-focused library: Re-inventing the library from the outside in.* Santa Barbara, CA: Libraries Unlimited.

Rubin, R. J. (1997). *Humanities programming: A how-to-do-it manual.* New York: Neal- Schuman Publishers.

RUSA-SUPS Services to Adults Committee. (1997). *Adult programming: A manual for libraries.* Chicago: Reference and Users Services Association, American Library Association.

Schull, D. D. (2004). The civic library: A model for 21st century participation. In Jaeger, P. T. and Bertot, J. C. (Eds.), *Advances in Librarianship* (Vol. 28, pp. 55–81). Bingley, UK: Emerald Group Publishing Limited.

Smallwood, C. (2010). *Librarians as community partners: An outreach handbook.* Chicago: American Library Association.

REFERENCES

Birge, L. E. (1981). *Serving adult learners: A public library tradition.* Chicago: American Library Association.

Carr, D. (2011). *Open conversations: Public learning in libraries and museums.* Santa Barbara, CA: Libraries Unlimited.

Carter, L. (2009, February 11). It's the collections that are special [Web log comment]. *In The Library With the Lead Pipe*. Retrieved from www.inthelibrarywiththeleadpipe.org/2009/its-the-collections-that-are-special/

Dana, J. C. (1928, November 15). Thoughts on the library and adult education. *Library Journal*, 53, 945.

Greene, M. (2007, September 1). *Strengthening our identity, fighting our foibles.* Retrieved from http://www.archivists.org/governance/presidential/ma-green2007.pdf

Holley, R. (2010, March/April). Crowdsourcing: How and why should libraries do it? *D-Lib Magazine, 16*(3/4). Retrieved from http://www.dlib.org/dlib/march10/holley/03holley.html

Kreisberg, A. (2014, Fall/Winter). Increasing access in 140 characters or less: Or, what are archival institutions doing on Twitter? *American Archivist, 77*, 534–57.

Lear, B. (2013). *Adult Programs in the Library* (2nd Ed.). Chicago: American Library Association.

Learned, W. S. (1924). *The public library and the diffusion of knowledge*. New York: Harcourt, Brace and Company.

Linard, L. (1987, Summer). Special collections in public libraries. *Library Trends, 36*(1), 179– 88.

Linderman, E. (2009, January/February). Archives in public libraries. *Public Libraries*, *48*(1), 46–51.

Matassa, F. (2014). *Organizing exhibitions: A handbook for libraries, archives and museums.* London: Facet Publishing.

(NARA) National Archives and Records Administration. (2009). *Preserving the past to protect the future: The strategic plan of the National Archives and Records Administration 2006–2016* (2009 Rev. ed.). Washington, DC: National Archives and Records Administration. Retrieved from http://www.archives.gov/about/plans-reports/strategic-plan/2009/nara-strategic-plan-2006-2016-final.pdf

(NARA) National Archives and Records Administration. (2014, March). U.S. National Archives and Records Administration fiscal year 2014–2018 strategic plan. Washington, DC: National Archives and Records Administration. Retrieved from http://www.archives.gov/about/plans-reports/strategic-plan/2014/nara-strategic-plan-2014-2018.pdf

Owens, T. (2012, May 20). *The crowd and the library.* Retrieved from http://www.trevorowens.org/2012/05/the-crowd-and-the-library/

Prentice, A. E. (2011). *Public libraries in the 21st century*. Santa Barbara, CA: Libraries Unlimited.

Robertson, D. A. (2005). *Cultural programming for libraries: Linking libraries, communities, and culture.* Chicago: American Library Association.

Schull, D. D. (2015). *Archives alive: Expanding engagement with public library archives and special collections*. Chicago: ALA Editions.

Stam, D. (2006, Spring). Bridge that gap! Education and special collections. *RBM: A Journal of Rare Books, Manuscripts, and Cultural Heritage*, *7*(1), 16–30.

Theimer, K. (2010). *Web 2.0: Tools and strategies for archives and local history collections*. New York: Neal-Schuman, 2010.

Theimer, K. (2011). *A different kind of web: New connections between archives and our users*. Chicago: Society of American Archivists.

Traister, D. (2000). Is there a future for special collections? And should there be? A polemical essay. *RBM: A Journal of Rare Books, Manuscripts and Cultural Heritage*, 1(1), 54–76.

Yakel, E. (2000, Spring). Thinking inside and outside the Boxes: Archival reference services at the turn of the century. *Archivaria, 49*, 140–60.

Chapter Fourteen

The Role, Impact, and Development of Community Archives in New Zealand

Sarah Welland

ABSTRACT

This chapter summarizes recent research into the role, impact, and development of New Zealand community archives carried out in 2014–2015. Three areas were addressed: the current state, areas of concern, and aspects that may impact community archives over the next decade. Stage 1 of the research involved case studies of five individuals with day-to-day responsibility for a small-community archives (interviewees), while Stage 2 used Delphi methodology to elicit feedback from fifteen archives experts. Findings showed that both interviewees and experts considered that community archives played an important role in collecting and looking after community memory, but this role was often adversely impacted by the small number of part-time staff, lack of funding, and few training and professional support initiatives. While interviewees' areas of concern were often similar to the future-impact categories forecasted by experts, the reality of day-to-day work in a community archive meant that interviewees viewed and addressed these concerns at a more fundamental level. As a result, beneficial strategic development of New Zealand community archives will require understanding and recognition by the wider heritage information industry to help address a variety of perceived issues.

INTRODUCTION

This chapter summarizes research carried out as a result of a scholarship from the Ian McLean Wards Memorial Trust.[1] Completed on a part-time basis from March 2014 to March 2015, the research provides deeper understanding of community archives in New Zealand through a detailed overview of three main areas:

- viewpoints relating to the role of community archives today;
- factors impacting what community archives can and cannot do currently;
- factors forecasted to affect the development of community archives over the next ten years.

Although there is evidence of occasional discourse about specific collections and more general issues (for example, Green and Winter, 2011; Hamilton, 2009; Love and Hall, 2012; Mellsop, 2010; Newman, 2011; Sullivan, 2012), the concept of "community archives" is one that many New Zealand information heritage professionals still find ambiguous. This has resulted in different levels of understanding pertaining to what community archives are, what they do, and how they do it. A range of other factors has also exacerbated these differences in understanding. These include the lack of a general definition describing New Zealand community archives, little focused discussion regarding local community archives in professional literature, few active community archives advocates, and patchy professional support.

DEFINITION AND SCOPE

While a key premise of community archives is to "give substance to a community's right to own its own memories" (Earles, 1998, p. 2), literature shows this can be demonstrated in a variety of ways, from small paper-based collections to cultural events (e.g., Bastian, 2013) and online communities of interest. Even a small country like New Zealand with a population of 4.4 million has a wide range of examples. They range from small collections run by community volunteers to government-funded local history repositories in public libraries or museums.

To date, no common definition exists for community archives in New Zealand. This research used a definition from Newman as a basis:

> Community archives are collections of archival records that originate in a community—that is, a group of people who live in the same location or share other forms of community of interest—and whose collection, maintenance and use involves active participation of that community. (Newman, 2010, p. 8)

To accommodate the scope of the research, certain concepts within this definition were further expanded or defined. *Community* included genetic or social relationships such as family, as well as identification with a specific culture, ethnic group, or race. It also included the concept of "self-defined" community (Flinn, 2007). *Collection* described the entire holdings of a community archives, as long as it included archival records. *Archival record* assumed the existence of a link between the record and the context of its creation and/or use that proved its archival value. This value could be historical, evidential, accountable, informational, social or "emotional, religious, symbolic [or] cultural" (Cook, 2012, p. 115).

The community archives within this research represented many of the themes currently associated with community archives in New Zealand. For example they:

- were controlled by a self-defined community;
- demonstrated some form of active community participation;
- required users to come to a physical place to access most of the collection;
- held a wide range of items from archival records to reference material and artefacts;
- operated as an in-house repository or as a collecting institution;
- represented common types, for example local history collections and heritage collections managed by cultural, political, hobby, history, sporting and other social or interest groups; and
- had one person with overall day-to-day responsibility for them.

The scope of the research meant that other common types of New Zealand community archives such as private archives, university archives, business archives, and digitized collections were not included. Collections under the direct control of any government agency or public sector organization and collections that had two or more paid staff members were also not covered.

SUMMARY OF METHODOLOGY

A qualitative research method was used to obtain a microcosm of the range of participant opinions about community archives. These opinions were gained by collecting and analyzing data from two groups across two stages.

Stage 1 analyzed interview transcripts from five individuals with day-to-day responsibility for a small community archives (interviewees). All worked part-time. Two were volunteers, two were paid to work as archivists, and one carried out occasional archival duties as part of a paid administration position. The community archives that these individuals worked within were deliberately chosen to demonstrate a sufficient range of shared characteristics and a suitable level of credibility. The following case types were used:

- a local history archive;
- a church archive;
- an interest group archive;
- an iwi (Māori tribe) archive (Māori are the indigenous people of New Zealand);
- a school archive.

Of these archives,

- three were from the North Island of New Zealand (which is more populous), and two from the South Island;
- three were urban, two were rural;
- collections varied in size from 98 linear feet (20 linear meters) of material to about 3,937 linear feet (1,200 linear meters) of material;
- three operated "in-house" from within a broader corporate structure, two were independently created by the community the collection served;
- four used volunteers; and
- none had any direct government funding.

Five face-to-face interviews were conducted over a period of eight weeks, with each interview taking between 20 and 180 minutes. These interviews were in a semi-structured format with open-ended questions that focused on four main areas:

1. physical context (location(s), storage, preservation, funding, and organizational affiliation);
2. intellectual context (how items were acquired, arranged, accessed and managed);
3. user context (who the users of the archives were and what items they used); and
4. personal viewpoints of the archives (what each individual thought about their collection and its role).

A key part of the data analysis was the division of onsite notes and interview transcripts into "conceptual categories" (Joe, Yoong, and Patel, 2013, p. 917). This grouped interviewee comments and onsite notes under category headings describing key aspects of the current environment. This process was carried out over three iterations with increasingly precise and specific categories being developed. Further analysis was also carried out by organizing relevant interviewee comments into nine categories representing areas of concern. These were identified through comments that indicated worry, frustration, awareness of a lack, or a desire to change the current state. The results were then compared with the categories developed in Stage 2.

Stage 2 involved the analysis of three rounds of Survey Monkey survey data from fifteen New Zealand archives and information heritage experts. Experts were purposively selected and all had demonstrable knowledge and experience in the field of archives or heritage management. Experts were asked to predict factors that they considered would impact community archives over the next ten years and give their feedback on statements that described the current state of community archives. The Delphi methodology was used for this stage because it "employs multiple iterations designed to develop a consensus of opinion concerning a specific topic" (Hsu and Sandford, 2007, pp. 1–2). It allowed for a range of comparative opinions to be gained from a number of experts without large expense in time or resources (Yousuf, 2007). It also provided a form of structured group communication (Okoli and Pawlowski, 2004) that enabled experts to submit responses, view summarized findings from the previous round, and keep or change their own viewpoints in the next round without being identified. Since the number of information heritage professionals working in New Zealand is small, individual anonymity was particularly valuable.

Round 1 of the survey required experts to list five factors that they considered will have a major influence on community archives over the next ten years, and rank them from 1 (the factor with the highest level of impact) to 5 (the factor with the lowest). Experts then had to provide their rationale for each factor and its associated ranking in an open-ended field. They were also required to choose one of three responses ("Agree," "Disagree," or "It depends") associated with sixteen statements describing possible characteristics of the current state of community archives in New Zealand, and give their rationale for each choice.

Round 2 provided an opportunity to clarify Round 1 results and gain further evidence of expert consensus or disagreement. Experts were asked to "Agree" or "Disagree" with the individual rankings of eleven categories that summarized the impact factors that they had identified in the previous round, explain their rationale for any ranking that they disagreed with, and suggest an alternative ranking. Experts also had to "Agree" or "Disagree" with a nonranked list of sixteen current-state statements adjusted in light of Round 1 comments, and suggest new impact categories or additional current state statements.

Round 3 was in a similar form again, but with rankings and statements adapted to take into account the previous round's feedback. While experts were asked to “Agree” or “Disagree” with each impact-category ranking and current-state statement, they did not have to explain their rationale for their choice. Instead, a free text field was provided at the end of the section for experts to document concerns with any particular ranking or statement, and to suggest alternatives.

RESULTS

Overall, experts considered that the eighteen statements in Round 3 provided a good overview of the current state of community archives in New Zealand. For ease of interpretation, these eighteen statements have been placed under nine headings. It is recognized that many of these statements can be placed in more than one category.

Role

- Community archives have a key role to play in creating and maintaining community memory. (100% agreement)
- Community archives have a key role to play in managing the evidence of their communities, although some community archives may understand it simply as “providing information of interest.” (100% agreement)
- Many community archives are viewed by trained and experienced archivists as valid archival repositories (that is, the archives are managed in ways that demonstrate suitable awareness of the key archival principles of provenance and original order), but not all. (92% agreement)

Governance

- In a majority of cases, the user community (including those responsible for governance) do not really understand the role and purpose of their community archives. (75% agreement)

Funding

- Although most community archives want to meet basic guidelines for storage, they do not always have the resources to do so. (100% agreement)

Repository management[2]

- Most community archives consider published and reference material as an integral part of the overall collection. (92% agreement)

- Most community archives store a wider variety of material than most other forms of archival repository. (75% agreement)
- Collection storage facilities range from excellent to poor, with most community archives having at least a couple of ongoing issues that could negatively impact the preservation of items; for example, they may have a lack of suitable environmental control or a lack of appropriate boxing. (92% agreement)
- Most community archives use pragmatic description techniques that are often based on decisions made "in-house." (100% agreement)
- Many individuals with day-to-day responsibility for community archives demonstrate a good level of awareness when it comes to the archival principles of provenance and original order, but there are also a number who do not. As a result, not all community archives follow these key principles when it comes to their accessioning and/or arrangement and description practice. (100% agreement)
- Many community archives have some form of supporting documentation in place regarding access, ownership, etc., but the currency, depth, and breadth of this information depends on the priorities of each individual archive. Some community archives do not have any documentation. (100% agreement)

Digital Archiving

- Most community archives lack the resources and facilities to effectively manage born digital archives. (100% agreement)

Community Engagement

- Many community archives get some form of active support from the communities from which they were created. However, the efficacy of this support depends on the level of stakeholder understanding and involvement, and the level of competition for community funding. (100% agreement)

Staffing

- Community archives are often dependant on one or two passionate individuals to lead and manage them. (100% agreement)
- Volunteers in community archives often carry out tasks to do with processing, storage, or basic preservation. Results can vary considerably, but most people with day-to-day responsibility for the collection consider this better than no progress at all. (100% agreement)

Training

- Most staff who manage community archives do not have archival qualifications, and while their understanding of foundational archival practices (boxing, listing, accessioning, etc.) may be sufficient, there can be evidence of a lack of in-depth training or mentoring when it comes to areas such as arrangement and description, appraisal, and preservation. (100% agreement)
- Community archives are not considered a priority when it comes to industry-based training or collaborative support initiatives. This is mainly due to a lack of resources rather than a lack of awareness. (92% agreement)

Table 14.1. Interviewee Areas of Concern

Key areas of interviewee concern relating to the management of community archives, in ranked order from 1 (the concern with the most comments from individual interviewees) to 9 (the concern with the fewest comments from individual interviewees).

Rank	*Area*	*Scope*
1	Repository Management	Concerns relating to day-to-day "business as usual" issues around the acquisition, processing, storage, and preservation of items.
2	Access	Concerns with aspects that impact upon the provision of equitable access to items within the collection.
3=	Governance	Concerns relating to the governing body and its understanding of archives management.
3=	Staffing	Concerns about the number and availability of paid and volunteer staff.
5	Marketing and community engagement	Concerns about the ability of a community archives to promote itself and its holdings, and to educate users and potential users about them.
6	Funding	Concerns relating to what is able and not able to be done with the resources allocated.
7=	Training	Concerns with the training of staff and volunteers and their level of archival, etc., knowledge.
7=	Wider environment	Concerns with more generalized population and cultural trends that could impact the development and use of community archives.
9	Digital archiving	Concerns with being able to store and manage electronic archives in the future.

Users

- Most community archives have a range of user groups. Common user groups include genealogists and local history enthusiasts, as well as the community itself. (100% agreement)

The community archives covered by the interviews tended to reflect these statements in their working context, and if it was not true for the collection itself, most of the interviewees knew of a similar situation elsewhere. Overall these community archives demonstrated:

- a key role in preserving community memory;
- a broad collection mandate that included a range of material kept as community memory;
- varied archival practices ranging from excellent to nonexistent;
- maintenance of the collection by one or two key individuals;
- user communities and governing bodies that did not always understand the role and purpose of community archives;
- a culture of pragmatic decision making on the part of staff;
- less than adequate resourcing that affected preservation and description practices to varying degrees;
- little professional support from, and few collaborative initiatives with, other heritage institutions and professional associations;
- staff with no archival qualifications and who lacked knowledge of archival principles and practices in some situations.

The interviewees shared similar concerns relating to the day-to-day management of "their" community archives, regardless of whether they worked in a paid or voluntary capacity (see table 14.1).

These areas of concern can be compared with the ten categories experts forecasted as having significant influence on community archives over the next ten years (see table 14.2). Note that the categories may overlap in some areas. *Funding* was the only category to have 100 percent expert agreement for its ranking.

A general comparison of areas that were covered by both groups, either as an area of concern or a category of perceived impact, showed that the perceived importance of each area was often viewed differently by each group (Graph 1). Note that while there was no one-to-one correlation of the two sets of data because two different data collection approaches were used, a general comparison of shared areas of concern was still possible.

Table 14.2. Expert Forecasted Future Impact Categories

The expert-forecasted future impact categories affecting community archives in the next ten years are ranked from 1 (the category with the most influence on community archives over the next ten years) to 10 (the category with the least).

Rank	*Future Impact Category*	*Scope*
1	Funding	Factors that impact the financing of community archives.
2	Digital archiving	Factors that impact the collection, creation, management, preservation, access, and use of digital content.
3	Collaboration	Factors that impact the ability of a community archives to collaborate with other agencies.
4	Staffing	Factors that impact the ability of the community archives staff to recruit and maintain appropriate numbers of skilled paid or voluntary staff.
5	Training and professional engagement	Factors that impact the training and education of a variety of people associated with community archives, including staff.
6	Standards	Factors that impact the establishment and maintenance of rules, standards, frameworks, specifications, guidelines, etc.
7	Wider environment	Factors that impact community archives from a general, nationwide perspective; for example, government legislation, aging population, and Web 2.0.
8	Governance and strategy	Factors that impact the governance of community archives.
9	Marketing and community engagement	Factors that impact the ability of a community archives to promote itself and its holdings, and to educate users and potential users.
10	Access	Factors that impact the ability of a community archives to give the community and other users equitable access to the collection and the items within it.

SUMMARY OF DISCUSSION

Overall, there were many areas of similarity between expert perceptions of the current state and areas of concern mentioned by interviewees. However, it was clear that both groups often perceived the importance of these areas quite differently. Expert concern tended to focus on areas of strategic development and the placement of community archives within the wider archival continuum. Interviewee concern was at a more fundamental level, focusing on issues that affected the collection, its management, and its role within a specific community. Key reasons for these differences were often dictated by the working context of the community archives. All interviewees worked part-time on the collection, and although each was dedicated, practices around storage, preservation, and arrangement and description were often compromised by a lack of suitable training, resourcing, and community support.

The issue of digital archiving is a good example. This was highly ranked by experts as a future-impact category, but digital archiving practices were not carried out to any depth within the case studies covered by the interviews. This was a situation that experts also recognized, with many stating that fundamental concerns such as funding and training needed to be addressed prior to digital solutions being developed. Collaborative initiatives were also seen by experts as a possible solution, but none of the interviewees had considered this in conjunction with digital-archiving practices. For them, collaboration was restricted to occasional informal training sessions with other community archivists. This lack of action, however, did not always indicate lack of understanding on the part of the archivist. Comments from two interviewees showed that at least some community archivists were aware of the importance of a more strategic focus that included digital archiving, even if they were not yet able to put it into practice.

Both experts and interviewees considered the role of community archives to be an important one in enabling community memory to be collected and looked after. Three specific roles were identified by one or both groups of participants:

- to preserve evidence of the history of a community (experts and interviewees)
- to enable and encourage the community to access its memory (interviewees)
- to support other broader community functions (interviewees)

While the preservation of the evidence of a community was discussed by both groups, experts saw the role from a top-down perspective. Community archives were often considered as part of the wider institutional spectrum that enabled different facets of societal memory to be collected, preserved, and remembered. Interviewees, on the other hand, viewed the role through a narrower lens that focused on the community itself. For them, the collection existed to tell the story of community *for* that community, rather than plugging memory gaps across wider society. As a result, the five community archives studied had a much broader collection mandate than many other types of archival institution because there was a perception that there was no backstop for community memory—if they didn't keep it, memory would be patchy or even lost completely.

While the role of archives in enabling a community to have equitable access to its memory was not specifically covered by expert comment, it was an area of clear focus for interviewees. For them, enabling and encouraging access was closely tied with helping community members use and understand the collection for themselves as prevailing community attitudes directly contributed to the current situation within, and the ongoing development of, community archives. For example, the one interviewee who stated that they were generally well funded credited it to the fact that a key person of influence had been involved in the management of archives in a previous role. As a result, the provision of access to the archival record was the second greatest area of concern for interviewees after that of repository management, because it not only showed up any gaps or compromises in existing archival processes, but also reduced the collections' ability to provide a primary service.

Four of the five interviewees also considered that one of the key roles of the community archives was to support other community functions by providing education and research services or administrative support. While none of the experts indicated awareness of this role, this is not surprising considering the overall trend by experts to focus on a broader society-wide perspective, and the lack of a current-state statement inviting expert discussion on this viewpoint.

Overall, experts tended to share a view that community archives were underresourced when it came to managing the evidence of their community—a perspective that tended to be borne out in reality. Most interviewees gave a range of examples of how a lack of funding had resulted in reduced training, restricted services, and delayed or frustrated plans in areas such as description, community engagement, preservation, and retrospective work.

Both experts and interviewees agreed that the archivist had ongoing influence on the management of the collection and how it was perceived and used by the community, regardless of whether or not this was demonstrated through appropriate resourcing. For example, all those interviewed stated that they were doing a number of things to market their collections within the resources they had available, even though they may not consider themselves natural advocators of their role or their collection. Both groups, however, also expressed concern about the wider lack of suitable training and staff archival knowledge. This was backed up by interviewee reports of a lack of support for ongoing professional development by governing bodies and few education and training opportunities that fit the budget and requirements of community archivists. It was also caused in some cases by a lack of awareness on the part of the archivist that training was even required. As a consequence, many experts doubted the ability of some community archivists to manage and preserve archival items in ways that reflected the key archival principles of provenance and original order—something a few of the interviewees also confirmed, either in terms of their own situation, or in situations they knew of elsewhere. While participation in formal archival education was not always essential, lack of suitable training was often one of the key causes of inappropriate or missing archival practices and a lack of awareness of broader issues affecting archives management.

The range of issues and concerns articulated by experts and interviewees indicated that community archivists in New Zealand may not always have the resources or knowledge to develop and conduct programs and initiatives that would change the status quo and that a more collaborative approach is required. Training and education solutions, for example, would require cooperative pooling of resources from the archives, museum, and library sectors, as well as from the community archives themselves.

Ideally, the industry needs to provide a framework of ongoing, articulate support that ranges from collaborative initiatives to informed and vocal advocacy. This framework should encompass respect for key archival principles, knowledge of the unique nature of archives, and understanding of the needs of community archives users. Archives professionals working in other archival repositories also need to recognize the unique range of issues faced by community archives. In collaboration with stakeholders from other heritage information communities, they need to work with community archivists to determine where development priorities lie and who is most able to help address them.

CONCLUSION

This chapter summarizes a range of concerns facing New Zealand community archives in 2015 and over the next ten years. It presents the different viewpoints that archives and information heritage experts and community archives staff have about these concerns. Many of these concerns are based on fundamental issues that are likely to require additional resourcing, as well as collaborative solutions from the wider information-heritage community. The provision of resourcing and solutions will help community archives not only meet the expectations of their role, but articulate it successfully.

The following recommendations were made for community archivists and the wider archives community in New Zealand:

1. Develop a broadly applicable definition of the term "community archives" for New Zealand archivists. This will help professional associations, archival institutions, archivists, and researchers discuss community archives.
2. Develop a formal statement about the role and purpose of community archives that is recognized by all professional associations in New Zealand that cover heritage information management.

3. Establish a community archives advocate group to act as a centralized voice and advocate for community archives and their ongoing development.
4. Develop voluntary baseline standards of practice for community archivists to address numerous industry questions relating to what should be managed, where, how, and who should manage them.
5. Develop a community archives toolkit for community archivists so that they can access and share current resources, articles, guides, and other "how to" documents.
6. Provide a communication space for individuals involved with community archives, providing online forums, webinars, and other information.
7. Champion a qualification suited for those working with community archives, such as the planned New Zealand qualification *Level 4 Certificate in Managing Heritage Information.* This will help to reduce the qualification gap between community archivists and archivists in other institutions, and increase opportunities for community archivists to staircase to other relevant information management qualifications.

NOTES

1. Sarah Welland was the recipient of the inaugural 2013 scholarship, which was granted in 2014. This New Zealand scholarship provides financial support for researchers and practitioners within the heritage information industry who wish to "to undertake research for a specific project advancing knowledge or improving practice relating to the recording, care, or conservation, of historical research materials" (Scholarship announcement, 2013, p. 1).

2. Both preservation and archival practice are covered by *repository management*, a catchall term that describes the day-to-day processes carried out on the collection that may affect the integrity and evidentiality of the record. Depending on the community archives, these processes may cover acquisition, storage, arrangement and description and preservation. The term *collection management*, often used by museums and libraries, would also be appropriate in some cases.

REFERENCES

Bastian, J. A. (2013). The records of memory, the archives of identity: Celebrations, texts and archival sensibilities. *Archival Science*, *13*(2–3), 121–31. doi:10.1007/s10502-012-9184-3

Cook, T. (2012). Evidence, memory, identity, and community: Four shifting archival paradigms. *Archival Science*, *13*(2–3), 95–120. doi: 10.1007/s10502-012-9180-7

Earles, K. (1998). Community archives: Introduction. *South Africa Archives Journal*, *40*. Retrieved from EBSCOhost.

Flinn, A. (2007). Community histories, community archives: Some opportunities and challenges. *Journal of the Society of Archivists*, *28*(2), 151–76. doi: 10.1080/00379810701611936

Green, S., and Winter, G. (2011). Looking out and keeping the gate open: Wairarapa archive, New Zealand's greatest little archive. *Aplis*, *24*(1), 23–31.

Hamilton, S. (2009). Gallopers and guano: Rescuing the archive of the Wellington Racing Club. *Archifacts, October 2008 to April 2009,* 101–12.

Hsu, C., and Sandford, B. A. (2007). The Delphi technique: Making sense of consensus. *Practical Assessment, Research and Evaluation: A Peer-Reviewed Electronic Journal*, *12*(10), 1–8. doi: ISSN 1531-7734

Joe, K, Yoong, P., and Patel, K. (2013). Knowledge loss when older experts leave knowledge-intensive organisations. *Journal of Knowledge Management, 17*(6), 913–27.

Love, H., and Hall, C. (2012). Ka Puta, Ka Ora: Digital archiving and the revitalisation of Taranaki reo. *Archifacts, October 2011 to April 2012*, 25–34.

Mellsop, S. (2010). From archivist to author: Writing the Dio difference. *Archifacts, October 2010*, 55–60.

Newman, J. (2010). *Sustaining community archives*. (Master's thesis, Victoria University of Wellington, Wellington, New Zealand). Retrieved from http://researcharchive.vuw.ac.nz/handle/10063/1398

Newman, J. (2011). Sustaining community archives. *Aplis*, *24*(1), 37–45.

Okoli, C., and Pawlowski, S. D. (2004). The Delphi method as a research tool: An example, design considerations and applications. *Information and Management*, *42*, 15–29. doi:10.1016/j.im.2003.11.002

Scholarship announcement: The Ian McLean Wards Scholarship: Support for research in librarianship, archives and records management. (2013).

Sullivan, E. (2012). Impact of the February 2011 aftershocks: Revisiting our heritage collections. *Archifacts, October 2011 to April 2012,* 73–92.

Yousuf, M. I. (2007). Using experts' opinions through Delphi Technique. *Practical Assessment, Research and Evaluation: A Peer-Reviewed Electronic Journal*, *12*(4), 1–8.

Part V

INFORMATICS IN CULTURAL STUDIES

Chapter Fifteen

Oliver Optic and Young America

Reading Library Shelves and Publishing Records for Insights into the Past[1]

Jennifer Burek Pierce and Mikki Smith

ABSTRACT

Oliver Optic, the pseudonym of William Taylor Adams, became an exemplar of librarians' complaints against series fiction, but their characterizations of Optic obscure his role in late-nineteenth-century American popular culture. Adams was a teacher interested in technology, whose literary marketing contributed to the success of his series for young readers and a popular, eponymous magazine. *Oliver Optic's Magazine* and Adams's series encouraged readers to know the nation's history while pursuing interests in technology and world travel. Young people also found in these outlets a means of communicating and connecting with their peers, turning their hands to literary production as well as its consumption. Numerous sources indicate youthful enthusiasm, parental approval, and library purchases of his books.

INTRODUCTION

Nineteenth-century author Oliver Optic, the pseudonym of William Taylor Adams, is now known primarily as an exemplar of librarians' complaints against series fiction. Objections to Adams's books, however, have deflected attention from the contents of library shelves and guardians' purchases for children. Discrepancies between public pronouncements and local actions invite attention to the broader cultural record surrounding the Oliver Optic phenomenon. Letters to publisher Lee & Shepard and Oliver Optic, orders and receipts, and library catalogues indicate that Adams's stories of travel and adventure reached a wide audience, cultivating young people's interest in the world around them, even as librarians told one another that Optic's books shouldn't be part of the children's collections then developing in U.S. public libraries (Pawley, 2000, pp. 90, 93).

Concerns among Adams's contemporaries about the effects of his adventure stories on young readers, particularly boys, are well documented. The phrase "Oliver Opticism" made its appearance in the library literature in 1879, when William P. Atkinson employed it in his address "Sensational Fiction in Public Libraries," in a special issue of *Library Journal* (Atkinson, 1879). Atkinson was far from alone in singling out the Optic novels as unsuitable reading matter, yet Optic's Young America Abroad and Starry Flag series were demonstrably popular. Adams's role as a figure engendering enthusiasm and opprobrium alike signals his significance in a world that was rife with change. His books and *Oliver Optic's Magazine: Our Boys and Girls* (1867–1875), together with the readership and the controversy they generated, document contemporary responses to profound cultural transformations that occurred during his lifetime. The Oliver Optic stories illuminated U.S. history while also drawing attention to technological novelties and inviting young people to explore the world. The immense appeal of the dynamic narratives helped Adams's words and ideas to become embedded in cultural institutions from libraries to the American family within their author's lifetime.

The books and eponymous magazine, which were marketed to families and enjoyed a large readership of boys and girls in their teens, represent a microcosm of significant cultural moments in the nineteenth century. Industrialization, railroads, wars, and the landscapes they changed figured in Adams's works for young readers. These publications invoked and involved numerous new technologies, from small printing presses operated by young people—the desktop publishing of its day—to steam locomotives operated by his young protagonists, as in *Through by Daylight* or *The Young Engineer of the Lake Shore Railroad*, an aspect of his work little noted in scholarship. He traveled extensively throughout his adult life; letters to his publisher in 1870 record the days when he was caught in Europe during the outbreak of the Franco-Prussian War and shuttled throughout the continent, looking for a way to return to the United States. His interest in international travel worked its way into his magazine and his fiction, for example, the aforementioned Young America Abroad series (1870s) and the All-Over-The-World Library series (1890s). This tendency inspired his contemporaries to note his extensive reliance on personal observations and research in his writing.

Preventing young people from reading such a topical and prolific author would have been difficult. He has been proclaimed "the great maker of books in series" and "one of the era's best-selling boys' authors" (Johnson, 2002, p. 155). His works were widely promoted, both by his own efforts and in the pages of unaffiliated publications, such as the student-authored *Harvard*

Advocate ("Books received," 1870). When Adams died in 1897, a local paper credited him with writing 1,723 short stories and 126 books. While different sources offer slightly varying counts for his publications, all concur that he was a highly prolific and profitable author (Johnson, 2002; Jones, 1985). Adams laid the groundwork for the success of Edward Stratemeyer and his "fiction factory," which published Nancy Drew, the Hardy Boys, and other long-running, popular series, so it is fitting that Stratemeyer completed the final Optic novel, *An Undivided Union* (1899), after Adams's death.

The reader-oriented departments of *Oliver Optic's Magazine* also provide evidence of Adams's status and influence among his young readers, as do materials held by the American Antiquarian Society (AAS). The Optic novels were first released by two other Massachusetts publishers, then reprinted by Boston publisher Lee & Shepard, which went on to become his primary publisher (Dorchester Atheneum, 2003). AAS holds the extant records of Lee & Shepard and public library catalogs from every state during this era; together these traces of the cultural record reveal that Oliver Optic's works were owned not only by individual readers but by libraries as well. While his aim was to promote the Oliver Optic brand published and distributed by Lee & Shepard, Adams simultaneously fostered a dynamic, multi-generational readership in libraries, homes, and wherever young people read. In turn, these young people—and sometimes their parents—wrote to Adams, a former schoolteacher, and his publisher with undeniable enthusiasm and devotion.

This chapter explores these themes as a way of evaluating Adams's appeal and availability to late-nineteenth-century readers. By looking at indications of his readership and how readers obtained his work, we can see his significance in creating and illuminating the dynamic and changing culture of the era. During Optic's rise, the United States saw an increase in its economic productivity and revenues, in its dealings with other nations, and in the scope of its own borders (Office of the Historian, United States Department of State, 2013). Although the sensational nature of Adams's adventure stories is generally cited as the reason for both their popularity among young readers and criticism of his books by librarians and other cultural gatekeepers, Adams—despite his intensely commercial sensibility—was consciously engaged in broader cultural work with regard to Young America in the last decades of the nineteenth century, akin to the intersecting developments in technology, commerce, and nationalism proposed in Zboray's *A Fictive People*. Where Zboray (1993) examined how, earlier in the nineteenth century, reading enabled "a new, modern definition of the American self" (p. xvii), Adams invoked the nation's past, emerging technologies, and the wider world as a means of encouraging young people to imagine themselves citizens in this changing world.[2]

WILLIAM T. ADAMS AND THE RISE OF OLIVER OPTIC

William T. Adams was born in 1822, in Medway, Massachusetts, a state that remained his home throughout his life, despite the many faraway places that informed the stories he wrote ("Death of 'Oliver Optic,'" 1897). Adams's reputation as a prominent and popular author of books for young people coincided, at least initially, with his career as a teacher and headmaster in Dorchester, Massachusetts ("Death of 'Oliver Optic,'" 1897); however, commercial success eventually prompted him to turn his full attention to the Oliver Optic enterprise. His voluminous authorship under that pseudonym spanned from the 1850s until his death in 1897. His reputation as someone who understood his readers because of his educational career nonetheless persisted throughout his life.

Adams led a many-faceted life. He was, in the words of one writer, "a skillful mechanic and a practical yachtsman" who once "spent all his spare time about the wharves and piers, where he acquired the nautical knowledge contained in his stories of the sea" ("William Taylor Adams," 1897, p. 205). This aspect of his life is reflected not only in his fiction but also in *Oliver Optic's Magazine*, which included discussions about boating and a multi-part glossary of nautical terms ("Cost of boats," 1867; "Nautical definitions," 1867). He was married, and he and his wife had two daughters. In his later life, he served in the Massachusetts state legislature, formally known as the General Court of the Commonwealth of Massachusetts. When he wrote and edited as Oliver Optic, his daily routine included lunch at his club and meeting with his publisher. The stories of his life crafted by dedicated memorialists after his death suggest a warm man with strong feelings for others.

That Adams traveled to generate content for both books and magazine pieces was well known. Beginning with those first published pieces, Adams drew on research, whether the lived experience of his own activities and travels or the knowledge he found in books. This characteristic of his work is evinced in prefaces, in letters to his editors from abroad, and in the text and illustrations of his books. Contemporary critics regarded him as a world traveler, seeing it as an essential aspect of his writing: "Many people received their impressions of Mexico and of European countries from his stories of travel and adventure" ("William Taylor Adams," 1897, p. 205). His first successful story, *Hatchie, the Guardian Slave*, written under the pseudonym Warren T. Ashton, resulted from a voyage to New Orleans, and in 1895, his plan to spend a month in the West Indies before continuing to Europe, made the pages of a prominent literary journal ("News and notes," 1895). His surviving correspondence with Lee & Shepard details the travails of his days in Europe in 1870, a trip noted by other scholars, which also provided fodder for the eponymous magazine (Kilgour, 1965).

It was as Oliver Optic, a pen name adopted in 1851 following the premiere of a Boston play with a similarly named character, that Adams became famous. Although Adams used a number of names during his long writing career, the pseudonym "Oliver Optic" was the one he used most often, and it became so entwined with his identity that he sometimes signed letters to his publishers, Lee & Shepard, "Yours ever Oliver Optic."[3] or with the initials "O.O." (Jones, 1985; Optic, 1870c; Optic, 1870d). When he died in March 1897, one local paper announced his passing with his pseudonym and declared, "Thousands of American Boys Will Learn of the Fact with the Keenest Sorrow" ("Death of 'Oliver Optic,'" 1897). These facts are only a few of the details that humanize a name that was, if not demonized in the professional library literature, then, for the most part, grudgingly acknowledged as that of a favorite children's author.

Relying on anecdotal characterizations of Adams as Optic misconstrues his role in late-nineteenth-century American popular culture. Rather than as a teacher interested in technology, whose keen and determined sense of literary marketing contributed to the success of his series for young readers, Adams appears as a hack writer in others' portrayals. For instance, Louisa May Alcott's *Eight Cousins* (1874), originally serialized in *St. Nicholas*, a competitor of *Oliver Optic's Magazine*, includes a scene in which a motherly character refers to books whose honorable, heroic characters make them appear better than sensational literature as "optical delusions" (p. 198). This cutting reference to Oliver Optic prompted a scathing editorial response to Alcott in *Oliver Optic's Magazine* ("Editorial," 1875) and anticipated librarians' debate over Optic's place in the public library: "a more difficult problem is raised by those books whose morality is ambiguous, 'written by men who mean well'" (Hendler, 2001, p. 86). Alcott's often quoted denunciation and related discourse about the effects of his writing suggest Optic was a contested, if not trivial, figure. While the controversy surrounding Adams's work may be all readers today know of Oliver Optic, it fails to adequately represent his centrality during the long nineteenth century.

Emerging professional librarians tended to side with Alcott rather than Adams, at least in print. Although at least a few librarians argued for collecting popular writers like Optic and Alger, the stronger professional voices warned against adding these authors' work to collections created with public funds (pp. 87, 89). Alison Marie Parker has also noted the considerable discussion of the role of series for boys by Optic and others in public libraries. Many voiced the opinion that these books didn't merit inclusion, while those who defended their purchase of these titles believed that they "had the potential 'to keep users from worse literature'" (Parker, 1997, p. 202). The cues provided by these contemporary librarians, sometimes cited for contrast with present-day collection of popular materials for young readers, give little sense of Adams as the peer, in terms of reputation and readership, of a subsequently canonized figure like Horatio Alger.

Some librarians of the era acknowledged Optic's popularity and endorsed it by placing his books on their shelves. In 1886, the San Francisco Public Library added "upward of 500 volumes of Oliver Optic's books to replace copies that had been worn out" ("Library notes," 1886, p. 121). The Massachusetts author was identified as leading the circulation of juvenile titles in other libraries ("Best reading," 1886; Pawley, 2000). A librarian in Lancaster, Massachusetts, reported that two dozen volumes by Optic added to the municipal library prior to a decision not to purchase his books anymore accounted for "'2 percent of the fiction circulated'" (Parker, 1997, p. 201). These indications of the way Optic inspired readers tended to appear in brief commentaries on collection maintenance, rather than in philosophical statements about collection development, where words opposing Optic were found.

True accolades, for the most part, are beyond the library literature, and well into the Progressive Era, praise could be found in magazines intended for serious adult readers. "When two men set out to change the trend of a city's growth, that is ambition," began a 1929 article in the *Nation's Business*. "If they accomplish it, it is success. If, to improve their real estate holdings, they establish a railway system that overshadows the original purpose, that is a good story." Such a story, the author concluded, was one Oliver Optic might have written (Corey, 1929, p. 31). This was not the only article to connect engineering achievements and the fiction Adams authored. In 1926, *Barron's* employed Optic's work as a trope for an American success story. "Oliver Optic never wrote a story half so dramatic as the biography of Samuel Insull would be," the author enthused years before the stock market crash of 1929, listing the man's immigration, employment by Thomas Edison, and subsequent leadership in the transportation industry ("Insull in transportation," 1926, p. 9). To journalists who covered American business in the early twentieth century, Optic's name invoked technical know-how and commercial success—two traits often missing from librarians' characterizations of his writing.

A laudatory, emotional obituary outlined his development as a writer from the 1840s when his first short stories appeared in periodicals to the profusion of short stories and books that sold more than two million copies before his death (Hayward, 1956). Contemporary reviews, like one published in 1895 in *The Bookman: A Literary Journal*, also dismissed the prevailing professional antipathy: "No boy or girl was ever really injured by a course of Optic, even though false ideas of juvenile superiority do crop out in his character-sketching." *The Bookman*'s reviewer confessed himself to be among "the old boys who recall with a thrill of pleasure Oliver Optic's first books, and remember how we held that new and novel writer as a name to conjure with" (Brooks, 1895). Far from decrying Optic as a poor writer or an untoward influence on the young mind, this writer identified himself as one of many enthusiastic readers and recollected, as it were, youthful emotion in later tranquility. Similarly, the *Harvard Advocate* had enthused about the Lake Shore Series, noting that its mature and capable protagonist "does just the right thing" in "every crisis." The *Advocate* advised readers that "The Lake Shore Series is good to put into the hands of one's younger brother," with the caveat that the younger readers should be told its hero "Wolf Penniman is a type; and that if one succeeds in doing a few things well as the hero does well in all things, he will do well indeed" ("Review of Brake up," 1870, p. 28). Like later journalists who would evoke Optic's name in nonfiction narratives about successful engineers and innovators, and unlike many librarians, these reviewers attributed to Adams the ability to tell a captivating human story that modeled an ideal professional life.

OLIVER OPTIC'S MAGAZINE: CONNECTING READERS TO THE WORLD AND ONE ANOTHER

Writing fiction was the primary way that Adams engaged readers, but he was also a skilled magazine editor, working in that capacity off and on for more than thirty years. He edited the monthly *Student and Schoolmate* (1855–1872) beginning in 1858, and Lee & Shepard's *Oliver Optic's Magazine: Our Boys and Girls* from its inaugural issue in 1867 to its demise in 1875 (Jones, 1985, pp. 9–10, 31–32). In both cases, Adams played an active editorial and authorial role, providing serialized stories in every volume, as well as other content. In his later years, Adams edited *Our Little Ones and the Nursery* (1880–1899), a magazine aimed at a younger audience than his previous serials (Jones, 1985, p. 67). His work in these outlets helped him to cultivate his readership within families and across generations and to interact with readers through their letters to the editor, which sharpened his sense of their collective interests. In his editorial capacity, he could also direct his readers' informal learning through the content he included in the magazine, the books he recommended, and the advice he provided in response to reader questions.

Whereas Adams had supplied one serialized story per volume for *Student and Schoolmate*, as editor of *Oliver Optic's Magazine*, he initially supplied four serial stories a year, or two per volume, and agreed not to publish in other juvenile periodicals. The latter point was highlighted by Lee & Shepard in its advertisements, signaling to readers that if they wanted to read the latest installments by their favorite author, they would need to subscribe (May, 1869). In 1871, Adams began publishing only two stories per year in the magazine. When a disgruntled subscriber suggested that this was because Adams feared he would run out of stories, Adams responded (referring to himself in the third person), "he thinks he has written too much for his health, and perhaps for his reputation; and he desires to be relieved of some portion of his work." He asserted that it was "quite impossible" for him to provide four stories per year to the magazine and finish the Young America Abroad series ("Pigeon-hole papers," 1871a, p. 202).

The magazine, initially published weekly in a twelve-page, two-column format, was offered at a subscription rate of $2.50 a year, or $1.25 a volume. Besides fiction by Adams, the magazine regularly contained work by Sophie May, the pseudonym of Rebecca Sophia Clarke, and Elijah Kellogg. The *North American Review*'s list of "Children's Books of the Year" from January 1866 (p. 236) indicates the status of these writers when *Oliver Optic's Magazine* debuted: the top three entries are Oliver Optic's Army and Navy Stories, Oliver Optic's Boat-Club Series, and Sophie May's The Little Prudy Stories. The criteria for inclusion on the list is not specified; however, based on the ambivalence expressed later in the same issue about Adams's fiction (pp. 247–48), it seems likely that this list is more an indication of successful sales and popularity than a recognition of literary merit. It is with these high-profile authors that the magazine launched, featuring an installment of Oliver Optic's "Starry Flag" and a short story by Sophie May, as well as a poem by Julia Ward Howe, a brief story titled "My First New Year's Day in America," a sketch on the gray squirrel by E. A. Samuels, and several departments that would become familiar to readers over the coming weeks, months, and years: "Original Dialogue," "The Orator" (complete with accompanying gestures), "The Playground" (which provided arguments, suggestions, and inspiration for indoor and outdoor play), and "Head-Work" (puzzles and games). The popular "Our Letter Bag" was not introduced until July 1867, and a second department devoted to readers' letters, "The Pigeon-Hole Papers," was launched in 1871, when the magazine shifted to a monthly publication schedule and more space was made available.

Adams's opinion pieces addressed world history, politics, and national and international current events, while also covering science and technology. For instance, Adams reported on electricity as an aspect of exhibits at the 1867 Paris Exposition: "Much space would be required to catalogue the various uses by which the ingenuity of man has made this powerful agent become a most useful servant." He then described a telegraph capable of delivering an exact copy—whether text or image—of the sender's message ("Cassell's telegraph," 1868, p. 176). The magazine published long expository pieces on topics such as electricity and silver mining, as well (Clarke, 1872, pp.

687–89; Hoyt, 1873, pp. 406–12). From an article recommending the best sewing machine to a five-part series on velocipedes to a long, detailed, and enthusiastic account of Adams's first encounter with a typewriter, the magazine provided young people with information about scientific and technological developments that were becoming or would likely become part of daily life for many Americans. Adams was so taken by the typewriter that he suggested parents should buy one for their children—at a cost of 125 dollars—as "it would teach spelling, punctuation, and the construction of sentences in the most delightful lessons" ("Sewing machines," 1867, p. 187; "The typewriter", 1875, p. 398; "Velocipedes," 1869). Many of Adams's readers were already involved in the "present juvenile mania for printing"—the production of amateur books and newspapers on small printing presses that became widely available after the Civil War—and this do-it-yourself spirit is reflected in another article instructing readers how to build a boat (Optic, 1869, p. 576; "How to build a boat," 1870, pp. 328–29; Smith, 2015). Articles about copyright and patents also help to imagine Young America as a generation of producers and innovators ("International copyright," 1867, p. 199; "Obtaining patents," 1869, p. 528; "Patents," 1869, p. 512).

In *Oliver Optic's Magazine*, in addition to the adventurous travels of fictional protagonists characteristic of many of his stories, Adams shared his extensive experience with and knowledge of railroads and steamers with his readers (see, for example, "An Ocean Steamer," 1867; Optic, "The City of Peking," 1874; "The New Tunnel," 1875). He also documented aspects of many of his personal vacations in the United States, Canada, and overseas. Between June 1870 and December 1871, the magazine published forty-one "Editorial Correspondence" columns that chronicled his travels in France, Italy, Germany, Spain, Russia, Turkey, and Greece (Optic, 1870b). Readers learned details about Adams's accommodations, the sites he visited, and the challenges he faced. Adams was in Munich when the Franco-Prussian War began, and from Dresden he informed readers, "here we are likely to stay longer than we desire, for his majesty the King of Prussia intends to whip the French if he can; and he has pressing need of all the cars and locomotives in his dominions to forward troops and war material to the Rhine, where death and desolation will soon rage" (Optic, 1870e, p. 688). Adams also included content by other writers about life in other countries. Mrs. J. P. Ballard's five-part series "Greenland and Iceland" delivered information through a running dialogue between two fictional characters, and Harriette B. Cotes depicted India from the perspective of a girl born there to British parents in the years before India's First War of Independence in 1857. This twenty-six part series, "Life in India," portrayed India as an exotic place, describing various animals and Hindu beliefs and customs (Ballard, 1867; Cotes, 1867–1868).

In addition to these longer series, the magazine provided other glimpses of the world, like a profile of Vienna, Austria, ahead of the World's Fair (Chase, 1873). Some pieces invited readers to reflect on American society, as in an excerpted letter that recounted a friend of Adams's travels in China. Noting the kindness with which he was treated despite the curiosity his presence aroused, the friend wrote:

> It was very different from the treatment the Chinese receive here (in California, and, we may add, Los Angeles in particular, since the recent massacre of Chinamen there). I was ashamed of my countrymen when I thought of their kindness to me. . . . So it is with our people, or, at least, a portion of them, who think that those who do not speak our language must be heathens, when, in fact, the heathen part comes on our side, not theirs. ("Pigeon-Hole Papers," 1871c, p. 834)

Adams also responded to readers' questions about travel, as when he tried to prepare young correspondent Katie to spend nearly two weeks on a steamer by discussing seasickness, the benefits of fresh air, and the best ways to pass the time ("Pigeon-Hole Papers," 1871a, p. 202).

Adams not only wanted his young readers to learn about other places; he expected them to become travelers, if they were not already. "One might well think," he editorialized in 1868, "after witnessing the immense operations of some of our principal railroad and steamboat lines, that the American people were like the particles in a pot of boiling water, hurled continually to every part of their sphere by the superabundant heat they contain." Later in the same paragraph, he referred to Boston as a "locomotive community." In that context, he asserted that people needed to travel "in order to keep their eyes wide open" (Optic, 1868, p. 576). To that end, he provided information to his young readers on booking travel, acquiring money abroad, sending and receiving mail while traveling, and passports (Optic, 1870d, p. 448). In his editorial work for *Oliver Optic's Magazine*, Adams attempted to prepare a generation of American youth to face what seemed to him an exciting, sometimes dangerous, changing world.

Estimated circulation numbers for *Oliver Optic's Magazine* range from 11,000 to 22,000, and neither of those numbers accounts for shared family reading or people accessing institutional subscription copies (Stoneley 2003, p. 38; Geo. P. Rowell & Co. 1875, p. 248; Geo. P. Rowell & Co. 1872, p. 288). The magazine's devoted and enthusiastic readership is evidenced by the amount of correspondence Adams received. Although the actual letters to the editor do not appear to have survived and Adams rarely printed the full text of correspondence in the magazine, "Our Letter Bag" and the "Pigeon-Hole Papers" do provide a glimpse into the lives and personalities of the magazine's young correspondents. One of the most noticeable ways in which this occurs is through the pseudonyms correspondents used to represent themselves. "Our Letter Bag" is filled with the names of fictional characters, predictably from Oliver Optic's books, but also from Charles Dickens (Artful Dodger, Oliver Twist) and Shakespeare (Yorick, Puck), and with examples of creative wordplay: B. Right, Lun A. Tic, M. A. Chine, Perry Winkle, N. O. Body, S. T. Upid. In one issue, Adams wrote, "Will Ku Klux Klan please to change his name? as we are a little afraid of a representative of that suspicious fraternity" ("Our letter bag," 1868, p. 415). Some pseudonyms reflect readers' other interests, for instance, in amateur printing (Punch, the printer; and Pica) (Smith, 2012; Smith, 2015).

Many of these correspondents to the magazine submitted puzzles or other creative work for publication, some of which was accepted, some critiqued, and some rejected without comment—all in the pages of the magazine for peers to read. Others wrote with questions. While the specific questions asked are sometimes impossible to determine from Adams's response, the gist is usually discernible. Where appropriate, Adams recommended book titles to readers for further research on a topic (not surprisingly, many Lee & Shepard titles were recommended), but at times he asked readers to respond. In one issue, reader questions included how to estimate the cost of travel to Europe and how to build a yacht ("Pigeon-hole papers," 1873b, p. 697). In another, a reader asked for help in identifying a coin ("Pigeon-hole papers," 1873a, p. 278). One young woman asked what she should talk about with young men, to which Adams responded, in part, "We advise Christabel to be herself, always and everywhere—talk about that which interests her and those with whom she converses," as opposed to the "talkists," who "must flatter vain and stupid people . . . and commend and admire even what she despises" ("Pigeon-hole papers," 1871b, p. 409). These few examples indicate readers' identification with Adams's stories and their concerns as young people navigating the social world.

As crowded and rich as the "Our Letter Bag" and "Pigeon-Hole Papers" are, the responses there represent only a small portion of the letters Adams received:

> We receive thousands of letters so commendatory of the Magazine, or of our own stories in it, or of independent books, that we cannot, of course, decently allude to them; at least not to those parts which affect our individual modesty. . . . [W]e only mention this subject to assure all our young friends that we are grateful to them for the many kind words they have spoken, though we fail to record them in the Magazine. ("Pigeon-hole papers," 1872, p. 759)

Adams nonetheless made exceptions to this, as when John shared his father's approval of the Young America Abroad series: "Pa . . . says I can learn more about England by reading [Optic's] 'Red Cross' than by studying the ordinary histories" ("Our letter bag," 1871, p. 689). Adams appreciated the compliment, which, as an adult opinion, potentially served to undermine his critics.

Adams, through his witty and sometimes acerbic responses to letters in the magazine, developed a strong rapport with readers. One reader, who identified himself in his letter as The Black Knight, appreciated "Our Letter Bag" because "while reading it I always fancy I can see the editor sitting with his boys and girls around him, dealing out to each one his replies to their ever-varying questions, and this with a spice and a freshness to it that is highly relished by every one that reads them" ("Pigeon-hole papers," 1872, p. 760). This sentiment is echoed by reader Thomas Troy, who described reading "Our Letter Bag" as being like "sitting down and chatting with family" ("Our letter bag," 1871, p. 688). Many readers became regular correspondents over the years, and their names or, more often, their pseudonyms became familiar. Correspondents to the magazine sometimes became correspondents with one another, based on shared interests and addresses, and these connections are another way in which Adams enlarged the world of his young readers (Smith, 2015).

Oliver Optic's Magazine ceased publication in 1875, before the founding of the American Library Association (1876) and subsequent debates in professional library literature about series fiction, including Optic's; however, the periodical is important for several reasons. First, many Optic stories referenced in those discussions were originally serialized in the magazine alongside a variety of other content, which is how many readers initially experienced them. Second, the magazine in the context of the body of his fiction invites a more complex analysis of Adams's project, beyond commercial success, and suggests a multidimensional figure. Finally, the magazine provides evidence that Adams's youthful readers were not passive consumers of sensational content but, rather, were actively engaged in the process of making sense of their reading and making connections with their world.

BUYING INTO OLIVER OPTIC: DOCUMENTING OWNERSHIP AND READERSHIP

Scholarship typically notes either the nineteenth-century popularity of books by Oliver Optic or repeats early professional diatribes by librarians as evidence of efforts at a sort of ill-considered cultural hegemony (Carrier, 1985; Young, 2013). Arthur P. Young's (2013) study of the circulation of Horatio Alger's books is distinctive in demonstrating that librarians' attempted "[c]ensorship activity, while drawing public attention, failed to significantly alter either library holdings or children's reading patterns" (p. 420), a trend also true of the Optic titles. In the years when "efficiency"-oriented technical training gave way to the idea, inspired by the turn-of-the-century child study movement, that children's librarians were educators and "cultural supervisors," however, anti-Optic rhetoric was pronounced (Eddy, 2006).[4] Multiple scholars have demonstrated the rise of reading during the antebellum years, and as literacy became more important and widespread in the decades that followed, librarians gave more attention to what ought to be read, particularly by the young (Gilmore, 1989; Zboray, 1993). Barbara Sicherman (2000) depicts the years following the founding of the American Library Association as a time when "librarians hoped to cultivate the 'taste for reading' and then channel it in proper directions" (pp. 291–92).

While some recent research reveals librarians' sincere interest in young users' enjoyment, the first professionals' critiques of popular series fiction endure in the scholarly literature (McDowell, 2009; Mitts-Smith, 2007). It is a truism that the librarians who first articulated the values of the profession in the United States did not believe series fiction belonged on library shelves. They characterized it as lacking seriousness, encouraging unrealistic expectations of life, and in the worst cases, sanctioning immoral behavior. From its founding, the American Library Association encouraged libraries to exclude series, whether sentimental or sensational, including those by Adams (Sicherman, 2000; Robbins, 2000). According to Sicherman (2000) and other historians, "It was a sign of the times that public libraries excluded not only dime novels but also Sunday school literature, the latter on grounds of shallowness and falseness to life" (p. 292). Dorothy Blythe Jones observed that assaults on Oliver Optic titles began at the 1876 meeting of the American Library Association and concluded that their complaints culminated in librarians' refusal to place his works on their shelves by the 1880s (Jones, 1985, pp. xv–xvi). In these meetings, even Samuel Swett Green, who would "have in every library a friend of the young," was only lukewarm in his public defense of Oliver Optic's tales, arguing that "comparatively few are deceived by these books" (Bernier, Chelton, Jenkins, and Pierce, 2010; Jones, 1985, p. xv). A comment like this conforms to now classic scholarly accounts of the origins of American public libraries as concerned with moral uplift and propriety, elements thought not to encourage the natural interests of younger users (Jenkins, 2000; Shera, 1965, pp. 216–17). In their discussions of the harm that could result from poor reading choices, librarians created a canon of this bad, even deleterious literature, generating lists of authors whose works were inappropriate for young readers. The names of the condemned included not just Oliver Optic, but Horatio Alger and G. A. Henty (Pawley, 2000, pp. 78, 80–81; Pierce, 2011). Then, after extensive efforts to identify unworthy books and articulate their pernicious effects, librarians proceeded to collect them.

As scholarship modifies our sense of the dominance of these voices, showing other trends and lines of thought, further scrutiny of the apparent antipathy to series fiction is warranted (Pierce, in press). The contents of nineteenth-century library catalogs and Lee & Shepard's files demonstrate that despite their public complaints, numerous libraries did, in fact, offer access to the disparaged titles. In this, the AAS documents contribute to a reassessment of Oliver Optic as an important cultural figure in his day, congruent with Christine Pawley's (2009) interest in organizations as a means of understanding historical reading practices. Holdings of Optic varied, and few libraries had anything like the entire corpus. Some, however, like the San Francisco Free Public Library, the Chicago Public Library, and the Elgin (Illinois) Public Library, recorded their ownership of multiple Optic series ("Catalogue of the Elgin," 1874; "Catalogue of the English," 1889; "Supplementary catalogue," 1889). The persistent presence of these volumes, along with other series, indicates that librarians recognized the allure of these works and by circulating them, contributed to their cultural resonance. John Cotton Dana voiced the view attributed to many of his peers when he stated that "any reading was better than no reading," since young people could be led from their passion for trash to higher things; yet the amount of popular fiction by Oliver Optic and his peers in many of these early public libraries belies the notion that series were barely tolerated (Pawley, 2007, p. 271).

The collection of nineteenth-century library catalogs held by AAS offers an important corrective to the long-standing notion that series fiction was omitted from libraries, in part because the catalogs come from institutions throughout the nation. While many reflect the holdings of public libraries, there are also records from subscription libraries, school libraries, and those whose status is somewhat ambiguous. Regardless of category, there is at least one nineteenth-century library catalog for every state at AAS, and most often in New England, more than one. In some instances, juvenile materials, as they were described, were separated from the rest of the library's holdings, while in others they were, if the nature of the catalogue is an accurate guide, integrated into the collection. The compilers of these catalogs often noted the volumes' imperfections, as in the case of the *Catalogue of English Prose Fiction and Juvenile Books in the Chicago Public Library*, which contains an acknowledgment that the anticipated inability to replace some volumes resulted in their omission ("Catalogue of the English," 1889, p. 3). Nonetheless, these lists of library holdings offer different information about collection practices from the proceedings of professional conferences or the landmark journal articles that have been used to characterize materials for young readers during this time.

One title to which Adams, as Oliver Optic, contributed was an anthology called *The Great Bonanza: Illustrated Narrative of Adventure and Discovery in Gold Mining, Silver Mining, Among the Raftsmen, in the Oil Regions, Whaling, Hunting, Fishing and Fighting.* While Optic's contributions were limited, Adams may have authored additional sections under other pseudonyms, like the three chapters contributed by "An Old Salt," a name that appears to echo Adams's Optic title, *Brave Old Salt, or, Life on the Quarter Deck: A Story of the Great Rebellion.* Overall, *The Great Bonanza* offers an example of both the marketing power of the Optic brand and the nature of content in series fiction. Published in 1876 by Lee & Shepard, the book was a veritable who's who of popular authors for young men. In addition to Adams, Ballantyne and others offered a set of loosely related stories and essays on the exploration—and exploitation—of the American West. The book certainly contained adventurous feats as promised in its subtitle, but it was a strange compendium, with some lyrical and romanticized passages and others that read more like an encyclopedia entry. Its title page called attention to its "200 illustrations" by equally prominent artists to market the book, itself a bonanza of content and potential sales.

The volume begins with a story by Capt. Charles W. Hall about two runaway boys who, inspired by "other boys we had read of 'to go and seek our fortunes,'" leave boarding school (Optic, 1876, p. 15). Subsequent chapters illuminate Pawley's contention that "In the minds of individual readers, as well as of those who helped shape their reading, the boundaries between literature, stories, information, and trash blurred and shifted, depending on circumstances of time and space" (Pawley, 2009, p. 86). The two boys undertake a "Vacation in Petrolia," a visit to an uncle in order to learn about drilling for oil. More than a fantastic adventure, this chapter is replete with technical details about the process, naming the parts necessary to the undertaking and their specifications. Illustrations in this chapter do not depict the boys amid a rugged and remote terrain; instead, items like drive pipes are diagrammed, complete with their patent numbers, as are other myriad pieces of machinery required for the process (Optic, 1876, p. 25). Dialogue in this chapter narrates the procedure of drilling, with attention to details like the consequences of hitting a rock and the uses of literacy in industry recordkeeping (p. 26). Later in the book, a chapter called "The Little Builders," written by Samuel Burnham, informs readers of the preceding technology-oriented narratives that "Man was not the first builder" (p. 209). An explanation, a precursor to a description of animals and their habitats, follows: "Long before houses, or tents, or huts, were built, long before there were men to need shelter, little animals, of different species, made their ingenious dwellings. . . ." (p. 209). The effects of "'clearing' the country" and beaver hunting, which resulted in the demise of the species, and the promise of its renewal, are among the facts presented (p. 209). Thus, threads of science and environmental awareness, coupled with a little disguised didactic impulse, are readily evident in *The Great Bonanza*, to which Adams contributed two of the twenty-four chapters. At least a few librarians added this blend of narrative and miscellany to their collections, signaling their recognition of the draw its authorship would have created.

It is also worth noting in this context that nineteenth-century library catalogs included other popular series, such as *Three Vassar Girls* by Elizabeth W. Champney and titles by Horatio Alger, Jacob Abbott, and R. M. Ballantyne. At the same time that sometimes substantial amounts of series fiction were available in libraries, these records reveal that Oliver Optic's magazine was not collected alongside the more reputable *St. Nicholas* magazine, with a library in Elgin, Illinois, being one of few that held both titles. Thus, while many librarians committed their budgets to Oliver Optic's books, some of which originated in serial form, his very popular periodical circulated largely outside this network (Kilgour, 1965, p. 83). Letters to Lee & Shepard, though, indicate that some school administrators ordered the magazine for their pupils (Christie, 1869).

The role of technical information in Adams's stories, and the way leading characters acquired it, has been rendered practically invisible to later critics, who have concentrated on the controversy surrounding his works rather than their content. All the complaints against runaways who made good and rags-to-riches heroes in these books emphasize literary quality and narrative arc, rather than mechanical know-how, although the latter abounded in Adams's work. Although his moral didacticism—the protagonist of the Lake Shore series and other characters learn the dangers of drinking and vow to live as temperance advocates—generated commentary then and now, his equally strong instruction in technical subjects has been largely ignored by scholars who have revisited his legacy. His Boat Club and Lake Shore series and the coauthored *Bonanza* anthology, as well as *Oliver Optic's Magazine*, demonstrated to young readers how boats, trains, and engineering operated. These features help explain extant public library circulation records from the nineteenth century that document adult borrowing of Oliver Optic's series, which has encouraged some scholars to suggest that lines between children's and adults' reading choices were blurred rather than distinct (Pawley, 2000, p. 107).

The files of Lee & Shepard at AAS contain letters like one from schoolmaster Charles E. Abbott, who in 1864 wrote to Adams's publishers telling them about his use of Optic books with his students, which inspired their own purchases: "I have quite a number of Oliver Optic's works for my pupils, and now one of my few scholars wishes to get these for his own library" (Abbott, 1864). Abbott was no isolated and indulgent adult. C. W. Ainsworth, who led reform schools in Iowa and Indiana, also sought Optic for his charges (Ainsworth, 1869a; Ainsworth, 1869b; Ainsworth, 1869c). Adults who were inclined to provide Optic books to others appear regularly in the Lee &

Shepard files, indicating these books were reviewed in periodicals like *The Sunday School Times* (Baker, 1870), ordered by libraries whose catalogues do not survive (Champney, 1868) and found in libraries the military provided for soldiers (Arnold, 1871) and owned by individual enlistees (Arnold, 1871; Baughman, 1869; Somers, 1864). Occasionally, a writer hints at an undeveloped regional market for the Optic titles (Hopkins, 1870).

Adult interest in Oliver Optic forms a significant strand of the surviving correspondence, showing that librarians who lambasted the author did not represent a universal view. While few adults seemed attracted to the technological and scientific information that can be found in Adams's writing, they were unreserved in their praise for this author and his influence on young people. Notably, the founder of a Pennsylvania library sought Oliver Optic's work as a substitute for the "kind of reading they are at now, . . . this abominable dime novel trash, and anything you will suggest about the selection of the books will be acceptable" (McKnight, 1868). Despite Alcott's much repeated complaint that his books weren't good for young readers, Adams, through *Oliver Optic's Magazine*, was credited with supporting a new free library run by a Children's Aid Society, ensuring that it was "well attended and is doing a great deal of good to which your magazine is ancillary" (Macy, 1867). Other institutions, like the Yonkers Military Institute, sent similar praise, calling *In School and Out* "an admirable book for boys" (Mason, 1864). Libraries established by the YMCA, missionary schools, and orphanages also regarded his work as ideal for young patrons (Rankin, 1871; Salter, 1870). Sometimes adults were motivated by nostalgia, as when Mrs. L. A. Wilkinson ordered *Sea and Shore, Or the Tramps of a Traveller*, recalling it as a title she once read and wanted to share with her children at Christmas (Wilkinson, 1876).

Fans' letters, sometimes written by his younger readers and sometimes by their guardians, reveal unchecked enthusiasm. There were autograph seekers (Elwell, n.d.; Fisher, 1884) and eager correspondents who acknowledged receiving letters from the famous author (Englebrecht, 1869), as well as fan mail that simply expressed interest in Oliver Optic's publications or anticipated sequels (Faunce, 1873; Keefer, 1865). One indulgent uncle recorded his nephew's determination that his friends should have copies of his favorite Optic books, as young Robert "was delighted with his Oliver Optics Library which I ordered for him at last Christmas, and has read the several volumes many times" (Fuller, 1862). More than one parent contacted Lee & Shepard on behalf of their children, though few with the open-handedness of T. Wilder Harris, who underwrote the purchases of "my Son, [who] wishes 'Down the Rhine,' and other books of you. Please sell him such as you can" (Harris, 1869). The words of Charles H. Hill, who noted that his son had part of an Optic series and now had "earned the money and wants the other two," represented a more typical purchaser (Hill, 1868). Sometimes a note of desperation appears, as when young C. W. McKisick penned a letter on his father's business stationery, seeking "the third book of the Young America Abroad by express COD and the rest of that series as soon as they are finished." He told Adams and his publishers that he owned "all the first series of *Young America Abroad* and though I have read a good many of his books I like them best of all." To his eager order he added a postscript: "Please send them as soon as you can for I want to read them mighty bad" (McKisick, 1873). His letter, and those of other readers, indicates something of the breadth and the tenor of the readership of Oliver Optic in nineteenth-century America. The books were found in private collections and circulating libraries, informing the experience of young people residing near Adams's home in Massachusetts and as far away as Hawaii, long before it became a U.S. territory.

While adults clearly read Oliver Optic titles, Lee & Shepard promoted Adams's potential as a children's author, and his books were advertised as "'among the most deservedly popular juveniles ever issued'" (Kilgour, 1965, p. 28). An obituary in *The Chautaquan* remembered him as "the favorite tale-teller of his majesty, the boy," and numerous other papers posthumously credited his importance to young readers ("William Taylor Adams," 1897, p. 205). Although older library borrowers borrowed his books for themselves or for their children, Adams's contemporaries knew him as a writer of stories for boys and girls. Thus, the many nineteenth-century libraries owning the Optic corpus did not have to worry that anxious parents might object to the titles made available to young readers. Children's guardians favored these titles, too.

CONCLUSION

Mothers and ministers bought Oliver Optic titles, and the surviving letters to Lee & Shepard indicate that although Adams's works are typically seen as written for boys, his audience was not limited to them (Wadsworth, 2001). Further, despite dramatic indictments of Oliver Optic in the professional literature, there are indications that numerous librarians incorporated substantive amounts of series fiction, particularly his work, into their collections and that when they did so, they responded to the enthusiasms of young readers and their guardians. Yet a considerable, nearly mythic view of the American public library as an entity that refused to collect works by Adams and his coterie persists (Pierce, 2007). Christine Pawley has demonstrated that writers like Adams, whose works were "'sometimes excluded from public libraries by reason of sensational or immoral qualities,'" were nonetheless found in the collection in Osage, Iowa (Pawley, 2000, p. 78). Our examination of Optic indicates that the phenomenon Pawley uncovered was widespread, that Optic was included in both librarians' lists of "excluded" authors and in their collections around the nation. Rather than the words of those who bought his works, which can be found in his publisher's files and the pages of his magazines, historians have focused on tales of exclusion, like the list put forth by the ALA Cooperation Committee, whose 1881 report Pawley cites, and the following recollection of an Optic fan: "Some years ago our Massachusetts State Library decided not to include the works of either juvenile writer [Optic and Horatio Alger] in its collection" (Hayward, 1956; Pawley, 2000, p. 78). Anecdotes like this, which strike present-day readers as overwrought and censorious, have diverted attention from the wider cultural resonance of the popular Oliver Optic titles published by Lee & Shepard.

The discourse surrounding the Optic empire suggests that contentions about moral uplift and censored reading as the driving impulses of youth services librarianship are one part of a more complex history of materials made available to young readers in the years following the founding of U.S. public libraries. Collectively, extant American public library records, publisher correspondence files, and other documents reposition the library collection with respect to its younger users and their demonstrable enthusiasm for tales incorporating technology and glimpses of a wider world. Multiple sources make evident that Optic titles had a place in U.S. public libraries and that librarians' public statements against series fiction were at odds with the endorsements of many adults, who encouraged children in their care to read the work of the man many knew as Oliver Optic.

Letters and, later, journalism show that Adams's readers remembered his stories fondly, sharing them with family and friends. The stories he wrote as Oliver Optic represented an expansive and changing American culture to avid young readers and, as a result, became tropes for subsequent discourse about these subjects. By focusing on technological innovation and expanding opportunities for travel, Adams committed the zeitgeist of the era to print, rendering it accessible to readers. His stories differed from classics that encouraged reverence for the world as it was, showing young readers that the world could be theirs. It was a message many carried into adulthood, as they ventured into college, careers, and families of their own.

NOTES

1. The authors wish to acknowledge and thank the American Antiquarian Society for its support of their research through the award of the Jay and Deborah Last Fellowship and Kate B. and Hall J. Peterson Fellowship, respectively.

2. For an extended discussion of child readers and citizenship in America through 1868, see: Weikle-Mills, C. (2013). *Imaginary citizens: Child readers and the limits of American independence, 1640–1868.* Baltimore: Johns Hopkins University Press.

3. Examples of the Optic signature may be found at Sept. 18, 1870, Dear Lee & Shepard . . . Oliver, Sept. 11, 1870, Dear Lee & Shepard, . . . Yours ever Oliver Optic.

4. On the origins of youth services librarianship, see also: Green, S. S. (1972). *The public library movement in the United States, 1853–1893*. Boston: Gregg Press. pp. 156–57.

REFERENCES

Abbott, C. E. (1864, February 4). [Letter to Lee and Shepard]. Lee and Shepard Papers, American Antiquarian Society, Worcester, MA.

Adams, W. T. (1853). *Hatchie, the guardian slave, or, the heiress of Bellevue. A tale of the Mississippi and the south-west.* Boston: B. B. Mussey and Co., R. B. Fitts. and Co.

Adams, W. T. (1866). *Brave old salt, or, Life on the quarter deck: A story of the great rebellion.* Boston: Lee & Shepard.

Ainsworth, C. W. (1869a, January 25). [Letter to Lee and Shepard]. Lee and Shepard Papers, American Antiquarian Society, Worcester, MA.

Ainsworth, C. W. (1869b, September 22). [Letter to Lee and Shepard]. Lee and Shepard Papers, American Antiquarian Society, Worcester, MA.

Ainsworth, C. W. (1869c, October 19). [Letter to Lee and Shepard]. Lee and Shepard Papers, American Antiquarian Society, Worcester, MA.

Alcott, L. M. (1874). *Eight cousins: Or, the aunt-hill.* Boston: Little, Brown and Company.

An ocean steamer. (1867, September 28). *Oliver Optic's Magazine: Our Boys and Girls, 2*, 520.

Arnold, R. (1871, December 6). [Letter to Lee and Shepard]. Lee and Shepard Papers, American Antiquarian Society, Worcester, MA.

Atkinson, W. P. (1879, September–1879, October). Sensational fiction in public libraries. *Library Journal, 4*. 359–62.

Baker, I. N. (1870, September 2). [Letter to Lee and Shepard]. Lee and Shepard Papers, American Antiquarian Society, Worcester, MA.

Ballard, J. P. (1867, May 25–1867, June 22). Greenland and Iceland. *Oliver Optic's magazine: Our boys and girls.*

Baughman, H. (1869, May 14). [Letter to Lee and Shepard]. Lee and Shepard Papers, American Antiquarian Society, Worcester, MA.

Bernier, A., Chelton, M. K., Jenkins, C. A., and Pierce, J. B. (2010, March 30). 200 years of young adult library services history: The chronology. *Voya*. Retrieved from http://www.voyamagazine.com/2010/03/30/chronology/

Best reading. (1886, May). *Library Journal, 11*, 142.

Books received. (1870, October 14). *Harvard Advocate, 10*(1), 10.

Brooks, E. S. (1895). On certain spring juveniles. *The Bookman, 1*, 405.

Carrier, E. J. (1985). *Fiction in public libraries, 1900–1950*. Littleton, CO: Libraries Unlimited.

Cassell's telegraph. (1868, March 14). *Oliver Optic's magazine: Our boys and girls*, 176.

Catalogue of the Elgin Public Library. (1874). Elgin, IL: The Advocate Power Print.

Catalogue of the English prose fiction and juvenile books in the Chicago Public Library (1889, January). Chicago: Library Rooms, City Hall.

Champney. (1868, May). [Letter to Lee and Shepard]. Lee and Shepard Papers, American Antiquarian Society, Worcester, MA.

Chase, M. G. (1873, May). Vienna. *Oliver Optic's magazine: Our boys and girls, 13*, 332–37.

Children's books of the year. (1866, January). *North American Review, 102*, 236–49.

Christie, A. A. (1869, February 23). [Letter to Lee and Shepard]. Lee and Shepard Papers, American Antiquarian Society, Worcester, MA.

Clarke, F. W. (1872, October). A talk about electricity. *Oliver Optic's magazine: Our boys and girls*, 687–89.

Corey, H. (1929, December). They turned a city around. *Nation's Business, 17*(3), 31.

Cost of boats. (1867). *Oliver Optic's magazine: Our boys and girls, 2*, 357.

Cotes, H. B. (1867, July 6–1868, February 8). Life in India. *Oliver Optic's magazine: Our boys and girls.*

Death of "Oliver Optic." Passed peacefully away at his home in Dorchester. (1897, March 28). *Sunday Herald*. Lee and Shepard Papers, American Antiquarian Society (Box 1, Folder 1), Worcester, MA.

Dorchester Atheneum. (2003, August 17). *William T. Adams, 1822–1897*. Retrieved from: http://www.dorchesteratheneum.org/page.php?id=51

Eddy, J. (2006). *Book women: Creating an empire in children's book publishing, 1919–1939*. Madison, WI: University of Wisconsin Press.

Editorial. (1875, September). *Oliver Optic's Magazine: Our Boys and Girls, 18*, 717–18.

Elwell, L. H. (n.d.). [Letter to Lee and Shepard]. Lee and Shepard Papers, American Antiquarian Society, Worcester, MA.

Englebrecht, C. F. (1869, August 11). [Letter to Lee and Shepard]. Lee and Shepard Papers, American Antiquarian Society, Worcester, MA.

Faunce, G. H. (1873, January 27). [Letter to Lee and Shepard]. Lee and Shepard Papers, American Antiquarian Society, Worcester, MA.

Fisher, M. (1884, November 10). [Letter to Lee and Shepard]. Lee and Shepard Papers, American Antiquarian Society, Worcester, MA.

Fuller, R. M. (1862, December 22). [Letter to Lee and Shepard]. Lee and Shepard Papers, American Antiquarian Society, Worcester, MA.

Geo. P. Rowell and Co.'s American newspaper directory. (1872). New York: Geo. P. Rowell & Co.

Geo. P. Rowell and Co.'s American newspaper directory. (1875). New York: Geo. P. Rowell & Co.

Gilmore, W. J. (1989). *Reading becomes a necessity of life: Material and cultural life in rural New England, 1780–1835*. Knoxville, TN: University of Tennessee Press.

Harris, T. W. (1869, December 20). [Letter to Lee and Shepard]. Lee and Shepard Papers, American Antiquarian Society, Worcester, MA.

Hayward, A. (1956, December 4). The rise of Oliver Optic. *Tel.* Lee and Shepard Papers, American Antiquarian Society (Box 1, Folder 1), Worcester, MA.

Hendler, G. (2001). Public sentiments: Structures of feeling in nineteenth century American literature. Chapel Hill: University of North Carolina Press.

Hill, C. H. (1868, October 6). [Letter to Lee and Shepard]. Lee and Shepard Papers, American Antiquarian Society, Worcester, MA.

Hopkins, C. E. (1870, June 18). [Letter to Lee and Shepard]. Lee and Shepard Papers, American Antiquarian Society, Worcester, MA.

How to build a boat. (1870, May 21). *Oliver Optic's magazine: Our boys and girls,* 328–29.

Hoyt, C. A. (1873, June). Silver mining. *Oliver Optic's magazine: Our boys and girls,* 406–12.

Insull in transportation: Electric railroads can make money! (1926, November 29). *Barron's,* 9.

International copyright. (1867, April 27). *Oliver Optic's magazine: Our boys and girls,* 199.

Jenkins, C. A. (2000). The history of youth services librarianship: A review of the research literature. *Libraries and Culture*, *35*(1), 103–40.

Johnson, D. (2002). From Abbott to Animorphs, from Godly Books to Goosebumps: The nineteenth-century origins of modern series. In L. C. Schurman and D. Johnson (Eds.) *Scorned literature: Essays on the history and criticism of popular mass produced fiction in America* (pp. 148–65). Westport, CT: Greenwood Press.

Jones, D. B. (1985). *An "Oliver Optic" checklist: An annotated catalog-index to the series, nonseries stories, and magazine publications of William Taylor Adams.* Westport, CT: Greenwood Press.

Keefer, E. (1865, July 24). [Letter to Lee and Shepard]. Lee and Shepard Papers, American Antiquarian Society, Worcester, MA.

Kilgour, R. L. (1965). *Lee and Shepard, publishers for the people*. Hamden, CT: Shoe String Press.

Library notes. (1886, April). *Library Journal*, *11*, 121.

Macy, J. (1867, January 29). [Letter to Lee and Shepard]. Lee and Shepard Papers, American Antiquarian Society, Worcester, MA.

Mason, B. (1864, May 2). [Letter to Lee and Shepard]. Lee and Shepard Papers, American Antiquarian Society, Worcester, MA.

May, S. (1869). *Dotty dimple at play*. Boston: Lee & Shepard. Retrieved from: https://books.google.com/books?id=558XAAAAYAAJ&dq=Dotty%20Dimple%20at%20Play&pg=PA1#v=onepage&q

McDowell, K. (2009). Toward a history of children as readers, 1890—1930. *Book History*, *12*, 240–65.

McKisick, C. W. (1873, January). [Letter to Lee and Shepard]. Lee and Shepard Papers, American Antiquarian Society, Worcester, MA.

McKnight, J. (1868, August 6). [Letter to Lee and Shepard]. Lee and Shepard Papers, American Antiquarian Society, Worcester, MA.

Mitts-Smith, D. (2007). L'heure joyeuse: Educational and social reform in post–World War I Brussels. *Library Trends*, *55*, 464–473. doi: 10.1353/lib.2007.0016

Nautical definitions. (1867, July 27–1867, August 17). *Oliver Optic's magazine: Our boys and girls*, 2, 373, 389, 405, 421.

News and Notes. (1895). *The Writer*, *55*, 42.

Obtaining patents. (1869, August 14). *Oliver Optic's magazine: Our boys and girls*, 528.

Office of the Historian, United States Department of State. (2013). *Milestones in the history of U.S. foreign relations*. Retrieved from: https://history.state.gov/milestones

Optic, O. (1868, September 5). Then and now, our little trip. *Oliver Optic's magazine: Our boys and girls,* 576–77.

Optic, O. (1869, September 4). Printing. *Oliver Optic's magazine: Our boys and girls,* 576.

Optic, O. (1870a, June 18). Editorial correspondence, II. *Oliver Optic's magazine: Our boys and girls,* 400.

Optic, O. (1870b, July 9). Editorial correspondence, V. *Oliver Optic's magazine: Our boys and girls,* 448.

Optic, O. (1870c, September 11). [Letter to Lee and Shepard]. Lee and Shepard Papers, American Antiquarian Society (Box 1, Folder 1), Worcester, MA.

Optic, O. (1870d, September 18). [Letter to Lee and Shepard]. Lee and Shepard Papers, American Antiquarian Society (Box 1, Folder 1), Worcester, MA.

Optic, O. (1870e, October 22). Editorial correspondence, XIX. *Oliver Optic's magazine: Our boys and girls,* 687–88.

Optic, O. (1871). *Through by daylight, or, the young engineer of the Lake Shore Railroad.* Boston: Lee & Shepard.

Optic, O. (1874, November). The City of Peking. *Oliver Optic's Magazine: Our Boys and Girls, 16,* 855–59.

Optic, O. (1899). *An undivided union.* Boston: Lee & Shepard Publishers.

Optic, O., et al. (1876). *The great bonanza: Illustrated narrative of adventure and discovery in gold mining, silver mining, among the raftsmen, in the oil regions, whaling, hunting, fishing and fighting*. Boston: Lee & Shepard.

Our letter bag. (1868, June 27). *Oliver Optic's magazine: Our boys and girls*, 415.

Our letter bag. (1871, October). *Oliver Optic's magazine: Our boys and girls, 10,* 688–89.

Parker, A. M. (1997). *Purifying America: Women, cultural reform, and pro-censorship activism, 1873–1933.* Urbana, IL: University of Illinois Press.

Patents. (1869, August 7). *Oliver Optic's magazine: Our boys and girls*, 512.

Pawley, C. (2000). *Reading on the middle border*. Amherst, MA: University of Massachusetts Press.

Pawley, C. (2007). Blood and thunder on the bookmobile: American public libraries and the construction of "the reader," 1950–1995. In T. Augst and K. E. Carpenter (Eds.), *Institutions of reading: The social life of libraries in the United States* (pp. 264–82). Boston: University of Massachusetts Press.

Pawley, C. (2009). Beyond market models and resistance: Organizations as a middle layer in the history of reading. *The Library Quarterly*, *79*(1), 73–93.

Pierce, J. B. (2007). "Why girls go wrong": Advising female teen readers in the early twentieth century. *Library Quarterly*, *77*(3), 311–26.

Pierce, J. B. (2011, July). *No more optical delusions: Science in the works of Oliver Optic*. Presented at the annual conference of the Society for the History of Authorship, Reading, and Publishing, Washington, D.C.

Pierce, J. B. (in press). The reign of children: The role of games and toys in American public libraries, 1876–1925. *Information & Culture*.

Pigeon-hole papers. (1871a, March). *Oliver Optic's magazine: Our boys and girls*, 201–2.

Pigeon-hole papers. (1871b, June). *Oliver Optic's magazine: Our boys and girls*, *9*, 408–9.

Pigeon-hole papers. (1871c, December). *Oliver Optic's magazine: Our boys and girls*, *10*, 833–34.

Pigeon-hole papers. (1872, November). *Oliver Optic's magazine: Our boys and girls*, 759–60.

Pigeon-hole papers. (1873a, April). *Oliver Optic's magazine: Our boys and girls*, *13*, 277–78.

Pigeon-hole papers. (1873b, October). *Oliver Optic's magazine: Our boys and girls*, *14*, 697–98.

Rankin, W. A. (1871, December 9). [Letter to Lee and Shepard]. Lee and Shepard Papers, American Antiquarian Society, Worcester, MA.

[Review of the book *Brake up; or the young peacemakers*]. (1870, March 18). *Harvard Advocate*, *9*(2), 28.

Robbins, L. S. (2000). *The dismissal of Miss Ruth Brown: Civil rights, censorship, and the American library*. Norman, OK: University of Oklahoma Press.

Salter, W. M. (1870, July 7). [Letter to Lee and Shepard]. Lee and Shepard Papers, American Antiquarian Society, Worcester, MA.

Sewing machines. (1867, April 20). *Oliver Optic's magazine: Our boys and girls*, 187.

Shera, J. H. (1965). *Foundations of the public library: The origins of the public library movement in New England, 1629–1855*. Chicago: University of Chicago Press.

Sicherman, B. (2000). The ideologies and practices of reading. In S. E. Casper, J. D. Groves, S. W. Nissenbaum, and M. Winship, (Eds.), *History of the book in America* (Vol. 3). Chapel Hill, NC: University of North Carolina Press.

Smith, D. M. (2012, March). *"For Minnie's Own Sake We Decline": Oliver Optic and the Young Women of* Our Boys and Girls. Paper presented at the meeting of the Northeast Modern Language Association, Rochester, NY.

Smith, D. M. (2015). *Print Networks and Youth Information Culture: Young People, Amateur Publishing, and Juvenile Periodicals, 1867–1890.* Unpublished doctoral dissertation, University of Illinois, Urbana-Champaign. In progress.

Somers, T. H. (1864, July 9). [Letter to Lee and Shepard]. Lee and Shepard Papers, American Antiquarian Society, Worcester, MA.

Stoneley, P. (2007). *Consumerism and American girls' literature, 1860–1940*. Cambridge, UK: Cambridge University Press.

Supplementary catalogue of books added to the San Francisco Free Public Library since May 1884 (No. 5, 1888). (1889). San Francisco: H. S. Crocker & Company.

The new tunnel. (1875, July). *Oliver Optic's Magazine: Our Boys and Girls*, *18*, 558.

The type-writer. (1875, May). *Oliver Optic's magazine: Our boys and girls,* 398.

Velocipedes. (1869, May 1–1869, May 29). *Oliver Optic's magazine: Our boys and girls,* 285, 301, 317, 333, 349.

Wadsworth, S. (2001). Louisa May Alcott, William T. Adams, and the rise of gender-specific books. *The Lion and the Unicorn*, *25*(1), 17–46.

Wilkinson, L. A. (1876, December 10). [Letter to Lee and Shepard]. Lee and Shepard Papers, American Antiquarian Society, Worcester, MA.

William Taylor Adams ("Oliver Optic"). (1897, May). *The Chautauquan*, *25*, 205.

Young, A. P. (2013). Banish the books: Horatio Alger, Jr., the censors, the libraries, and the readers, 1870–1910. *Children's Literature Association Quarterly*, *38*, 420–34. doi: 10.1353/chq.2013.0058

Zboray, R. J. (1993). *A fictive people: Antebellum economic development and the American reading public*. New York: Oxford University Press.

Chapter Sixteen

New Mediations of Native Cultural Heritage

The Case of the TimeTraveller™ Machinima Project

Iulian Vamanu

ABSTRACT

Since the early 1990s, indigenous artists have adapted new media technologies to create innovative forms of art and to promote the cultural heritage of their tribes and Nations within the broader society. This process of art creation has involved both a critical and an affirmative dimension: not only have Native artists addressed stereotypical representations of Native heritage circulating in the mainstream media and Academia, but they have also proposed imaginative stories of Native lives and cultures. My study explores these two dimensions in the case of TimeTraveller™, a recent machinima series conceived and produced by Mohawk artist Skawennati. This project plays on the time-travel theme to imagine what Native life and heritage may look like in the future. Based on a discourse-analytic approach of the series and of the artist's scholarly and interview statements, the study claims that TimeTraveller™ challenges what I call the "Discontinuity narrative"—a major stereotypical scenario that downplays Native peoples and their cultural heritage as inexistent, thereby contributing to the erasure of Indigenous presence in North America. The study shows how TimeTraveller™ proposes powerful counter-narratives to this stereotypical narrative and how the availability and use of new media technology for artistic purposes contributes to a redefinition of the very meaning of Native cultural heritage.

INTRODUCTION AND BACKGROUND

The invisibility of Indigeneity is a predicament deplored by both researchers of the phenomenon and activists (Hopkins, 2011; Mithlo, 2008; Nason, 2000;

Rickard, 2007; Smith, 2009). It conveys the notion that Native peoples and their heritage are still present in our societies, albeit in highly inconspicuous ways. Prominent Indigenous curator Jolene Rickard traced the cause of this situation back to what she called the "ongoing erasure of Indigenous presence in the Americas since contact" (Rickard, 2007, p. 91). In other words, she associates the idea of American Indian peoples and their heritage being invisible nowadays with a certain visual understanding of presence: what is present is usually out there for us to see, yet there are situations in which presence is less obvious or even downright unrecognizable. Critical efforts—by scholars, artists, and activists—focus on identifying and addressing the processes through which Native presence is erased and, thus, made invisible. Some of the most interesting such mechanisms are of symbolic (or discursive) nature; after all, one of the key insights of discourse theory—the theory that claims that social phenomena are constructed discursively—is that any discourse constitutes veritable spaces of visibility for some objects, while at the same time leaving other objects invisible. What is visible exists, what is invisible (or erased) is, if not theoretically at least practically, inexistent.[1]

Presence understood as visibility is usually a spatial term: something that is present occupies a certain place in the world, has a location in space such that one can usually distinguish it. Yet presence can also be a temporal notion. In this less common sense, something (a community, cultural and heritage objects and practices, etc.) may be said to be actual, to exist "in the present," that is, the "right now" dimension of time. To frame the presence of Indigenous heritage—the object of interest in this study—as a temporal phenomenon amounts to conceiving it in terms of possible links between various constructions of the three basic temporal axes (i.e., the past, the present, and the future). French cultural theorist Michel de Certeau proposed a similar approach when he emphasized the different ways in which time (i.e., the relationships between past, present, and future) is assumed to function in historiography and psychoanalysis:

> Psychoanalysis recognises the past in the present; historiography places them one beside the other. Psychoanalysis treats the relation as one of imbrication (one in the place of the other), of repetition (one reproduces the other in another form), of the equivocal and of the *quiproquo* (What "takes the place" of what? Everywhere, there are games of masking, reversal, and ambiguity). Historiography conceives the relation as one of succession (one after the other), correlation (greater or lesser proximities), cause and effect (one follows from the other), and disjunction (either one or the other), but not both at the same time. (de Certeau, 1986, p. 4; author's italics.)

Just like de Certeau's historiography, we can argue that the dominant discourse within which we operate in the Academy, popular culture, and media encourages a view of the flow of time (that is, of how people understand time in their everyday life) in terms of the three well-known, yet discrete, components: past, present, and future. These are assumed to be discontinuous moments of time, that is, separated from one another in such a way that the present cannot exist unless the past is left behind, and the future becomes reality by negating the present. I claim that this assumption about the segmentation of time into three self-sufficient temporal stages enables the production and circulation of various types of stereotypes about Indigenous peoples and their heritage.

Native curators and artists have attempted to address such stereotypes in their art and scholarly works and, thus, to critically and creatively redefine Native cultural heritage in the context of the emerging digital environment. Since the early 1990s, indigenous artists (K. C. Adams, Dana Claxton, Stephen Foster, Skawennati Tricia Fragnito, Ahasiw Maskegon-Iskwew, and Archer Pechawis, among others) adapted new media technologies to protect and promote the cultural heritage of their tribes and Nations within the broader society (Guglietti, 2009; Hopkins, 2006, 2008; Lewis, 2004, 2012, 2014; Lewis and Fragnito, 2005, 2012; Loft, 2005, 2009; Todd, 2006). As Lewis and Fragnito (2012) claim, "the era of networked digital media presents a unique opportunity for Aboriginal people to present a self-determined image to the world" (p. 206). This process of generating new art forms involves a *critical* dimension whereby artists point to and address stereotypical representations of Native heritage circulating in the Academy, popular culture, and media, as well as an *affirmative* dimension whereby artists tell imaginative stories: "what stories do we want to tell? First and foremost, we are imagining Native people in the future. Who will we be? What past achievements will we be proud of? How will we participate in contemporary society? What technologies will we be using? How will we contribute to their development, their look and feel, and their use?" (Lewis and Fragnito, 2012, p. 207).

METHODOLOGICAL CONSIDERATIONS

To explore the *critical* and *affirmative* dimensions of Indigenous art creation, my study focuses on TimeTraveller™, a digital project which has been designed, written, directed, and edited since 2007 by Skawennati Tricia Fragnito, a Mohawk new media artist from Canada, with the help of executive producer Jason Edward Lewis, a Cherokee media artist and professor of computational arts at Concordia University in Canada.[2] The project runs seventy-five minutes in nine short machinima films about Hunter, a skillful, young Mohawk living in 2121.[3] Bored by the consumer-driven society in which he lives, Hunter uses immersive technology (in the form of a sophisticated pair of glasses) to travel through time and experience significant moments in the past history of North American Native peoples (e.g., the Minnesota Massacre in 1875, the occupation of Alcatraz Island in 1969, and the Oka/Mohawk Crisis at Kanesatake in 1990); his goal, in his own words, is to "learn more about [his] heritage" (Episode 9). Based on this reconstructed look of the past, TimeTraveller™ "paint[s] at least one possible future history" (Lewis, 2012, p. 20) of Indigenous peoples (e.g., a hypothetical Manito Ahbee intergalactic powwow at the Olympic Stadium in Winnipeg in 2112). Reflecting on this futuristic work, the creator and the producer of this unique project suggest that "[t]hese past, present and future imaginaries provide us with a palette to work through questions about historical accuracy and perspective, speculative history, the dreams of and goals for the near and far future we have for our peoples, and the contingencies of intellectual 'proof'" (Lewis and Fragnito, 2012, p. 207). It is precisely one of the goals of my study to show how the notion of Native cultural heritage is redefined through such new media art projects.

I analyzed the visual and textual contents of a set of documents in order to explore whether and, if so, how, they address a major stereotypical narrative about Indigenous peoples and their heritage, which I found to be of particular interest to Native curators and artists and which I labeled the "Discontinuity narrative" (Vamanu, 2014). Grounded in a particular assumption about the past as a discrete temporal unit, namely one that is disconnected from the present and the future, this narrative downplays, and even rejects, Indigenous peoples and their heritage as inexistent, thereby contributing to the erasure of Indigenous presence in North American societies.

The documents I analyzed are the following: the nine episodes of the machinima series produced by Skawennati (together with Lewis), seven of their relevant scholarly publications (two cowritten articles, two articles by Skawennati, and three articles by Lewis), one publicly available interview in which Skawennati elaborates on her artistic vision and projects, as well as an open-ended in-depth interview I conducted with her in 2010 (as part of my research for my doctoral dissertation). I aimed to reconstruct the strategies by means of which they respond to what they perceive to be a major threat to Indigenous heritage. Such strategies constitute part of what discourse research calls "phenomenal structure" (Keller, 2013, p. 114) of a phenomenon (Indigenous heritage, in this case).[4]

FINDINGS AND INTERPRETATION

My study claims that the TimeTraveller™ machinima series challenges the "Discontinuity narrative" by proposing three powerful counter-narratives to it. Moreover, it shows how the availability and use of new media technology for artistic purposes supports these counter-narratives and contributes to a redefinition of the very meaning of Native cultural heritage.

The Discontinuity Narrative

A widely spread stereotype about Indigenous peoples and heritage informs, at least in part, the academic disciplines (like anthropology, art history, and historiography) and most of the popular culture and media; I called it "the Discontinuity narrative" (Vamanu, 2014). According to its raw scenario, "real" or "pure" Indian peoples and cultures existed only in the past: "there are no more Indians [today]—they all died;" moreover, Indian cultures are "a relic of the past" (Nason, 2000, pp. 37–39) and were replaced by the "dominant, mainstream American" culture (Dartt-Newton, 2012). In "freezing [Indian peoples and cultures] in the past" (Hopkins, 2011, p. 13), academia and the media have achieved a consistent negation of "the reality of a continuing Indian presence" in North America (Nason, 2000, p. 37).

A major problem associated with this symbolic construction of the Indian past is that it produces concrete material effects. For instance, many museum exhibits focusing on American history and civilization are organized along the lines of this problematic narrative and, thus, contribute, in turn, to the reinforcing of the stereotype. As Chumash museum curator and artist Deana Dartt-Newton puts it, such exhibits "portray . . . a chronological trajectory where the Indians are only at the beginning of the story—literally placed at the entry of the exhibit spaces, but left behind in every way" (Dartt-Newton, 2012). In consequence, visitors are led to believe that Indigenous peoples and their heritage is a closed chapter in the history of the Americas.

The Discontinuity narrative is grounded in the seemingly sound reasoning scheme according to which the past is isolated from both the present and the future, and Indians and their cultures belong to the past. Hence, there is no way they may exist in the present, let alone claim a presence for themselves in the future. Roughly put, what belongs to the past stays in the past.

Indigenous curators and artists devised three main lines of response to undermine this narrative and its underlying reasoning scheme: critiquing fake images of the past, focusing attention on the present, and imagining possible futures for Indigenous peoples and their heritage. I claim that, and, in what follows, show how, the TimeTraveller™ machinima enacts all these lines of response; moreover, I illustrate how representations of the three seemingly discrete moments of time blend together in imaginative ways.

Critique of Fake Images of the Native Past

One of the three strategies Indigenous curators and artists employ to challenge the Discontinuity narrative involves the questioning of the dominant stereotyping view of the Indian past—one that pervades both the academy and popular culture, including virtual environments. As the creator and the producer of the TimeTraveller™ machinima series note: "Representations of Indigenous characters in video games are rare and, in the few instances where such characters appear, are based on stereotypical caricatures flowing from deep ignorance about both the history and present reality of Indigenous people" (Lewis, 2014, p. 64). Specifically, the anti-Discontinuity strategy consists of a critique of the distorted representations of Indians peoples and their heritage circulated though the Academy and media. This critique may take the form of "a story featuring Indians as actors on the world stage and not merely victims, . . . a story of . . . the greatest mass human extinction in history, and the countless ways Indians survived and triumphed in the face of adversity (Smith, 2005, n.p.).

The TimeTraveller™ series embeds many examples of this strategy. For instance, in its first episode, the protagonist (Hunter), who—we remember—lives in one of *our* futures, decides to use a time-traveling technology that has just been made available and is advertised on the television as follows:

> Travelling through time these days is easy, thanks to TimeTraveller™! Witness important historical events or interact with the people who made them happen. You can even customize your own events and visit with your great-great-great-great-grand mother. . . . All customized characters must have existed. It's easy and fun. (Episode 1.)

After listening to the advertisement, Hunter makes the following comment to clarify to us the marvels this new immersive technology can achieve: "It takes all the known facts about a particular event in history—a speech, a battle, a day-in-the-life of [someone]—and recreates it for you in living color. It's basically like going into a full-on, 3D chat room and hanging out with famous dead people, like Geronimo" (Episode 1). Any time traveler is, thus, able to witness events in either a fly-on-the-wall or an interactive mode. If in the former mode, they may get to know the historical characters involved (their thoughts, feelings, and so on), but they obviously cannot change the course of history. From this point of view, the time traveler is the perfect participant observer, as he or she can learn how historical events actually unfolded, but without disturbing the "field" through his or her sheer presence, as it usually happens in ethnographic undertakings.

Prodded by his long-standing interest in the art of combat, in which he claims to display the same proficiency as his ancestors—from whom he learned the relevant skills—Hunter embarks on a first such endeavor and visits (in Episode 1) the scene of the only massacre perpetrated, according to Google-based statistics, by Indians themselves, rather than by the British colonists, as the story goes. As he confesses, he is interested in participating in "some good old-fashioned killing." Hunter first arrives at the scene of what looks like a propaganda session, in which white officers seated on benches are briefed about an alleged massacre of Minnesota white farmers. We are in 1862, and Hunter summarizes what he sees in a fly-on-the-wall mode as follows:

> This one Sioux hunter dares his friend to kill this white farmer, so the friend kills the farmer's whole family. Then all the Sioux go on a rampage and kill hundreds of settlers: they cut off people's heads, rape women, torture children, and loot a few towns. It really gets the audience riled up. This ridiculous, unsophisticated agitprop has done the trick. And if I was one of these guys [i.e., the soldiers on the benches], I'd be ready to kill the savages too. But I'm not buying it. If there's one thing every Indian knows, it's this: when it comes to history, always get a second opinion. (Episode 1.)

It is precisely this advice that Hunter is bent on following and, equipped with his miraculous glasses, pays a visit to the four Sioux tribesmen who took part in the bloody events at the farm (in Acton Township, Minnesota, year 1862). He is now willing and able to interact with them (speaking and understanding their language, feeling what they feel), so he decides to switch from the fly-on-the-wall to the interactive mode of the glasses. It does not take too long for him to learn that the Indian Federal Bureau agents did not pay them their due rent (as stipulated in the two treaties from 1851), so they are not able to buy food. The group decides to visit a local farmer to ask for food, under the assumption that this neighbor will act as a good Christian. However, they soon face an angry farmer with a rifle in his hands, shouting in a raspy voice: "Get off my land!"—after which he withdraws behind his house's door. The rather bemused and amused Sioux depart, but are stopped on their way by the farmer and three other persons (two men and one woman). They loom menacingly from the house's open doors and windows, pointing their rifles at the Indians. The farmer thunders again, "Nobody threatens me on my own land! Go back to where you came from!" After a moment of loaded silence, one "grumpier" Sioux opens fire, kills the farmer, after which the situation degenerates into what Hunter calls, "a classic case of 'kill or be killed.'" The farmer's acolytes are killed in the brawl. A girl is later found dead in the house, clearly a collateral victim, much to the distress of the Sioux warriors. Hunter reports that a full-fledged massacre against the Sioux ensues, which he can luckily shun. He concludes:

> This little skirmish kicked off an all-out war: the Dakota Sioux vs. the United States. My crew plus hundreds of their fellow tribesmen were accused of treason. Of them, thirty-seven Indians were hung in the largest mass execution in America ever. In other words, we're the worst bunch of criminals this country has ever seen. Maybe our problem is bad press. (Episode 2.)

This kind of story, presented in the form of a machinima (as an interactive media combining film and game features), challenges received (and, as a rule, distorted) narratives about Native peoples and their heritage in a very innovative fashion. As the creator and the producer of TimeTraveller™ emphasize, the series "paints a picture that consciously seeks to perturb accepted history" (Lewis, 2012, p. 23). The notion of "paint[ing] a picture" should be taken literally: this machinima reconstitutes, in the form of a visually compelling and entertaining narrative, the Indians' version of how various (often unfortunate) events in the American history most likely unfolded. We, spectators, know that what we see is fiction, yet this fiction captures how things may have looked from the point of view of the Native themselves: we actually receive the events through the eyes, ears, and mind of the Mohawk protagonist and can, thus, identify better with his point of view.

(Re)focusing Attention on the Present

At the same time as they are reshaping the past from the perspectives of the Native peoples, Indigenous curators and artists are pressing for a reinvigorated attention to a "dynamic present" (Rickard, 2011, p. 472), more specifically to "a different kind of today, where [Indians] are present in the world like everyone else," since they have always been "trying to be part of the world" (Smith, 2009, p. 101). This redirection of attention to the significance of the present often involves a continuously renewed, though by no means easy, strategy of projecting into the public sphere Native images of Indians living in the present. Focusing on such multimodal media as the museum exhibitions, Chumash curator Deana Dartt-Newton recommends that Indigenous curators focus on depicting Native peoples in all their appearances—whether or not they "look 'Native,'" whether or not they are engaged in "'traditional' cultural practices"—on addressing "the actual history of place in text panels," and on "show[ing] maps of displacement of local people and discuss[ing] what this meant for identity and cultural knowledge for the people" (Dartt-Newton, 2012).

This present-oriented strategy is well illustrated by the creator and the producer of the TimeTraveller™ machinima. The sense that Indians are actually part of the present is reinforced, first, by the fact that the Hunter character addresses us, the viewers, as if we were part of a conversation with him happening right here and right now; and second, by the fact that we "see" him actually living in one of our possible futures (i.e., in the twenty-second century) and being able to travel back to our present (i.e., in the twenty-first century). The first episode actually opens with a scene in which Hunter presents himself as a Mohawk living in the present (in fact, *his* present, which is, in fact, one of our possible futures): "My name is . . . Hunter. I'm a Mohawk, not a Mohican, ok?

We survived" (Episode 1). What strikes us immediately is the performative assertion that the Mohawk people managed to survive. More precisely, Hunter's talking to us is the best proof that he (and his people) have existed all along (in *our* and *his* present). This form of self-presentation is obviously meant to make a head-on critical statement about the Discontinuity narrative, which, we intuit, runs tacitly in the background. The same statement is made even more explicit in a brief dialogue between Hunter and his new girlfriend, Karahkwenhawi, a Mohawk girl living in *our* present (i.e., 2011), but who has the opportunity to travel through time. After she reaches the future (i.e., Hunter's present) and learns that the major Nations have separated from Canada and formed independent confederacies, she exclaims: "I thought you said there weren't any Indians around these days. We're stronger than ever." To this, Hunter responds: "I never said that. I said I wanted to learn more about my heritage" (Episode 9). Here is an indirect acknowledgment of the fact that even Indians living in the future (*our* future, which is *their* present) are still decoupled from their heritage and in need of reconnection with it.

Refocusing attention to the present involves emphasizing the "spilling over" of past realities into the present. One such type of continuity the TimeTraveller™ makes obvious is that of family lines. Specifically, it plays with the notion of generational survival and continuity: Hunter's travels through time are ways for him to see Mohawk families evolve. For instance, he travels to Kanehsatake (Canada), during the famous Mohawk Crisis of 1990 over land ownership, and meets a young Mohawk and her six-year-old daughter named Karahkwenhawi. He helps them during the evacuation process of the Treatment Center, where the fifty Mohawk warriors established their headquarters. We encounter Karahkwenhawi and her mother again after twenty years, in 2011, and we also see the young woman in 1969 (still *our* past), as well as in 2112 and 2121 (*our* possible future).

By allowing the characters to jump from one moment of history to another, the time-traveling device makes family ties that bind Indigenous people across time more palpable. It also relativizes the discreteness of the three temporal moments.

Imagining the Indian Future: "But the Best Stuff Is the Future, My Future"

Arguably, the most innovative strategy for addressing the Discontinuity narrative emphasizes less (or at least not directly) the past or even present-day Indians and their heritage, and more the Indians conceivably living in the future. The reason may be that, as a rule, Indigenous curators and artists have preferred to focus on contesting dominant views of the Indian past or on drawing attention to the predicament of present-day Indigenous peoples. They have barely dealt with the issue of the future as a horizon for reflecting on possible ways in which Indigenous peoples and their heritage may exist (Lewis, 2014). In this respect, the creator and the producer of the TimeTraveller™ series occupy a key position, as they display a keen interest in the affordances of the new media technologies for addressing the issue of representation of Indigenous peoples and their heritage in the future. In this context, the word "representation" refers both to the way Indians are being depicted in the old and new media and to the extent they are present at all in the collective imaginaries of the future (as reflected, for instance, in science-fiction literature, film, and gaming). On the one hand, Lewis and Skawennati are uneasy about the almost total absence of Indian traces in the collective futuristic imaginaries, irrespective of the medium of expression through which these imaginaries are made available to us. As the two authors claim, "we do not tend to spend much time imagining what our communities will be like in one hundred, five hundred, or a thousand years. . . . Our absence from the future imaginaries of the settler culture should worry us. Absence implies non-existence, or, at the very least, non-importance" (Lewis, 2014, pp. 56–58). What seems to be at stake here is a most concrete and worrisome effect this type of invisibility can have on the present: "A people that are absent in the future need not be consulted in the present about how that future comes about" (p. 58). On the other hand, Lewis and Skawennati point to the availability of new media technologies—included under the label of "cyberspace"[5]—which present Native artists and curators, first, with opportunities for making the imaginaries of the future more inclusive and, second, with means for controlling the media representations of Indigeneity (i.e., what defines Indigenous peoples and their ways of being in the world).

Indians in(to) the Future

Lewis (2014) approaches the first of the two above-mentioned goals by means of a metaphor: their aim as new media artists is to "tell a story [that reflects] on how [Indians] might sail the sea of cyberspace as a means of dreaming forth a future" (p. 58). The metaphor of sailing (presumably unknown) waters is apposite in this context: it brings forth a sense of a medium that enables exploration and discovery, but also the grounding or instituting of new dwellings, new forms of life, and new communities, among other things. Just like the imaginary domain, cyberspace is as open and rich in possibilities as the seas. In addition, this metaphor cannot but conjure up the imagery of the Spanish, British, and French colonizers who "discovered" and explored/exploited the two Americas. However, the implication seems to be that, possibly for the first time, American Indians themselves are ready to engage in a kind of activity that is both similar and different: it is structurally similar in that it takes the form of exploration; but it is different because the aim is no longer colonization in the traditional sense. Lewis makes this point even clearer in an interview, where he claims that,

> Cyberspace has no native population that might contest the notion that it is *terra nullius* and thus subject to control by the first immigrants who might claim it. The resources in cyberspace are not timber, game and gold; they are processing power, bandwidth, networks and data, which, in dutiful accordance with Moore's Law, increase at a dizzying rate. The stakes are not those of survival, but of prosperity. And we're not just colonizing the place, we're making it up as we go. (Lewis, 2004, n.p.)

In this quotation, Lewis suggests that cyberspace constitutes a territory with practically unlimited resources; anybody can be an "explorer"—using these resources not so much to colonize (in the traditional sense of the word), as to actually create that territory. In this respect, competition may refer less to fighting for resources, and more to the excess of creativeness generating prosperity in an overly accommodating and presumably democratic environment.

Controlling Media Representations of Indigeneity

As far as the second goal is concerned, the two authors suggest that, "as a new territory, as a new frontier," the cyberspace allows Native artists and curators to generate, among other things, adequate representations of Indigeneity—"to assert control over how we represent ourselves to each other and to non-Aboriginals" (Lewis and Fragnito, 2005, p. 29). This possibility takes on imperative accents, which is all the more important, because, even when figuring in futuristic scenarios, Natives are represented distortedly, "based on stereotypical caricatures flowing from deep ignorance about both the history and present reality of Indigenous people" (p. 64).

Skawennati claims that—in contrast to the past, when Indigenous peoples were in front of, rather than behind the camera—the present is a horizon opening up new possibilities: specifically, the new immersive technologies constitute "one of the first media that aboriginal peoples have a chance to be in on a ground floor," a media within which they can represent themselves. The ideal is, in this case, to create "more representations of ourselves across cyberspace" (Skawennati, personal interview, August 20, 2010). The two authors are confident that present-day Indigenous media artists and curators are skillful enough to achieve this representational goal. In this respect, both artists invoke the notion of adaptability: they claim that, as a matter of fact, Natives have always been able to resist attempts by the majority to dissolve their identities (by assimilation or even by annihilation), and have rather adapted themselves quite proficiently to new (and often hostile) circumstances. Borrowing and adjusting new technologies to their specific needs is a good example of successful adaptation. In this respect, Fragnito (2002) is amazed about the fact that,

> in the year 2000, despite numerous attempts to the contrary, First Nations people still exist as distinct nations and are stronger than ever. The strength of a people is a function of their adaptability. Technologies and customs brought to us by Europeans—such as writing, law and a thing called art—did not serve to assimilate us. Instead, we absorbed them and have learned to use them to our advantage. We have our own writers to tell our stories. We understand the law and go to court to regain title to our lands or to ensure the correct interpretation of our treaties. And we have our own artists, whose images and ideas reflect our contemporary world. (p. 229.)

In the context of this felt need by Native peoples to write their own stories, the creator and the producer of TimeTraveller™ emphasize that futuristic representations of Natives in the cyberspace will need to represent the Indigenous peoples no longer as "just survivors," but rather as "fully participating, empowered members of society, of contemporary, thoroughly modern, futuristic society" (Fragnito, nd). Their machinima series actually illustrates well the shift from the survival to the empowerment model. For instance, Hunter presents himself as follows:

> Like my father and my father's father, I can use a bow and arrow like nobody's business. I can also paddle a canoe faster than most speedboats. . . . And like the legends say, I can walk the high steel without a worry. Hell, I can do gymnastics up there. All these traditional skills would've made me one serious breadwinner once. . . . But today, in an over-mediated, hyper-consumerist North America, where there isn't enough room for everybody, I have to be content with being a ruthless, efficient, cold-blooded killer. And that pisses me off. (Episode 1.)

As these facts—conveying the notion of a continuity of warrior traditions and practices—are disclosed to us, we actually see Hunter skillfully handling various types of weapons, from more traditional (e.g., bow and arrows) to more futuristic ones (e.g., a Star Wars type of force light saber). In what recalls a piece of social Darwinist ideology, he portrays himself as an example of the citizen fit for the society in which he lives, applying the traditional skills of his tribe to new and sophisticated weapons.

Another illustration of the empowerment representational imperative centers on the now twenty-six-year-old Karahkwenhawi and her travel to the future. While doing research on Kateri Tekakwitha—a seventeenth century Mohawk Catholic saint—at Francis Xavier Mission, in Kahnawake, she perceives, for a brief moment, an apparition of Hunter, whom she recognizes as her protector during the Mohawk war from 1990. Hunter disappears, but not before his glasses drop inadvertently to the floor. Karahkwenhawi retrieves them, (expectedly) puts them on, but notices they are not usual glasses. Hence, she will attempt to figure out how they work and how to use them to find Hunter. She manages to voyage to the future (2112), more precisely to the Olympic Stadium in Winnipeg, where she participates in a lavish Manito Ahbee intergalactic powwow. The ceremony includes a fashion show where young Native girls display clothing with Indigenous themes. The general tone is celebratory, especially since the host reminds the Indigenous audience that powwows were once forbidden in the public space, but that their ancestors managed to survive and to find ways to continue convening secretly.

Blending of Genres and Temporal Dimensions

One cannot miss, in this context, the fact that the futuristic machinima technology employed in the TimeTraveller™ project allows for surprising types of blending (e.g., of genres and of temporal dimensions). Its rhetorical function in the story is to render the portraits of future Indians more palpable.

First, the series builds on a blending of genres. For instance, traditional Native and cyber-punk motives fuse together in providing a possible face of the culture within which Indians of the future may live. This is obvious in people's way of dressing and sporting their hair in the Winnipeg scene (Episode 4).

Second, the series also plays on an obvious blending of temporal dimensions that well serves the critique of the Discontinuity narrative. For instance, Hunter addresses us, the spectators, as his contemporaries. Yet, we know that he is a Mohawk living in one of our possible futures. He travels to his past (*our* present) to meet Karahkwenhawi (when she is young), as well as to our (and his) past, to meet Karahkwenhawi (when she is only a girl) and her mother. Moreover, the young woman is also able to travel to, and actually live in, the future. The three temporal dimensions melt together into the present time of our participation, as spectators, in Hunter and Karahkwenhawi's time-traveling endeavor. There is at least one telling scene in this respect: in the last episode of the series, we follow Karahkwenhawi, who traveled to the future to meet with Hunter. While walking through a futuristic-looking museum, where early twenty-first century Indigenous artifacts are exhibited, she experiences a moment of illumination: "As I stood there I felt all of time collapsing into one moment, and I knew I was where and when I was supposed to be" (Episode 9). The scene is important because it gives voice to a fundamental Indigenous (Mohawk) experience of temporality as nondiscrete, that is, as fusing together the past, present, and future.

Heritage and Love

Moreover, I argue that this notion of temporality, in which past, present, and future fuse together, provides the background against which two major themes, namely heritage and love, intersect. Hunter puts it clearly, more than once, that he is interested in learning more about his heritage. Yet, what he actually finds, in moving back and forth through time, is love. Karahkwenhawi too is looking (for Hunter) and finds him in *her* future; yet what she also finds is something possibly more surprising, namely love. In fact, a whole episode (Episode 8) is devoted to the development of the relationship between the two young Mohawks, which shows that this theme is central to the series. In what I believe is another key scene in this series, we are brought back to 2011 and can see the young woman approaching her mother in the kitchen of their house, where she explains to her how the TimeTraveller™ glasses function and, finally, discloses Hunter's invitation: "They're glasses from the future. Hunter lives in year 2121, . . . I can use them to visit Hunter in the future. Mum, he's asked me to come and live with him in the future. . . ." (Episode 9). After the young woman confesses to her mother her love for Hunter (and, implicitly, her desire to move to *his* present to live with him), her mother exclaims, "I guess it's true what they say, then: Be careful what you wish for!" (Episode 9).

For both Hunter and Karahkwenhawi, then, searching for heritage (as their way to develop a better understanding of themselves as Mohawk people) unfolds as an experience of discovering love. Thus, what emerges from this series is that heritage means more than just history and traditional artifacts. Heritage also involves patterns of relationship people have with themselves and with the others—patterns they learn from ancestors and teach to their descendants in an unbroken generational chain. This notion of heritage resonates well with a claim Skawennati made when I asked her about her view of Aboriginal cultural heritage. She said that heritage is "something that we carry within ourselves, that we know. . . . It's what I grew up knowing. It's almost so inside of me that it's very hard to define." Mohawk heritage encompasses such things as "the way we talk to our children, [and] the expectations we have of them and of ourselves" (Skawennati, personal interview, August 20, 2010). In other words, the heritage of a community should be assumed as including not only traditional objects and practices, but also ways of being in the world exemplified by its members. Love, courage, and humor are perennial features describing human beings and their relationships, yet the challenge is to capture their possible nuances in the lives of Indians from the future. I believe the TimeTraveller™ machinima has taken up this challenge successfully.

CONCLUSION

I started this study based on the premise that a major stereotypical narrative about Indigenous peoples and their heritage circulates through the Academy, popular culture, and media; in a previous work, I had labeled it the "Discontinuity narrative" (Vamanu, 2014). This is a narrative grounded on the Western European assumption that time is constituted by a concatenation of three distinct moments (past, present, and future). In a map of the dominant understandings of the relationships between the three temporal moments, the past is construed as absent from the present (and, hence, from the future). Projected stereotypically onto Indigenous peoples and their heritage, the Discontinuity narrative downplays, and even rejects, Indigenous peoples and their heritage as inexistent, thereby contributing to the erasure of Indigenous presence in North American societies.

Based on this premise, I explored the efforts of such Indigenous curators and artists as Skawennati Tricia Fragnito and Jason Edward Lewis to address this stereotypical scenario, which they find detrimental to the well-being of Native communities and their heritage. The two artists employ new media technologies and scholarly venues to critique fake images of the Indian past, to refocus attention on the present, and to imagine versions of a possible "Indian future." The third strategy is their most innovative: Skawennati and Lewis deplore the absence of Indigenous peoples from the imaginaries of the future and suggest that (and show how) new media technologies provide Native artists and curators with the means to make the imaginaries of the future more inclusive (and populate the cyberspace with American Indian characters) and to control the representations of Indigeneity in the virtual environment. They argue that Native peoples have always adapted new technologies to the purposes and ideals they happened to espouse in the past and, thus, managed not only to survive but, more importantly, to thrive in often hostile environments. Through their TimeTraveller™ machinima series, which is a work of fiction blending genres and temporal dimensions, Skawennati and Lewis aim to project a compelling picture of a possible Indian future. The notion of temporality this digital project privileges—that is, one in which past, present, and future fuse together, rather than subsisting in isolation from one another—provides the background against which its two authors explore two major interrelated themes: heritage and love. Indigenous heritage is recast as including not only the usual items (such as traditional artifacts and practices) but also ways of being in the world that have defined and soldered generations of American Indians (Mohawk, in this case).

NOTES

1. Kendall and Wickham (1999) emphasize Foucault's idea that "scientific discourse has already made the objects of science visible. This is not an alternative route to a pure pre-discursive realm of existence. These visibilities are not reflections of the pure forms of objects, but rather the result of temporary discursive luminosity; they allow a thing to exist only as a flash, sparkle or shimmer" (p. 40).

2. The episodes of this series are available at: http://www.timetravellertm.com/episodes

3. The word "machinima" refers to "films made by real-time three-dimensional computer graphics rendering engines" (Ng, 2013, p. xiv).

4. Phenomenal structure is a theoretical concept by means of which one can capture the referential aspect of a discourse, that is, the manner in which that discourse refers to an object or topic by thematizing or problematizing it in specific ways. The "theme" or "referential relationship" is constituted through a process of selection of elements, as much as by their combination into a specific formation, hence the notion of "phenomenal structure" (Keller, 2013, p. 114).

5. Under the label "cyberspace," the two authors refer to "the websites, chat rooms, bulletin boards, virtual environments, and games that make up the internet" (Lewis and Fragnito, 2005, p. 29).

REFERENCES

Dartt-Newton, D. (2012, Winter). Deana Dartt-Newton, Chumash/California/Mayo: Interview with Elayne Janiak. *Contemporary Indigenous North American Artists*. Retrieved from http://contemporarynativeartists.tumblr.com/post/19052879352/deana-dartt-newton-chumash-californio-mayo-cochimi

de Certeau, M. (1986). *Heterologies: Discourse on the other* (B. Massumi, Trans.). Manchester, UK: Manchester University Press.

Fragnito, S. T. (n.d). Skawennati Fragnito interviewed by the Indigenous Arts Network. Retrieved from http://Indigenousartsnetwork.ca/artists/skawennati_tricia_fragnito/interview/

Fragnito, S. T. (2002). Five suggestions for better living. In L. Jessup and S. Bagg (Eds.), *On Aboriginal representation in the gallery* (pp. 229–37). Ottawa, ON: Canadian Museum of Civilization.

Guglietti, M. V. (2010). Aboriginal Internet art and the imagination of community. In K. Howley (Ed.), *Understanding community media* (pp. 133–42). Los Angeles: Sage Publications.

Hopkins, C. (2006). Interventions in digital territories. In D. Claxton, and S. Loft (Eds.), *Transference, tradition, technology: Native new media: Exploring visual and digital culture*. Alberta, AB: Banff Centre Press.

Hopkins, C. (2008). Making things our own: The Indigenous aesthetic in digital storytelling. In D. Butt, J. Bywater, and N. Paul (Eds.), *Place: Local knowledge and New Media practice* (pp. 93–102). Newcastle, UK: Cambridge Scholars Publishing.

Hopkins, C. (2011). Why can't beauty be a call to action? In S. Farrell-Racette (Ed.), *Close encounters: The next 500 Years*. Winnipeg, MB: Plug In Editions.

Keller, R. (2013). *Doing discourse research: An introduction for social scientists*. London, UK: Sage Publications.

Kendall, G., and Wickham, G. (1999). *Using Foucault's methods*. London, UK: Sage.

Lewis, J. E. (2004). Terra Nullius, Terra Incognito. *BlackFlash*, *22*(1).

Lewis, J. E. (2012). Time travelers, flying heads, and second lives: Designing communal stories. *Interactions*, *19*(2), 20–23.

Lewis, J. E. (2014). A better dance and better prayers: Systems, structures, and the future imaginary in Aboriginal new media. In S. Loft, and K. Swanson (Eds.), *Coded territories: Tracing Indigenous pathways in new media* (pp. 48–77). Edmonton, AB: University of Alberta Press.

Lewis, J. E., and Fragnito, S. (2005). Aboriginal territories in cyberspace. *Cultural Survival Quarterly*, *29*(2), 29.

Lewis, J. E., and Fragnito, S. (2012). Art work as argument. *Canadian Journal of Communication*, *37*, 205–12.

Loft, S. (2005). Aboriginal media art and the postmodern conundrum: A coyote perspective. In D. Claxton, and S. Loft (Eds.), *Transference, tradition, technology: Native new media: Exploring visual and digital culture*. Alberta, AB: Banff Centre Press.

Loft, S. (2009). Indians in space: Curating media art by Indigenous artists. *ARC Speaker Series*. Available at: http://sarweb.org/?iarc_lecture_steven_loft-p:past_events

Mithlo, N. M. (2008). *"Our Indian princess": Subverting the stereotype*. Santa Fe, NM: School for Advanced Research.

Nason, J. (2000). "Our Indians": The unidimensional Indian in the disembodied local past. In W. R. West, Jr. (Ed.), *The changing presentation of the American Indian: Museums and native cultures* (pp. 29–46). Washington, DC: The Smithsonian Institution Press.

Ng, J. (2013). *Understanding machinima: Essays on filmmaking in virtual worlds*. London, UK: Bloomsbury Academic.

Rickard, J. (2007). Absorbing or obscuring the absence of a critical space in the Americas for Indigeneity: The Smithsonian's National Museum of the American Indian. *RES: Anthropology and Aesthetics*, *52*, 85–92.

Rickard, J. (2011). Visualizing sovereignty in a time of biometric sensors. *South Atlantic Quarterly*, *110*(2), 465–82.

Smith, P. C. (2005). *Presenting evidence*. Retrieved from http://www.paulchaatsmith.com/presenting-evidence.html

Smith, P. C. (2009). *Everything you know about Indians is wrong*. Minneapolis: University of Minnesota Press.

Todd, L. (1996). Aboriginal narratives in cyberspace. In M. A. Moser, and D. MacLeod (Eds.), *Immersed in technology: Art and virtual environment* (pp. 179–94). Cambridge, MA: MIT Press.

Vamanu, I. (2014). *North American indigenous curators' constructions of indigenous knowledge: Applying the sociology of knowledge approach to discourse*. (Doctoral dissertation). doi:10.7282/T3862J2X

Index

About the Editor

Dr. Jennifer Weil Arns holds a BA from the Maxwell School of Citizenship at Syracuse University with a minor in economics, a master's degree in library and information science from the University of California at Berkeley, a master's degree in public administration from the Kennedy School of Government at Harvard University, and a doctoral degree in information and library science from the University of North Carolina at Chapel Hill. Prior to obtaining her PhD, she was a senior evaluator at the U.S. General Accounting Office, where she managed and contributed to program evaluations related to information policy.

Her current research and teaching focus on cultural institutions as social and economic units and the contributions these make to the health and prosperity of their communities. She is the past chair of the American Library Association Research Roundtable and a current member of the American Library Association Committee on Archives, Libraries, and Museums. She has also chaired the University of South Carolina School of Library and Information Science Research and Doctoral Committee and is the author and co-principal investigator of the school's IMLS-funded *Cultural Heritage Informatics Leadership (CHIL): An Experiment in Responsive Doctoral Education* project. Based on The Responsive PhD model developed by the Woodrow Wilson Fellowship Foundation, this new curriculum requires interdisciplinary coursework and field placements specifically designed to explore the common threads that unite museums, libraries, and other cultural institutions. Her international presentations include the Inclusive Museum and International Federation of Library Associations conferences. Her interest in the arts and humanities is long-standing, and her memberships include the Columbia Museum of Art, the Boston Museum of Fine Arts, and the Peabody Essex Museum.

Contributors

Daniel Gelaw Alemneh is the Digital Curation Coordinator for Digital Libraries at the University of North Texas Libraries and an Adjunct Professor in the College of Information, University of North Texas. Daniel's research and scholarship generally focuses on digital resource lifecycle management, and many of his publications are available at http://digital.library.unt.edu/explore/collections/UNTSW. Daniel is actively involved in various professional societies—serving on program committees and editorial boards of several international publications/conferences and as a manuscript reviewer.

Tatjana Aparac-Jelušić is Professor at the Department of Information sciences at the University of Zadar. As Dean of the PhD program since 2008, she has supervised over 200 diploma papers, twelve Master in Science, and seven PhD theses of Croatian and Slovenian LIS students. She has served on the Editorial Boards of several journals, including Information Processing Management until 2008, Alexandria, Journal of Documentation, JALISE (since 2013), and Bibliotekar (Serbia). She is the past chair of the ASIS&T European Chapter and Euclid. Tatjana has authored one book, six chapters in books, over 100 research and professional papers (in Croatian and English), over thirty reviews and opinion papers, and edited twenty-four books. She has also served as Co-Director of the LIDA Conference, member of PC for CoLIS, ECDL, QQML2009, and reviewer for ASIS&T, ALA, ECDL and other international conferences. She received the Thompson/ISI Outstanding Teacher of Information Science 2006 given by ASIS&T.

Shimelis Assefa is Associate Professor in the department of Research Methods and Information Science in the Morgridge College of Education, University of Denver. His research interests focus on interrelated topics that shed light on the role, value, and impact of information systems and services in organizations. More specifically, he is interested in knowledge production, knowledge diffusion, and knowledge structure as well as learning technologies, scholarly communication, value creation, and innovation systems. He has published widely in peer-reviewed journals and presented at regional, national, and international conferences.

Brenda Reyes Ayala is currently an Information Science PhD candidate at the University of North Texas. Currently she works as a Research Assistant at the University of North Texas Libraries, and as a Support Engineer for the Internet Archive's Archive-It team. Previously she worked at the National Library of Spain as a web archivist and usability specialist. She holds a Bachelor's in Technical Writing from Carnegie Mellon University and a Master's in Human-Computer Interaction from Georgia Institute of Technology.

David Carr studied, wrote, and consulted about the commonalities of museums and libraries, and was an advocate for cultural institutions as places for addressing the unfinished issues of adult life. For many years he practiced and taught librarianship, specializing in collections, adult reading, and reference work in humanities and social sciences. His essays appeared in two collections, *The Promise of Cultural Institutions* (AltaMira, 2003), and *A Place Not a Place* (AltaMira, 2006), and his most recent book, *Open Conversations: Public Learning in Libraries and Museums*, was published by Libraries Unlimited/ABC-CLIO in 2011. David received a BA from Drew University, an MA from Teachers College, Columbia University, and MLS and Ph.D. degrees from Rutgers University. He continued writing about adult reading and his museum observations over three decades up to his untimely death in 2016.

Mary Carroll is the Associate Course Director in the School of Information Studies at Charles Sturt University. Prior to employment at CSU she was an Early Career Development Fellow at RMIT University, Melbourne. Her research focuses on the provision of information and its relationship to access and equity both in contemporary society and historically.

Carla Colombati is Librarian at The Humanistic Library of University of Teramo. Her main interests focus on research and scholarship, learning and training, digital libraries, social networks and tools, and user experience in libraries.

Michael A. Crumpton, MLS, SPHR, is the Assistant Dean for Administrative Services at the University of North Carolina at Greensboro. He is an adjunct instructor for the Department of Library and Information Studies at the University of North Carolina at Greensboro and is the former Director of Library Services for Wake Tech Community College and Access Services Manager at the Public Library of Cincinnati and Hamilton County. His published works includes monographs; "Handbook for Community College Librarians", Library Unlimited, 2013, Strategic Human Resource Planning for Academic Libraries, Chandos Publishing, 2015, as well as several other chapters and articles not currently in this institutional repository: http://libres.uncg.edu/ir/uncg/clist.aspx?id=1946

Elena De Carolis is Chief Librarian at Federico Caffè Library, Department of Economics and Law, Sapienza University of Rome. Her research interests include information literacy, lifelong learning, and open access.

Agnese Galeffi is a visiting professor of Cataloguing and Classification at the Vatican School of Library Science and member of the IFLA Cataloguing Standing Committee and FRBR Review Group. Her interests include: cataloguing (theory, rules, standards and formats), search tools and discovery systems, data visualization, and interfaces.

Mary Anne Kennan is a Senior Lecturer in the School of Information Studies at Charles Sturt University, where much of her research is in the area of the social studies of scholarly communications, e-research and data management. She teaches an introduction to information science, research data management and research methods.

Timoty Leonardi is the Library and Museum Manager at the Fondazione Museo del Tesoro del Duomo e Archivio Capitolare of Vercelli. He is currently a member of the Bernstein Project Council (Bernstein, The memory of paper), the Società Storica Vercellese Executive Board, and the SiBEP Executive Board (Sistema delle Biblioteche Ecclesiastiche Piemontesi).

Paul F. Marty is a Professor in the School of Information at Florida State University. He has a background in ancient history and computer science engineering, and his Ph.D. is from the Graduate School of Library and Information Science at the University of Illinois at Urbana-Champaign. His research and teaching interests include museum informatics, technology and culture, information science, and innovation and design. He has served on the editorial boards and committees of national and international organizations including Museum Management and Curatorship, Museums and the Web, and the Museum Computer Network.

Sigrid McCausland is a Senior Lecturer in the School of Information Studies at Charles Sturt University, specializing in records and archives management. She is Joint Secretary of the International Council on Archives section on Archival Education and Training. Her current research focuses on advocacy, public programs and managing and providing access to analogue and digital community cultural heritage.

Giovanni Michetti is Assistant Professor in Archival Science at Sapienza University of Rome. His research area is focused on contemporary and digital archives. His main research interests are records management, archival description and digital preservation. He has been involved in international initiatives on digital preservation, such as ERPANET and CASPAR, and is currently a research member of the InterPARES Trust project. He works actively in the standardization area: he is the Chair of the Subcommittee "Archives and Records Management" and Vice-Chair of the Committee "Documentation and Information" in the Italian Standards Organization (UNI), as well as the Italian representative within a few ISO working groups on records management. He has authored articles and essays on scholarly journals, as well as the Italian translations of EAD (Encoded Archival Description) and OAIS (Open Archival Information System).

M. Cristina Pattuelli is an associate professor at the School of Information at Pratt Institute, New York, where she teaches courses on knowledge organization, cultural heritage, and art documentation. Her current research explores the intersection between cultural heritage and information access, description and design. She is the director of the Linked Jazz Project that investigates the application of Linked Open Data technology to cultural heritage resources. She is a frequent consultant to libraries, archives, and museums on similar topics and related projects. She was recently awarded the Jesse H. Shera Award for Distinguished Published Research, the OCLC/ALISE Library and Information Science Research Grant, and the American Library Association, Carroll Preston Baber Research Grant. She received her Ph.D. in Information and Library Science from the University of North Carolina at Chapel Hill and holds degrees in Philosophy and in Cultural Heritage Studies from the University of Bologna, Italy.

Jennifer Burek Pierce is associate professor in the School of Library and Information Science at The University of Iowa. Her books include *What Adolescents Ought to Know: Sexual Health Texts in Early 20th Century America* (UMass Press, 2011) and *Sex, Brains, and Video Games: A Librarian's Guide to Teens in the 21st Century* (ALA Editions, 2009). She developed the Youth

Matters column for American Libraries, to which she has recently returned as a contributing author, and has also written for The Chronicle of Higher Education. At Iowa, she serves on advisory boards for the Iowa Initiative for Sustainable Communities and the University of Iowa Press.

Bob Pymm is an adjunct Senior Lecturer in the School of Information Studies at Charles Sturt University, Wagga Wagga, Australia, teaching in the areas of collection development and preservation. He also coordinates a specialist online audio-visual archiving program with research interests in this field.

Abebe Rorissa is an Associate Professor in the Department of Information Studies, University at Albany, State University of New York. He currently serves on program committees and the editorial boards of several international journals, publications, and conferences. His leadership positions include the Association for Information Science and Technology (ASIS&T) SIG Cabinet Steering Committee, Chair and Officer of ASIS&T's SIG III, and the ASIS&T Board. A multidisciplinary scholar, he has published extensively in leading international journals, and his research interests include multimedia information organization and retrieval, scaling of users' information needs/perceptions, and the se/acceptance/adoption and impact of information and communication technologies. His honors include University at Albany Provost's Fellowship and the ASIS&T SIG Member of the Year Award.

Maria Luisa Russo is a specialist in preservation, conservation, and valorization of library and archive materials. She has been working as an advisor for book conservation in several institutions, and since 2015 she has co-managed the project "Safeguarding the manuscripts of Timbuktu" of the University of Hamburg—Centre for the Study of Manuscript Cultures. She is enrolled in the PhD Literary archives program at the University of Turin.

Diantha Dow Schull is founder and principal, DDSchull Associates, LLC, providing advisory services to libraries, museums, and foundations. Her previous positions include president of Libraries for the Future, director of interpretive programs at the Library of Congress, director of exhibitions at the New York Public Library, and assistant director of the Museum Aid Program of the New York State Council on the Arts. She is a frequent speaker at professional conferences and author of numerous articles and books including *Archives Alive: Expanding Engagement with Public Library Archives and Special Collections* and *50+ Library Services: Innovation in Action.*

D. M. ("Mikki") Smith is a doctoral candidate at the Graduate School of Library and Information Science at the University of Illinois, Urbana-Champaign. Her areas of interest include children's literature, print culture, and library history. Her dissertation, *Print Networks and Youth Information Culture, 1867–1890*, explores the dynamics between periodicals created for young people and those created by them, and examines the ways in which print networks supported peer networks and an information culture among young readers in the United States in the late nineteenth century. She was a Kate B. and Hall J. Peterson Fellow at the American Antiquarian Society in 2012–2013.

Anna Maria Tammaro is Professor at the University of Parma in the International Master DILL Digital Library Learning, joint course together with Tallin University. Her main research interests focus on international dimension of LIS education and Digital Library. She is Chair of IFLA Section Library Theory and Research and past Chair of the IFLA Division IV (2011-2013) and Education and Training Section (2007–2011), past member of IFLA Governing Board (2007–2009; 2011–2013). She is currently studying data curation and interdisciplinary research and education for digital libraries. She holds a Ph.D. in Information Science from University of Northumbria.

Iulian Vamanu is an Assistant Professor in the University of Iowa School of Library and Information Science. His main research interests are: knowledge organization, cultural heritage informatics, information behavior, and information ethics.

Sarah Welland is a lecturer in Information and Library Studies, Open Polytechnic of New Zealand, and a consultant specializing in government recordkeeping. She has extensive knowledge of and experience in the records, archives and information management industries, and manages her community's local history collection on a volunteer basis. Her research interests are recordkeeping education, archival theory and community archives.

CPSIA information can be obtained
at www.ICGtesting.com
Printed in the USA
BVHW030207050123
655625BV00001B/2

9 781442 263703